The Interpersonal Communication Reader

Joseph A. DeVito

Hunter College of the
City University of New York

Allyn and Bacon

Boston ■ *London* ■ *Toronto* ■ *Sydney* ■ *Tokyo* ■ *Singapore*

Senior Editor: Karon Bowers
Editor in Chief, Social Sciences: Karen Hanson
Editorial Assistant: Sarah Kelly
Executive Marketing Manager: Lisa Kimball
Editorial-Production Administrator: Annette Joseph
Editorial-Production Service and Electronic Composition: Nesbitt Graphics, Inc.
Composition Buyer: Linda Cox
Manufacturing Buyer: Julie McNeill
Cover Designer: Kristina Mose-Libon

Library of Congress Cataloging-in-Publication Data
The interpersonal communication reader / [edited by] Joseph A. DeVito.
    p.   cm.
   Includes bibliographical references and index.
ISBN 0-321-08352-0 (alk. paper)
1. Interpersonal communication. I. DeVito, Joseph A.,

BF637.C45 I646 2001
153.6—dc21   2001022103

Printed in the United States of America

10 9 8 7 6 5 4   RRD-VA 06

The Interpersonal
Communication Reader

Contents

part one
Foundations of Interpersonal Communication

Welcome to
The Interpersonal Communication Reader

This collection of readings is designed for the interpersonal communication course—a course concerned with explaining the theory and research in interpersonal communication and its very practical skills. The readings included here will enable you to explore numerous interesting topics and will prove especially useful when you read the articles in conjunction with the relevant chapters in your interpersonal communication text. Suggestions for coordinating the readings with your textbook are provided in the grid presented on pages xii–xiii.

The Articles

The articles are, for the most part, relatively brief—far shorter than the traditional textbook chapter or unit, so you'll be able to read one, two, or three articles in conjunction with your regular textbook chapter or unit. The articles come from a wide variety of sources addressed to the educated consumer of research rather than to the communication researcher or theorist. They are all eminently suited to college students beginning their study of interpersonal communication.

The articles complement rather than duplicate what is already available in your textbook. For example, feedback, gossip, and apologies are frequently mentioned in textbooks but are usually given no more than a few paragraphs. Here, you'll have the opportunity to pursue these topics, and many like them, in greater depth.

The articles span the entire breadth of interpersonal communication, focusing on the basic concepts and principles of interpersonal communication, verbal and nonverbal messages, and interpersonal relationships. The articles emphasize the practical skills of interpersonal communication and relationships but are clearly based on theories and research findings in interpersonal communication and related fields.

As you read these articles, you'll find that they offer you insights into a wide variety of topics in interpersonal communication. They are extremely well written and interesting to read. The most important characteristic of the articles in this collection is that they effectively address real-life practical needs of people seeking to become better interpersonal communicators.

Learning Aids

The articles are presented with a variety of learning aids, which makes reading them an interactive experience with immediate and practical payoffs. Six types of sidebars are included throughout the readings. These sidebars are integrated into the articles, and placed next to the discussion to which they are most applicable.

- **Brain Talk** sidebars offer suggestions for thinking about interpersonal communication more critically and more creatively. They identify and illustrate such creative and critical thinking concepts as stereotyping, self-serving biases, polarization, overattribution, and the dangers of anecdotal evidence.

- **Cultural Analysis** sidebars ask you to analyze the influence of culture on different aspects of interpersonal communication and encourage you to more carefully examine your own cultural beliefs and values about interpersonal communication and relationships.

- **Ethical Judgments** sidebars ask you to consider the ethical implications of communication behaviors discussed in the article; for example, the ethics of assertiveness, lying, and gossip.

- **Communicating Skillfully** sidebars ask you how you'd communicate in a situation related to the major concepts of the article. These questions bring together the substance of the article with your own communication understanding and skill.

- **Explaining Ideas** sidebars ask you to describe one or more of the concepts discussed in the article, usually as these concepts relate to your own interpersonal interactions; for example, your use of feedback, your competency in small talk, or the benefits you'll derive from interpersonal relationships.

- **Evaluating Ideas** sidebars invite you to analyze the usefulness of a concept or of the article as a whole and ask, generally, if you would take issue with anything the author says or would want to amend or add anything to the substance of the article; for example, to the author's classification of lies, communication analyses, or explanations of relationship myths.

Each of the articles is prefaced with a brief headnote identifying the theme and major topics of the article. Each headnote contains a *"Want to learn more?"* section that offers suggestions for pursuing the topic of the article and lists other works by the author.

Your feedback is important in making future editions of this reader more useful to students like you. I hope you'll take a few minutes to share your thoughts. The feedback form is available on the Web (www.ablongman.com/devito). If you prefer, please send your comments directly to me at jdevito@shiva.hunter.cuny.edu. I look forward to receiving your comments.

Acknowledgments

My first debt is to the authors who allowed me to print from their works. Without their willingness—and, of course, their written works—this reader could not have been constructed. I especially want to thank Karon Bowers, senior editor for communication, and Jennifer Harper, project manager, for their expertise, support, and goodwill. I also want to thank the following individuals who reviewed the manuscript and provided helpful comments: Marion E. Boyer, Kalamazoo Valley Community College; Kenneth N. Cissna, University of South Florida; Alice L. Crume, SUNY Brockport; Paulette Grotrian, Washtenaw Community College; Glenn Austin Johnston, Texas State Technical College–Harlingen; Cindy Kistenberg, University of Houston–Downtown; Jay R. Martinson, Olivet Nazarene University; Robert L. Walsh, Mitchell Community College; and Kent L. Zimmerman, Sinclair Community College.

Interpersonal Communication Textbooks and The Interpersonal Communication Reader

	Adler, Ronald B. and Neil Towne, *Looking Out/Looking In*, 9th ed. Fort Worth, TX: Harcourt Brace, 1999.	Adler, Ronald B., Lawrence B. Rosenfeld, and Russell F. Proctor II, *Interplay: The Process of Interpersonal Communication*, 8th ed. Fort Worth, TX: Harcourt Brace, 2001.	Beebe, Steven A., Susan J. Beebe, and Mark V. Redmond, *Interpersonal Communication: Relating to Others*, 3rd ed. Boston, MA: Allyn & Bacon, 2002.	DeVito, Joseph A. *Messages: Building Interpersonal Communication Skills*, 5th ed. Boston, MA: Allyn & Bacon, 2002.	DeVito, Joseph A. *The Interpersonal Communication Book*, 9th ed. Boston, MA: Allyn & Bacon, 2001.	Trenholm, Sarah and Arthur Jensen, *Interpersonal Communication*, 4th ed. Belmont, CA: Wadsworth, 2000.	Verderber, Kathleen S. and Rudolph F. Verderber. *Inter-Act: Interpersonal Communication Concepts, Skills, and Contents*, 9th ed. Belmont, CA: Wadsworth, 2001.	Wood, Julia T. *Interpersonal Communication: Everyday Encounters*, 2nd ed. Belmont, CA: Wadsworth, 1999.
PART ONE Foundations of Interpersonal Communication								
1. Elgin	1	1	1	1	1, 2	1	1	1
2. Satir	1	1	1	1	1, 2	1	1	1
3. Marano	2	10	2	1, 8	1, 14	2	9	2
4. Gabor	9	12	8	12	5	9	10	8
5. Forgas	3	4	3	2	4	6, 8	2	3
6. Stone, Patton, & Heen	3	3	3	3	6	6	2	3
7. Stettner	7	7	5	4	7	6	7	6
8. Alessandra & Hunsaker	7	7	5	4	1, 7, 8	6	9, 14	6
9. Kaplan	5	5, 11	6	4, 8	8, 22	4	9	6
10. Elashmawi & Hunter	9	2	4	9	3	13	1	3, Epilogue

	Adler, Ronald B. and Neil Towne, *Looking Out/Looking In*, 9th ed. Fort Worth, TX: Harcourt Brace, 1999.	Adler, Ronald B., Lawrence B. Rosenfeld, and Russell F. Proctor II, *Interplay: The Process of Interpersonal Communication*, 8th ed. Fort Worth, TX: Harcourt Brace, 2001.	Beebe, Steven A., Susan J. Beebe, and Mark V. Redmond, *Interpersonal Communication: Relating to Others*, 3rd ed. Boston, MA: Allyn & Bacon, 2002.	DeVito, Joseph A. *Messages: Building Interpersonal Communication Skills*, 5th ed. Boston, MA: Allyn & Bacon, 2002.	DeVito, Joseph A. *The Interpersonal Communication Book*, 9th ed. Boston, MA: Allyn & Bacon, 2001.	Trenholm, Sarah and Arthur Jensen, *Interpersonal Communication*, 4th ed. Belmont, CA: Wadsworth, 2000.	Verderber, Kathleen S. and Rudolph F. Verderber. *Inter-Act: Interpersonal Communication Concepts, Skills, and Contents*, 9th ed. Belmont, CA: Wadsworth, 2001.	Wood, Julia T. *Interpersonal Communication: Everyday Encounters*, 2nd ed. Belmont, CA: Wadsworth, 1999.
PART TWO Messages in Interpersonal Communication								
11. Tingley	5	2, 5	6	5	9, 10, 11	13	4	3, Epilogue
12. Lazare	9	12	6	8	14	12	4	9
13. Westen	8	9	6	8	14	2, 4, 11	4	4
14. Blum	6	6	7	6	3	5	5	5
15. Wainwright	6	6	7	6	3	5	5	5
16. Heldmann	10	8	5	11	4, 12	16	10	9
17. Ford	10	8, 12	8	7	6	13	10	5
18. Baldrige	9	10	11	8	4, 12	5	5	4
PART THREE Interpersonal Relationships								
19. McCarthy, Gilmour, & Gotlib	8	9, 10	10	10	10, 11	7, 8, 9, 10	12	10, 11
20. Sternberg with Whitney	8	9, 10	9	10	10, 11	7, 8, 9, 10	12	11
21. Creighton	10	12	8	11	12	13	11	9
22. Zunin & Zunin	9	11	10	10, 11	5, 11	14	8	8
23. Fitzpatrick	8	9	10, 11	10	10	15	13	11
24. DeVito	9	10	8, 10	10, 11, 12	10, 11, 21	12, 13	13	7, 9, 11

The Interpersonal
Communication Reader

part one

Foundations of Interpersonal Communication

Communication is power. Those who have mastered its effective use can change their own experience of the world and the world's experience of them.

—Anthony Robbins

1

How to Use Communication

In this article Suzette Haden Elgin, perhaps best known for her *The Gentle Art of Verbal Self-Defense,* offers four reasons why good communication is so important. Reviewing these reasons provides an effective backdrop for the learning of interpersonal communication skills to be covered in later articles. These reasons, although couched in the context of talking with children, are applicable to all forms of communication and, in fact, are the same reasons for studying interpersonal communication.

Want to learn more? Take a look at some of Elgin's other books, for example, *The Gentle Art of Verbal Self-Defense* (New York: Barnes and Noble, 1985), *Success with the Gentle Art of Verbal Self-Defense* (Englewood Cliffs, NJ: Prentice-Hall, 1989), and *The Gentle Art of Verbal Self-Defense at Work* (Englewood Cliffs, NJ: Prentice-Hall, 2000).

Cultural Analysis

What emphasis does your culture place on communication? On teaching the skills of effective communication to its members?

I'm not going to tell you that good communication is important because it's part of being a better person, or part of moving humanity toward moral and intellectual superiority, or anything else of that kind. These statements may be true. Good communication and language skills may be the heart of all ethics and esthetics and philosophy. But I'm not a philosopher, or a theologian, or even an image counselor. I am a practical person who has spent her life dealing with the same problems *you* have to deal with. I'm going to give you four practical down-to-earth reasons why you aren't safe saying, "Oh, it's only talk! We have lots more important things to worry about than *talk!*" If that ever was true, it's true no longer. And here are the reasons why.

Reason One: Language and Health Are Tightly Linked

We're used to being told that we can't expect to stay fit and healthy unless we pay close attention to a long list of hazards and risk factors in our lives. Cholesterol. Nicotine. Power tools. Overweight. Alcohol. Speedometers. Exercise. Germs—our germs and other people's. The list goes on and on. Sometimes it seems as though there's nothing on this earth that isn't a threat. What we *haven't* been told—because until quite recently nobody knew it—is that these hazards aren't the ones we most need to worry about.

Suzette Haden Elgin, "The Four Reasons Why Good Communication Is So Important," *The Gentle Art of Communicating with Kids.* (New York: Wiley, 1996), pp. 2–7. Copyright © 1996. Reprinted by permission of John Wiley & Sons, Inc.

As long as researchers were only able to look at the health histories of relatively small groups of people, tracked over only a few years, the items on that list *did* seem to be our main concern. But once we had computers powerful enough to look at health histories of *hundreds of thousands of people over many decades of their lifetimes*—a recent development—we suddenly realized that we'd been missing the most important patterns. The research we're able to do now shows us clearly and dramatically that the real hazards to our health, for all diseases and disorders and accidents across the board, are simply these two: hostility and loneliness.

You're in far more danger from exposure to hostility and loneliness than from exposure to the things you're used to worrying about. The more extensive your exposure, the more often it occurs, the longer and more chronic it is, the greater the danger you face. And hostility and loneliness can't be considered separately, because there's no quicker way to become a lonely person than to be a hostile one.

Very few human beings express their hostility by blowing things up and burning things down. Ninety-nine percent of us, whatever our age, express hostility primarily through our *language.* The only way we can reduce the hostility and loneliness that threatens us is by using language that will reduce and defuse hostility in our lives and help us build strong social networks. And nothing we can do to guard the health and fitness of our children is as important as seeing to it that their *language* environment doesn't poison them and make all our other efforts worthless.

You can give a child the very best diet, the finest medical care, the most abundant opportunities for games and sports, all the traditional advantages. But if that child spends his or her young life in an environment where people do nothing but blame and argue and plead and threaten and put one another down from morning till night—or where the most frequent kind of language is silence—you've wasted your time and money and energy. That child will not be healthy, and neither will anybody else who has to live in that environment.

Reason Two: Verbal Violence and Physical Violence Are Tightly Linked

I said above that most human beings express hostility primarily through language, and that's accurate. It's a sad comment on our society that a large number of human beings also express hostility with *physical* violence, which is now an epidemic in the United States. However, almost nobody past the age of diapers just walks up to another person and starts hitting. First there are angry words; first there is an argument; only then does the hitting begin.

You may think you can blame your high taxes and high cost of living on politicians and incompetent bureaucracies. You would be wrong. Those things are expensive, but they aren't where most of our money goes. *Most of our money is spent protecting society against physical violence and dealing with its consequences.* Most of our money goes for insurance and law enforcement and metal detectors and judges and prisons and emergency de-

Explaining Ideas

How would you explain the language that you were exposed to growing up? Were you exposed to, for example, language that blames, argues, pleads, threatens, and puts others down? Were you exposed to language that was positive, supportive, and empowering? Are these forms of language that you grew up with a part of your current interpersonal communication system?

Communicating Skillfully

What would you say to the person who argues that many famous and competent people have been poor communicators and offers in support three well-known examples?

partments and all the rest of the things we have to have to survive the physical violence in this country. If we could get physical violence—which begins, 99 percent of the time, with *verbal* violence—under control, we would have plenty of money for everything else we need. The cure for our raging national debt and deficit isn't a balanced budget amendment, it's language used in such a way that verbal violence is dealt with effectively while it's still verbal, so that it *doesn't* escalate to physical violence.

The cure for violence, and the chance for everyone (not just the very wealthy) to have a comfortable and decent lifestyle, has to begin with the language used in the home. No other solution exists that has even a modest hope of success.

Reason Three: Good Communication Skills and Success Are Tightly Linked

There was a time when people could assume that their children—if they finished high school and acquired "work ethic" habits such as showing up on time—would be able to go get a decent job and make a pretty decent living. People knew that youngsters might take a few "trial" jobs in their teens but would soon settle into a field where they could either hang on to their position (and count on a regular package of benefits and a series of raises over time) or advance steadily to a higher position. Job changes would be few, and a career change after thirty would be almost unheard of. Parents could assume that their adult children would work in situations where they were well known and others had time to get to know them and understand their personal foibles and problems. In that world, there was plenty of time to work everything out, there was job security, and all that mattered was the motivation to do a job well.

That world is gone. So far as anyone can tell, it's gone forever. We live in a world now where earning a decent living means being ready to change jobs—and careers—at the drop of a hat, not just once or twice but many times. A world where machines constantly replace human beings by doing the work humans used to do. We've seen whole populations of workers—telephone operators and backup musicians and assembly-line workers and typists—disappear from the workforce, replaced by machines. We live in the world of outsourcing and downsizing, of temporary workers and independent contractors.

It's not enough today to be willing and able to work hard; it's not enough to have one set of well-honed skills. Today's successful adult must have the ability to move into a group of total strangers and quickly establish good relationships with them that will last as long as the job (or the job training) does. And this must be done over and over again, with new groups, until retirement.

The one crucial factor for doing that is good communication skills. And that one factor is rapidly dividing our population into two groups: the Haves, who can expect roughly the sorts of opportunities their parents had;

Brain Talk

When confronted with a problem, a useful creative thinking tool is to ask yourself how different people would see the problem and deal with it. Sometimes it helps to ask how famous people throughout history would look at the problem or how people from different fields (e.g., psychology, communication, sociology, or computer science) would respond to the problem. When the problem is an interpersonal one, it helps to ask how your partner or friend sees the problem. Conducting a mental role-playing where you imagine your partner commenting on the problem often yields amazing interpersonal insight.

Explaining Ideas

How would you describe "good" e-mail, chat room, and newsgroup communication?

and the Have-Nots, who can expect only low-wage and low-status jobs for their entire working lives, followed by retirement into poverty. There's no middle ground any more, and language skills determine which of the two extremes children will fall into as adults.

It's nice to be able to give your children training in tennis and golf and ballet and piano and figure skating. These skills can be a big help in adult life. But *nothing* will help kids as much, and go as far toward making them successful and independent adults, as good language skills. And nobody but parents and primary caregivers can provide *that* training during the formative years when children are best equipped to learn language skills.

The teachers in our schools don't have time to do this. They have to deal with thirty or more children at once, many of whom have special needs (including the inability to speak the teacher's language). The television set—which demonstrates that the person with the meanest mouth always gets the biggest laughs, and where "talk" shows are not talk but no-holds-barred verbal slugfests—is not going to provide that training. Certainly other *children* can't be expected to do the job! It has to be done by the only people who have years of one-on-one time with the children—the people, usually parents, they live with. Your time with your kids may be limited, but you have more of it than anyone else does, and it's a precious resource that you *cannot* afford to waste.

Reason Four: Communication Skills Are Your Family Inheritance

You may not be able to leave your children a large fortune; most of us can't. We do the best we can, and often our best doesn't include mansions and yachts. But there's one legacy that all parents do leave to their kids, whether they want to or not: *the family communication strategies.*

If your children are past the toddler stage, you may be prepared to tell me that they'd rather be drawn and quartered than use the language they hear *you* use. They don't want to talk the way you talk. They think your vocabulary and your conversational style are stuffy or nerdy or worse. I understand that, and I think it's true a great deal of the time, especially for adolescent children. But what the kids are rejecting is the parts of your language behavior they're *consciously aware of*—and that's a long way from being all there is.

Behind and/or beneath such matters as your word choices and the rules you follow to put your sentences together, there's a whole lot more to your grammar, including the *strategies* you use when you communicate. Strategies for heading off arguments or for provoking them. Strategies for convincing others to do what you want them to do and persuading them not to do things you're opposed to. Strategies for circling the truth when you don't want to tell it and finding out if others are doing that to *you*. Strategies for negotiating agreements. Strategies for rewarding and punishing. Your children may use different words and slang and different styles, but unless

Evaluating Ideas

How would you evaluate Elgin's effectiveness in explaining and illustrating these four reasons? For example, are you convinced that good communication and success or verbal and physical violence are closely linked?

Ethical Judgments

Can you identify specific examples of parent-to-child communication that you'd consider unethical? For example, are parents ethical when they push a child into certain careers and away from others? When they teach their children prejudices against members of other races or religions?

something unusual happens in their lives they will use the communication strategies they learned from observing *you.*

When the strategies you model for your children are good ones, it will mean more to them and do more for them than any other inheritance can, in the long run. If, on the other hand, the strategies you show them are the kind that turn a home into a combat zone or a misery zone, they'll inherit that from you, too—and they will probably go on and hand it on down to your grandchildren. You can write a will to keep your kids from inheriting money you think would be put to better use somewhere else. But there's not one thing you can do to set aside your communication strategies so that your children won't carry them on into adult life. That will happen, and it gives new meaning to the field of estate planning.

These four basic units of information about the importance of communication work together: Whatever you do about any one of them will have consequences for the other three. That makes things easier.

2

How to Give and Receive Information

In this article, Virginia Satir, one of the world's most insightful family theorists and one who makes communication the central concept in her approach to theory and therapy, reviews essential concepts in interpersonal communication and provides a unique introduction to the study of interpersonal communication and its most important skills.

Want to learn more? If you enjoy this article and want to read more by Satir, read the other chapters in *Conjoint Family Therapy* or try her classic *Peoplemaking* (Palo Alto, CA: Science and Behavior Books, 1972). Useful overviews of the communication process include Dominic A. Infante, Andrew S. Rancer, and Deanna F. Womack, *Building Communication Theory*, 3rd ed. (Prospect Heights, IL: Waveland Press, 1997); Em Griffin, *A First Look at Communication Theory*, 4th ed. (New York: McGraw-Hill, 2000); and Stephen W. Littlejohn, *Theories of Human Communication,* 6th ed. (Belmont, CA: Wadsworth, 1999). Visit a search engine or an online bookstore and request material on *communication process, communication theory,* or *interpersonal communication.* Or, try the Allyn & Bacon Web site at www.ablongman.com.

1. What do we mean by "communication"? Isn't studying how people communicate almost like studying how they walk across a room? Doesn't this amount to ignoring the deeper processes which psychiatry should deal with?

    a. The word "communicate" is generally understood to refer to nonverbal as well as verbal behavior within a social context. Thus "communication" can mean "interaction" or "transaction." "Communication" also includes all those symbols and clues used by persons in giving and receiving meaning.

    b. Taken in this sense, the communication techniques which people use can be seen as reliable indicators of interpersonal functioning.

    c. As an aid to therapy, a study of communication can help close the gap between inference and observation as well as help document the

---

Virginia Satir, "Communication: A Process of Giving and Getting Information," *Conjoint Family Therapy*, 3rd ed. (Palo Alto, CA: Science and Behavior Books, 1983), pp. 79–93. Reprinted by permission of Science and Behavior Books.

relationship between patterns of communication and symptomatic behavior.*

2. People must communicate clearly if they are going to get the information that they need from others. Without communication we, as humans, would not be able to survive.

   a. We need to find out about the world. We learn to differentiate and relate ourselves to objects by learning how to label them and by learning, through words and experience, what we can expect from them.

   b. We need to find out about other people and about the nature of relationships.

      • What, for example, are the socially approved ways to act, ways expected by others?

      • What behavior will please or displease others?

      • Why do others respond as they do? What are they after? What are their intentions toward us? What are they reporting about themselves?

      • How do we appear to others? How do others see us, evaluate us, react to us?

   c. We receive this vital information in two basic ways:

      • We ask for verbal responses.

      • We also observe nonverbal behavior.

3. People must communicate clearly if they are going to be able to *give* information to others. We need to let others know what is going on inside us.

   a. What we have learned or what we think we know.

   b. What we expect of others.

   c. How we interpret what others do.

   d. What behavior pleases us, displeases us.

   e. What our own intentions are.

   f. How others appear to us.

4. Let us examine in this chapter the difficulties posed by simple verbal communication.

   a. For one thing, the same word can have different meanings, different *denotations.*

      • For example, if B asks us "What class are you in?" it is not clear whether he is asking us what we are taking in school or what social standing we have.

---

*Jackson, Riskin and I demonstrated this several years ago in a paper analyzing five minutes of a taped family conversation that was sent to us by Dr. Lyman Wynne without identifying data. Don D. Jackson, J. Riskin, and Virginia Satir (1961). A Method of Analysis of a Family Interview. *Arch Gen Psychiat.* 5:321–339.

- In the United States, "Let's *table* that motion" means "Let's put it aside." In England, the same phrase means "Let's bring it up for discussion."

b. For another thing, the same word can have different *connotations*.

- For example, "mother" is a woman who bears and/or rears a child (denotation). But "mother" can be a warm, accepting, nurturing woman or a cold, demanding, unresponsive woman (connotation).

- When B uses the word "mother," what connotation does the word carry for him?

c. What compounds the problem is that words are abstractions, symbols that only stand for referents.

- The symbol is not the same as the "thing" or "idea" or "observation" for which it stands (although we often behave verbally as if symbols are literally what they symbolize). Very often the symbol and its meaning are assumed to be synonymous.

- Also, words are at different levels of abstraction. We have words about objects, words about relationships between objects, words about inner states, words about other words, words about words about words.

- As words become more abstract, their meanings can become increasingly obscure.

- Finally, there are many aspects of experience which are not describable by words.

Communicating Skillfully

How would you communicate your denotative meaning for *love, family,* and *death* to someone who was just learning English? How would you communicate your connotative meaning for these same terms? From this experience, why would you say communication problems more often center on differences in connotation than in denotation?

5. This elementary "meaning of words" aspect of communication is very important because people so often get into tangles with each other simply because A was using a word in one way, and B received the word as if it meant something entirely different.

a. An excellent example of this might be when A says, "I was only a *little* late," and B says, "You were *not!*"

b. Because words themselves are often unclear, it is important for people to clarify and qualify what they say, and to ask others to do the same when they find themselves puzzled or confused.

6. Words are tools which people use to give and get information. If a person fails to realize that words are only abstractions he will tend to overgeneralize, and he will fall into the error of making the following assumptions:*

a. He will assume that one instance is an example of all instances. He will be unclear, particularly in his use of who, what, where, and when.

- He may use the concept *who* as follows:

---

*I am indebted here to William Pemberton's article, "Non-Directive Reorientation in Counseling". W. H. Pemberton (1959). Non-Directive Reorientation in Counseling. *Etc.* 16:407–416.

"*Everybody* is like that."

"*Nobody* likes me."

"*All women* are …"

"*Men* are …"

- He may use the concept *what* as follows:

"*Nothing* turns out right."

"*Everything* is all fouled up."

- He may use the concept *where* as follows:

"*Everywhere* I go, that happens."

"*Nowhere* is it any different."

- He may use the concept *when* as follows:

"*Never* is it any different."

"*Always* this happens to me."

b. He will assume that other people share his feelings, thoughts, perceptions:

"How can you like fish!"

"Why didn't you do it the *right* way?"

"Of course he wouldn't want that!"

c. He will assume that his perceptions or evaluations are complete:

"Yes, I already know about that."

d. He will assume that what he perceives or evaluates won't change:

"That's the way she is."

"I've always been that way."

"That's life."

e. He assumes that there are only two possible alternatives when assessing perceptions or evaluations; he dichotomizes or thinks in terms of black or white:

"She either loves me or she doesn't."

"That will either make him or break him."

"You're either for me or against me."

f. He assumes that characteristics which he attributes to things or people are part of those things or people:

"That picture is ugly."

"He is selfish."

"She is hostile."

g. He assumes that he can get inside the head of another. He operates as if from a "crystal ball" and he acts as a spokesman for others:

"I know what you're thinking."

"I know what she *really* means."

"I will tell you what she was feeling."

"This is what he was going through."

h. He also assumes that the other can get inside his head. He assumes that the other also has a crystal ball. He allows the other to be a spokesman for him:

"She knows what I think."

"You know what I *really* mean."

"He can tell you what I went through."

7. If the receiver of these messages is as dysfunctional a communicator as the sender, he will respond by either agreeing or disagreeing.

a. If he agrees, clear communication will not have taken place, since he cannot be sure what it is to which he is agreeing. He may say:

"That picture *is* ugly, isn't it."

"She *is* selfish, isn't she."

"Yes, she *was* feeling such and such."

"Yes, women *are* like that."

"That certainly *is* the right way."

b. If he disagrees, he still cannot be sure with what he is disagreeing. However, the fact that he does disagree can stimulate either him or the sender to clarify their messages later. He may say:

"That picture is *not* ugly. It is beautiful."

"She is *not* selfish. She is very generous."

"No, she was *not* feeling that. What she was feeling was …"

"No, women aren't like that. They're …"

"No, that isn't the right way. *This* is the right way."

8. If the receiver, in this interchange, is a functional communicator, he will not stop either to agree or disagree. He will first ask the sender to clarify and qualify. He may say:

"What do you mean when you say that picture is ugly?"

"What does she do that strikes you as selfish?"

"How can you tell what I'm thinking? You aren't me."

"What do you mean, 'everybody' is like that? Do you mean your wife, your boss, or who?"

"Do you mean *all* women or just the women you have known?"

"What doesn't turn out right? What in particular?"

"Where, exactly, have such things happened to you? At home? At work?"

"Why does it surprise you that I like fish? *You* don't, but that doesn't mean *I* don't."

Communicating Skillfully

Can you identify situations in which you've communicated dysfunctionally? What happened? How might you have communicated more functionally in these situations?

Explaining Ideas

How would you describe dysfunctional communication in Internet chat groups? What are some of the more obvious types of dysfunctional chat-group communication? Can you provide specific examples?

"What do you mean by doing something the 'right' way? Do you mean *your* way, or what?"

9. Once the sender receives such requests to clarify and qualify, how does he respond to them?

a. If he is a functional communicator, he may say:

"Let me try to re-state that another way."

"Maybe I should give some examples."

"I operate from a certain assumption on this, I guess. Here's what I must be assuming …"

"I overgeneralized, didn't I? I'll try to pin that down a bit more."

"I'm giving my impression. Maybe you don't share it. How do you see it?"

Cultural Analysis

What added difficulties in verbal communication come into play when communication is intercultural? Can you create a real or hypothetical scenario to illustrate such difficulties?

b. If the original sender is a dysfunctional communicator, he can respond to requests to clarify or qualify in a multitude of different ways. But all these ways tend to shut out feedback from the other.

• He may openly rebuff such requests:

"You know perfectly well what I mean."

"I couldn't be any clearer."

"You heard me."

• He may restate his case without altering it:

"As I said, women are …"

• He may re-emphasize his case, without altering it:

"Women are not only X, they are also Y."

"That picture is not only ugly, it is positively revolting."

• He may accuse the questioner:

"Why get so 'picky'?"

"You don't understand plain language."

"Must you 'peel and shred'?"

• He may evade the questions.

10. If the original sender responds in a functional way to requests for clarification and qualification, then the receiver of his message has a better idea of what is being discussed. He may then say:

"Oh, that's what you meant! I misunderstood you."

"Well, we have different ideas about that. Let's see how we arrived at them."

"I don't share your experiences, I guess."

"Yes, I've had similar experiences, but I came to slightly different conclusions. Here's what I decided …"

"Maybe we are hung up on words. Here's what I mean by …"

11. If the sender had clarified and qualified his messages in the first place, the interchange would have had less chance of going awry. He might have said:

"Many people, at least the ones I have known, seem like that."

"This often happens to me, particularly at work."

"I find it hard to see how anyone could like fish. Maybe that's because I hate it."

"This way has worked for me. Maybe it would for you."

"I wouldn't *expect* him to want that. I wouldn't want it myself."

"I would call her selfish, but then she is probably different with other people. How is she with you?"

"To me, women are such and such. Do you agree?"

"I got the impression, from what you said, that you meant to do such and such. Did I size you up right?"

12. In summary, a person who communicates in a functional way can:

a. Firmly state his case,

b. yet at the same time clarify and qualify what he says,

c. as well as ask for feedback,

d. and be receptive to feedback when he gets it.

13. If verbal communication is to be reasonably clear, both the sender of a message and the receiver have the responsibility to make it so.

a. Mutual clarification and qualification cuts down on generalizations.

- It enables both parties to be specific and to give evidence for their assertions.

- It enables one person to check out his "reality" against the other person's "reality."

b. It also helps to separate the perceiver from what is being perceived.

- It cuts down on the tendency to project one's own wishes, thoughts, perceptions, onto others.

- It cuts down on the efforts of one person to speak for another.

14. Of course, none of us communicates this ideally or intellectually.

a. We all generalize when we communicate.

b. Anyone who perpetually clarified and qualified would seem just as dysfunctional as the person who rarely did so. He might even lead the receiver to wonder if there was anyone in the interaction to interact *with*.

c. A sender who perpetually asked a receiver for feedback would put himself

Ethical Judgments

Do you have an ethical obligation to make yourself and your messages clear to a listener? Is it unethical to be purposely indirect or ambiguous? For example, would it be unethical for you to talk in vague and ambiguous terms so as to prevent a reporter from uncovering potentially embarrassing personal information? Would it be unethical to talk in vague terms to prevent police from researching a crime about which you have knowledge, but don't want to discuss because you don't want to get involved?

in the position of being inundated by it and never formulating his own case.

d. A receiver who perpetually asked a sender to clarify would seem testy, uncooperative, and irritating.

15. Generalizations are dangerous, if overused, but they are also indispensable shortcuts.

a. They help us organize our experience.

b. They help us talk about a multitude of different observations all at once.

c. They free us from the necessity of evaluating every new event afresh.

d. Theory itself is a body of generalizations. As such, it has been a useful tool in all the sciences.

16. But the person who communicates dysfunctionally behaves as though he is not aware of the fact that he generalizes or that he operates from assumptions.

a. He rarely checks out or specifies how he or others are using words.

b. He overgeneralizes.

c. His communication techniques only serve to becloud meaning, and he seems to have no way to get back on the communication track when he gets off of it.

17. Dysfunc nal people also send incomplete messages.

a. They do not complete their sentences, but rely on the receiver to fill in:

"He isn't very ... *you* know."

"As you can see ... well, it's obvious."

b. They use pronouns vaguely. (Such communication problems repeatedly show up in family therapy.)

W: We went and so they got upset.

Th: Wait a minute. *Who* went *where? Who* got upset?

W: Oh, well, Harry and I went to his mother's house, see—Harry's mother's house. The kids wanted to go but Harry and I wanted to go alone. So the kids cried as we left the house.

c. They leave out whole connections in their messages.

Th: (to wife) I'm sorry I was late to our appointment today.

W: Oh that's all right. Mark was running around the block.

Filled in, such a message becomes:

Oh that's all right. My dog got out of the house (my dog's name is Mark) and was running around the block. I had to run after him. It took some time to catch him. So I was late to our appointment, too.

d. Often, they do not send a message at all but behave, in relation to others, as if they had. (This comes up repeatedly in therapy, and is usually related to an inside wish which never gets into words.)

M: They never help around the house.

Th: Now you mean the kids?

M: Yes.

Th: Have you told them what you want them to do?

M: Well, I think so. They're supposed to know.

Th: But have you *told* them?

M: Well, no.

W: We had no bread for dinner. He forgot.

Th: You mean your husband?

W: Yes.

Th: (to husband) Did you know that you were out of bread in the house?

H: No, heck no, I didn't....

Th: Do you remember her telling you?

H: No. No, she never told me. If I had known, I would have picked some up on the way home.

Th: Do you remember telling him that you were out of bread and asking him to pick some up?

W: Well, maybe I didn't. No, maybe I didn't. But you'd think he'd know.

e. Here is an example that also includes a tangle over the definition of a word:

H: She never comes up to me and kisses me. I am always the one to make the overtures.

Th: Is this the way you see yourself behaving with your husband?

W: Yes, I would say he is the demonstrative one. I didn't know he wanted me to make the overtures.

Th: Have you told your wife that you would like this from her—more open demonstration of affection?

H: Well, no, you'd think she'd know.

W: No, how would I know? You always said you didn't like aggressive women.

H: I don't, I don't like *dominating* women.

W: Well, I thought you meant women who make the overtures. How am I to know what you want?

Th: You'd have a better idea if he had been able to *tell* you.

18. As I said before, absolutely clear communication is impossible to achieve because communication is, by its very nature, incomplete. But there are degrees of incompleteness. The dysfunctional communicator leaves the receiver groping and guessing about what he has inside his head or heart.

a. He not only leaves the receiver groping and guessing; he operates from the assumption that he did, in fact, communicate.

b. The receiver, in turn, operates from what he guesses.

c. It is easy for them to misunderstand one another.

d. It is difficult for them to arrive at planned goals or outcomes.

e. People need to have a means for completing their communication as much as possible if they are going to arrive at successful joint outcomes, from accomplishing the mundane work of everyday life and seeing that the bread gets on the table, to being able to enjoy mutually satisfying sexual relationships.

Evaluating Ideas

How effectively does Satir explain dysfunctional communication? Do you have any questions about dysfunctional communication that Satir doesn't address? Try finding answers to your questions by reviewing the research recorded in *ERIC, Psychlit,* or *Sociofile* databases.

19. This is not to say that all incomplete messages are dysfunctional ones. They may be functional and amusing.

a. Codes, for instance, are intentionally incomplete messages.

- They represent shared shortcuts in meaning.
- People who share a code share something special together.

b. But the users of a code must be clear about its meaning. When they get off the communication track through using codes, they must be able to get back on the track by being able to determine when the game is over.

c. When people have shared experiences, they tend to condense many of them into codes. Therapists do this with patients. "Oh, that's all right, Mark was running around the block," became a code between the family and me, a code which I referred to when family members failed to complete their messages. I also used it to demonstrate that codes *can* be used functionally, if everyone concerned is clear about the meaning. This code got shortened to "Remember Mark" or even just "Mark."

d. There is a story about codes, which I often tell to patients when they get off the communication track with each other:

A reporter visited an old men's home and noticed a group of men sitting in the living room. One of the men said "27" and everyone went "ha ha ha." Then another said "15" and everyone went "ha ha ha." Then another said "36" and there was silence.

"What's going on here?" the reporter asked the director, who was showing him around. "You hear all these numbers and then everyone laughs."

"Oh," the director said, "you see, these men have been here for a long time and they know each other's jokes so well that instead of telling them over and over again, they just give the number."

"Well," the reporter asked, "what happened to number '36' then?"

"Oh that fellow!" the director answered, "He never *could* tell a joke."

3

How to Be Popular

In this article, Hara Estroff Marano identifies eight qualities that make people popular and argues that popularity is not something you're born with but something you have to learn.

Want to learn more? Two useful paths for becoming more popular are (1) understanding your own shyness and learning to deal with it and lessen it and (2) acquiring specific skills for communicating more confidently. To learn more about your own shyness see, for example, Virginia Richmond and James C. McCroskey, *Communication: Apprehension, Avoidance, and Effectiveness*, 5th ed. (Boston: Allyn & Bacon, 1998.) Also, look through the ERIC database for articles on "communication apprehension" and "shyness." To acquire some useful specific skills for communicating in social situations see, for example, Lillian Glass, *Attracting Terrific People: How to Find—and Keep—the People Who Bring Your Life Joy* (New York: St. Martin's Griffin, 1997) and Dianna Booher, *Communicate with Confidence: How to Say It Right the First Time and Every Time* (New York: McGraw-Hill, 1994).

If you were ever the last person picked for a team or asked to dance at a party, you've probably despaired that popular people are born with complete self-confidence and impeccable social skills. But over the past 20 years, a large body of research in the social sciences has established that what was once thought the province of manna or magic is now solidly our own doing—or undoing. Great relationships, whether friendships or romances, don't fall out of the heavens on a favored few. They depend on a number of very sophisticated but human-scale social skills. These skills are crucial to developing social confidence and acceptance. And it is now clear that everyone can learn them.

And they should. Recent studies illustrate that having social contact and friends, even animal ones, improves physical health. Social ties seem to impact stress hormones directly, which in turn affect almost every part of our body, including the immune system. They also improve mental health.

Hara Estroff Marano, "The Eight Habits of Highly Popular People," *Psychology Today* (January/February 2000), 40, 42, 43, 44, 78. Reprinted with permission from *Psychology Today*, Sussex Publishers, 1998.

Having large social networks can help lower stress in times of crisis, alleviate depression and provide emotional support.

Luckily, it's never too late to develop the tools of the socially confident. Research from social scientists around the world, including relationship expert John Gottman, Ph.D., and shyness authority Bernardo Carducci, Ph.D., show that the most popular people follow these steps to social success:

1. Schedule Your Social Life

It is impossible to hone your social skills without investing time in them. Practice makes perfect, even for the socially secure. Accordingly, the well-liked surround themselves with others, getting a rich supply of opportunities to observe interactions and improve upon their own social behaviors.

You need to do the same. Stop turning down party invitations and start inviting people to visit you at home. Plan outings with close friends or acquaintances you'd like to know better.

2. Think Positive

Insecure people tend to approach others anxiously, feeling they have to prove that they're witty or interesting. But self-assured people expect that others will respond positively—despite the fact that one of the most difficult social tasks is to join an activity that is already in progress.

3. Engage in Social Reconnaissance

Like detectives, the socially competent are highly skilled at information gathering, always scanning the scene for important details to guide their actions. They direct their focus outward, observing others and listening actively.

Socially skilled people are tuned in to people's expression of specific emotions, sensitive to signals that convey such information as what people's interests are, whether they want to be left alone or whether there is room in an activity for another person.

To infer correctly what others must be feeling, the socially confident are also able to identify and label their own experience accurately. That is where many people, particularly men, fall short.

Explaining Ideas

How would you explain "social reconnaissance"? Can you give specific examples of how social reconnaissance might be used by someone who has just started a new job or entered a new school?

Good conversationalists make comments that are connected to what is said to them and to the social situation. The connectedness of their communication is, in fact, one of its most outstanding features. Aggressive people actually make more attempts to join others in conversation but are less successful at it than the socially adept because they call attention to themselves, rather than finding a way to fit into ongoing group activity. They might throw out a statement that disrupts the conversation, or respond contentiously to a question. They might blurt something out about the way they feel, or shift the conversation to something of interest exclusively to themselves.

"You don't have to be interesting. You have to be interested," explains John Gottman, Ph.D., professor of psychology at the University of Washington. "That's how you have conversations."

4. Enter Conversations Gracefully

Timing is everything. After listening and observing on the perimeter of a group they want to join, the socially competent look for an opportunity to step in, knowing it doesn't just happen. It usually appears as a lull in the conversation.

Tuned in to the conversational or activity theme, the deft participant asks a question or elaborates on what someone else has already said. This is not the time to shift the direction of the conversation, unless it comes to a dead halt. Then it might be wise to throw out a question, perhaps something related to events of the day, and, if possible, something tangentially related to the recent discussion. The idea is to use an open-ended question that lets others participate. "Speaking of the election, what does everybody think about so-and-so's decision not to run?"

"People admire the person who is willing to take a risk and throw out a topic for conversation, but you have to make sure it has general appeal," says Bernardo Carducci, Ph.D., director of the Shyness Research Institute at Indiana University Southeast. Then you are in the desirable position of having rescued the group, which confers immediate membership and acceptance. Once the conversation gets moving, it's wise to back off talking and give others a chance. Social bores attempt to dominate a discussion. The socially confident know that the goal is to help the group have a better conversation.

5. Learn to Handle Failure

It is a fact of life that everyone will sometimes be rejected. Rebuffs happen even to popular people. What distinguishes the socially confident from mere mortals is their reaction to rejection. They don't attribute it to internal causes such as their own unlikability or inability to make friends. They assume it can result from many factors—incompatibility, someone else's bad mood, a misunderstanding. And some conversations are just private.

Self-assured people become resilient, using the feedback they get to shape another go at acceptance. Studies show that when faced with failure, those who are well-liked turn a negative response into a counterproposal. They say things like, "Well, can we make a date for next week instead?" Or they move onto another group in the expectation that not every conversation is closed.

And should they reject others' bids to join with them, they do it in a polite and positive way. They invariably offer a reason or counter with an alternative idea: "I would love to talk with you later."

6. Take Hold of Your Emotions

Social situations are incredibly complex and dynamic. One has to pay attention to all kinds of verbal and nonverbal cues, such as facial expression and voice tone, interpret their meaning accurately, decide on the best response for the scenario, and then carry out that response—all in a matter

Cultural Analysis

Did your culture teach you anything about "talking to strangers," "becoming popular," or "emphasizing the positive"?

Communicating Skillfully

You're with a group of close friends from one of your classes and you see another student from the class sitting alone, looking rather lonely. What might you do to make this other student feel more comfortable?

Communicating Skillfully

You see a few students from your interpersonal communication course talking in the cafeteria and, since you're new to the school and don't know anyone, you decide to join them. You approach them and cheerfully introduce yourself, "Hi, I'm Joe; I'm in your interpersonal class." In response, someone nods weakly, another smiles just barely, and the third continues talking totally ignoring your comment. What would you do?

Ethical Judgments

Do people have an ethical obligation to be inviting to others?

Cultural Analysis

Would these characteristics of popular people function differently in individualist cultures (cultures that stress the autonomy of the individual) and in collectivist cultures (cultures that stress the individual's responsibility to the group)? Would such characteristics be used differently in "masculine" cultures (cultures in which men are viewed as assertive and strong, and women are viewed as modest and tender) and "feminine" cultures (cultures in which both men and women are encouraged to be modest, oriented to the quality of life, and tender)?

Ethical Judgments

Can you identify examples of people trying to make themselves popular that you would consider unethical and that should be avoided on moral grounds?

Evaluating Ideas

Which one of these habits do you think will prove the most helpful to you personally?

of microseconds. No one can pay attention to or correctly interpret what is going on, let alone act skillfully, without a reasonable degree of control over their own emotional states, especially negative emotions such as anger, fear, anxiety—the emotions that usually arise in situations of conflict or uncertainty.

Recently, studies have found that people who are the most well-liked also have a firm handle on their emotions. It isn't that they internalize all their negative feelings. Instead, they shift attention away from distressing stimuli toward positive aspects of a situation. In other words, they have excellent coping skills. Otherwise, they become overly reactive to the negative emotions of others and may resort to aggression or withdraw from social contact.

7. Defuse Disagreements

Since conflict is inevitable, coping with confrontations is one of the most critical of social skills. It's not the degree of conflict that sinks relationships, but the ways people resolve it. Disagreements, if handled well, can help people know themselves better, improve language skills, gain valuable information and cement their relationships.

Instead of fighting fire with fire, socially confident people stop conflict from escalating; they apologize, propose a joint activity, make a peace offering of some kind, or negotiate. And sometimes they just change the subject. That doesn't mean that they yield to another's demands. Extreme submissiveness violates the equality basic to healthy relationships—and a sense of self-worth.

As people gain social competence, they try to accommodate the needs of both parties. Managing conflict without aggression requires listening, communicating—arguing, persuading—taking the perspective of others, controlling negative emotions, and problem solving. Researchers have found that when people explain their point of view in an argument, they are in essence making a conciliatory move. That almost invariably opens the door for a partner to offer a suggestion that ends the standoff.

8. Laugh a Little

Humor is the single most prized social skill, the fast track to being liked—at all ages. Humor works even in threatening situations because it defuses negativity. There's no recipe for creating a sense of humor. But even in your darkest moments, try to see the lighter side of a situation.

How to Assert Your Rights

In this article, Don Gabor discusses one of the most difficult types of interpersonal communication—namely, asserting your rights. Here Gabor discusses the values of assertiveness, provides an interesting self-assessment so you can evaluate your own tendency toward assertiveness, and offers a six-part strategy for becoming more assertive in your communications.

Want to learn more? If you enjoy this article try other paperback books by Gabor, for example, *How to Start a Conversation and Make Friends* (New York: Simon & Schuster [Fireside], 2001) and *How to Talk to the People You Love* (New York: Simon & Schuster [Fireside], 1989). If you want to learn more about assertiveness try Madelyn Burley-Allen's *Managing Assertively: How to Improve Your People Skills* (New York: Wiley, 1983) or Dena Michelli's *Successful Assertiveness* (Hauppauge, NY: Barron's Educational Series, 1997). You'll be able to find more recent works by visiting an online bookstore and requesting books on *assertive communication* or *assertiveness*. If you want to review research on assertiveness, the best online databases for this topic are *Psychlit, Sociofile,* and *ERIC*.

Are you a wimp when it comes to standing up to a conversational bully? Are you afraid to say no to even the most outlandish requests? Do you cringe at the thought of confronting someone who is making your life miserable? If you allow aggressive sales people, manipulative relatives, or hostile coworkers to take advantage of you, then it's time for you to learn how to tap the power of assertive communication skills.

What does it mean to be assertive? To begin with, this often misused term does *not* mean being aggressive. Speaking assertively means that you can make a positive statement or request and then be ready to respond to a possible objection, refusal, or disapproval from the listener. When you make an assertive statement, it suggests that you have high self-esteem, strong beliefs, and will assume personal responsibility for your words and actions. It is your assertiveness and persistence—*not* how aggressively you speak or act—that reflect your confidence.

What Can Assertive Communication Do for You?

Mastering the art of assertive communication can help you in many ways. You have your own goals, needs, and priorities, which may lead to conflict with others around you. Assertive communication allows people with different viewpoints and goals to minimize friction by reaching mutually acceptable compromises.

By using both assertiveness and tact in stressful conversations you can get your points across to others without resorting to shouting or insensitive comments. When you speak assertively, others are more likely to listen and respect your feelings, opinions, judgments, and viewpoints. Plus, they will be more open to changing their behavior or how they treat you.

As you may have guessed, assertiveness skills and self-esteem are closely linked. There is no doubt that your self-esteem suffers whenever your boss, coworkers, relatives, friends, or business associates coerce you into doing something you'd rather not do. On the other hand, your self-esteem and confidence increase when you assertively stand up for yourself—at home, at work, or in the business world.

How Assertive Are You?

Take this short quiz and find out. Use the scale below. Write 0, 1, 2, 3, or 4 in the space after each question, then total your score. See the evaluation at the end of the quiz to rate your assertiveness skills.

0 = Never   1 = Rarely   2 = Sometimes   3 = Frequently   4 = Always

1. Do you get tongue-tied or offended if someone questions your judgment, decisions, opinions, or feelings? _____

2. Do you let others take advantage of your good nature or make you feel guilty for not coming to their rescue? _____

3. Do you get stuck with unpleasant jobs at work because you're afraid to say no to your supervisor or coworkers? _____

4. Do you avoid making personal decisions or pursuing your dreams because you might be criticized by your friends or family? _____

5. Do salespeople talk you into purchasing products or services that you never planned on buying and don't really need? _____

6. Is it difficult for you to criticize other people's actions, even when they affect you adversely? _____

7. Do you avoid telling friends and family why you are angry? _____

8. Do you have difficulty expressing your opinions and feelings in groups or on a one-to-one basis? _____

9. Do you avoid complaining to managers about poor customers service in restaurants or other businesses? _____

10. Do you remain nearly silent in conversations so that you won't say the wrong thing or offend the other person? _____

Score:

0–10 YOUR ASSERTIVENESS SKILLS ARE EXCELLENT: Congratulations! You are a confident individual who knows how to stick up for yourself in any demanding conversation. Keep up the good work!

11–16 YOUR ASSERTIVENESS SKILLS ARE GOOD: All right! You are your own person most of the time, but you still allow yourself to be manipulated under more stressful circumstances.

17–25 YOUR ASSERTIVENESS SKILLS ARE FAIR: Not too bad! You speak your mind about half the time, but frequently think of what you could have said after the conversation is over.

26–34 YOUR ASSERTIVENESS SKILLS NEED MORE PRACTICE: You don't stand up for yourself enough. People know that if they push you long enough and hard enough, you'll cave in and do what they want. You need to use the power of persistence.

35–40 YOU NEED TO LEARN BASIC ASSERTIVENESS SKILLS: People see you as a pushover and take full advantage of you—only because you let them. You can change that perception if you make it your goal to become an assertive communicator.

Develop Assertiveness Skills at Any Stage of Your Life

Assertiveness skills are easy to learn and make a big difference in how you feel about yourself and how others treat you. After using the following six-step assertiveness strategy, take this quiz again and see how much better you do. It does take practice to become an assertive communicator, but the boost it gives your self-esteem makes it well worth the effort!

A Six-Step Assertiveness Strategy

The following six-step assertiveness strategy provides an example that shows how to handle a difficult conversation. Although all six steps are illustrated in this example, it is not always necessary to use all of them, and you can change the order to suit your own particular situation. Keep in mind, however, that it is vital to get to the "bottom line" of what you want to say *before* the other person pleads innocence, counterattacks, or changes the subject.

In addition, avoid starting the conversation if you sense that your emotions are bubbling just below the surface or you feel so angry, you are just waiting to explode. Instead of facing off in a verbal duel, take a short walk and spend several minutes breathing deeply to regain control of your feelings before approaching the other person. Even though you may still be angry or annoyed, speaking calmly improves your ability to communicate, encourages receptivity in others, and allows both of you to remain dignified and tactful.

Situation: You and a coworker share a ride to your place of employment. Your coworker is frequently not ready when you drive up to his house in the morning, and he is frequently late in picking you up for work. Your coworker's

> **Explaining Ideas**
>
> How would you explain the communication of some of the popular characters on television sitcoms in terms of assertiveness? (e.g., the characters from *Ally McBeal, The Practice, ER, NYPD Blue,* or *Friends*)? Who's the most assertive character on each of these shows? Who's the least assertive character? What specific communication patterns do these actors use that made you judge their characters as assertive or not assertive?

tardiness has caused you to be late several times, and today you got reprimanded by your boss. Yes, it does take courage to confront someone, so begin by reinforcing your right to address and resolve issues that affect you.

Step 1: Repeat Your Assertiveness Rights to Yourself
Before you confront your coworker, say the following to yourself:

"I have a right to think, feel, and the act the way I do."

"I have a right to change my mind."

"I have a right to be treated with respect."

"I have a right to say no."

"I have a right to act on my own behalf."

Step 2: Request a Private Moment
In a calm tone tell your coworker:

"I need to talk to you about a problem. Do you have a few minutes?"

Step 3: Briefly Describe the Problem Behavior
Continue talking in a firm, but friendly tone:

"I like sharing rides to work with you, but over the last few weeks, I've been late to work at least half a dozen times because either you haven't been ready to leave on time when I pick you up or you have arrived late when it's your turn to drive and pick me up."

Step 4: Say How the Problem Behavior Adversely Affects You
Stick to the point. Let the tone, not the volume, of your voice convey your concern. Say:

"Arriving twenty to thirty minutes late causes me major problems because it puts me behind schedule for the whole day. Plus, this morning my boss gave me an 'official warning,' as she put it, because I was late for the sixth time this month!"

Step 5: State What the Particular Behavior Is You Want to Change
Keep your voice firm and your body language open. Get to the bottom line and emphasize key words such as "leaving between seven-thirty and seven forty-five," "carpool with me," "not ready," and "getting to work on your own." Say:

"Maybe you're not worried about staying on good terms with your supervisor, but I am with mine. So, from now on, I'm LEAVING at our regular time— BETWEEN SEVEN-THIRTY AND SEVEN FORTY-FIVE A.M. If you still want to CARPOOL WITH ME, that's great, but if you're NOT READY to go by then, you can plan on GETTING TO WORK ON YOUR OWN."

Communicating Skillfully

Your boss at work consistently ignores your contributions at meetings. Comments that you made ten minutes earlier are responded to as wise and insightful when made by others, while your comments were listened to politely and ignored. At your next meeting you decide that you'll be more assertive. What specifically would you say?

Step 6: Repeat Your Position and Ask for a Response
Smile and gesture with your hands open, palms facing upward. Say:

"You know, I enjoy your company, but I can't afford to arrive late to work anymore. So what do you want to do—keep riding to work together or commute on our own?"

HANDLING RESISTANCE WITH THE "BROKEN RECORD" TECHNIQUE
Hopefully your coworker will agree to get his act together and be on time from now on. You must be prepared, however, for a more common response, such as feeble excuses, arguments, or accusations that attempt to minimize the situation. They might sound like this:

"Hey, I haven't been late all that many times!"

"I remember you were late once too!"

"We were stuck in traffic last week. You can't blame that one on me!"

"Your supervisor really has you under her thumb, doesn't she?"

"She's just trying to make you jump and let everyone know that she's in charge."

"It's just a lot of hot air. Don't worry about it."

"Tell her it's my fault and she'll let you off the hook."

"Don't be so paranoid! This job isn't that great anyhow."

Don't argue—simply repeat your bottom line like a "broken record." While you might be tempted to defend yourself against accusations such as ***"Why do you want to be on time? Are you bucking for a promotion?"*** your best bet is to use the highly effective "broken record" assertiveness strategy. This assertiveness skill consists of repeating more or less the same answer over and over again without further elaboration—like a broken record—until the other person accepts your position and deals with the issue. Keep your voice and body language friendly, but get to the point as quickly as you can. It might sound something like this:

"I can see how you might think that, but let me repeat what I said. From now on, I'm leaving at our regular time—between seven-thirty and seven forty-five a.m. If you still want to ride to work together, you're going to be ready to go by then or plan on getting to work on your own. So what do you want to do, keep riding to work together or commute on our own?"

WHEN SAYING NO ONCE, TWICE, OR EVEN THREE TIMES DOESN'T WORK You can use the "broken record" technique for rude people who do not know how to take no for an answer. Whether you are refusing food, alcohol, drugs, a date, or anything else, the "broken record" technique of saying no is very effective. Here is another example:

Him: *"Hi there. Hey, you need a drink!"*

Her: *"No, thank you. I don't care for anything to drink right now."*

Him: *"How about a wine cooler? They're really good!"*

Her: *"Thanks for asking, but I don't care for anything to drink right now."*

Him: *"Oh, come on. Here, take this beer."*

Her: *"No, thank you, I'd rather not. I don't care for anything to drink right now."*

Him: *"Why not, are you afraid you might like it?"*

Her: *"I just don't care for anything to drink right now. Do you have a problem with that?"*

Him: *"One lousy drink isn't going to hurt you. Come on, loosen up a little and have some fun!"*

Her: *"No, thanks. I really don't care for a drink right now."*

Him (frustrated): *"Well, then, I'm leaving!"*

Talk Assertively, Not Aggressively

Aggressive statements often contain criticisms and accusations, while assertive statements reveal a speaker's feelings and wishes. The following "Don't Say" examples are aggressive and can provoke arguments. If they are replaced by the more open-minded and assertive "Do Say" examples, there is a better chance that the listener will be more open and thus respond positively.

You Don't Say . . . Or Do You?

Don't Say ...	Do Say ...
"You should know how I feel."	*"I'm upset because...."*
"You shouldn't feel bad."	*"How do you feel about the situation now?"*
"Why do you always blame me when something goes wrong?"	*"I'd like to tell you my side of the story."*
"What makes you so smart?"	*"You've made a good point."*
"I told you so."	*"It could happen to anyone."*
"How could you be so stupid as to think that?"	*"I don't see the situation the way you do, but I respect your opinion."*

Some More Assertiveness Tips

Beware of always having to get your way. Flexibility and compromise are as important as assertiveness in any conversation. Say,

> *"I'm willing to talk about it."*

When someone attempts to control your behavior through guilt-inducing statements or threats, say,

> *"I do not respond to or appreciate this kind of manipulation."*

Evaluating Ideas

How useful do you think these six steps will be to enabling someone to become more assertive? Would you add or amend anything the author has said here?

Ethical Judgments

Is assertiveness always ethical? Can you identify specific examples of situations in which it would be unethical to be assertive? Try looking at this question from the point of view of both individualist cultures (where competition and individualism are emphasized) and collectivist cultures (where cooperation and group identity are emphasized). Would members of these cultures answer this question differently?

When someone asks you something and expects a quick response, give yourself a moment or two to gather your thoughts. Say,

> "*Let me think about what you've said for a moment before I give you my answer.*"

When you find yourself under pressure from someone asking you to do something you don't want to do, stand up straight, look him or her in the eye, and with a firm voice repeat as often as necessary:

> "*I understand what you are asking me to do, but the answer is no.*"

Begin your assertiveness training right now by repeating this statement to yourself several times a day:

> "*I have the right to think and feel the way I do, and if other people can't accept that, it's their problem, not mine!*"

Assertiveness Gets Results

You may be surprised to find out how effective assertiveness statements are—as long as you are fair and say them clearly and calmly. Most people feel embarrassed to hear that they were tactless or caused you a problem. If the other person cares about you at all, he or she will quickly apologize and bend over backward to make amends. When this happens, show that you know how to accept an apology and say,

> "*Thanks! I appreciate your listening to me. As far as I'm concerned, the case is closed.*"

Cultural Analysis

Does your culture have different rules of assertiveness for men and for women or are men and women expected to be similarly assertive or nonassertive? If your culture does have different rules, can you identify situations in which one sex is expected to be assertive and the other sex is expected to be unassertive?

5

How to Make the Right Impression

This lively article discusses self-presentation, the process by which you try to present a positive image to others. The article identifies several self-presentation strategies and offers a wealth of insights into how you can present a more positive, more attractive, more appealing image to others.

Want to learn more? See Edward E. Jones, *Interpersonal Perception,* (New York: Freeman, 1990) for a thorough and research-oriented look at how we perceive other people. The *Psychlit* database contains a wealth of research material on person perception.

Most of us care deeply about the way other people see us. The desire to create a positive impression, to present ourselves to advantage is almost universal. If we present ourselves successfully, not only will others think more positively of us, but ultimately, our self-image and self-esteem will also improve. Successful self-presentation will almost always be incorporated into our self-image: we become the people we make others think we are.

Self-presentation is a particularly important skill in modern industrialized societies. For most of our history, human beings have lived their entire lives within the confines of small, familiar groups, such as the extended family, the tribe or the village. There was little mobility, and most relationships lasted a lifetime. The emergence of industrialized mass societies during the past few hundred years, however, has created a very different social setting. In this "society of strangers" frequent, short and superficial encounters between people of no shared past or future are increasingly the norm. The ability to create a positive impression on strangers is thus of particular importance in this age, and is likely to play a growing role both in our working, and in our private lives.

Actors on a Stage

Just as professional actors prepare for their performances, learn their roles and use "props," people in everyday life seem to use similar skills to stage their self-presentations. This is suggested by the so-called "dramaturgical" model that has become influential in the study of self-presentation. According to this model, we prepare for our performances backstage (in our bathroom and in front of the mirror in the bedroom) the same way as actors do. We select our costumes for the day with no less care, and seek to convince our audience, be they friends or strangers, of our authenticity. Selecting a wallpaper, office decor or furniture for our house is similar to stagecraft: we aim to construct a stage for our social life. People also use a "mask" or "face," different from their private selves, to present themselves in public. Accent, dress, mannerisms, vocabulary can all be part of the "face" we present to the world.

The Skill of Self-Presentation

To fail in a performance leads to loss of face, which upsets the pattern of social intercourse. When somebody acts out of role, we no longer know what to expect. Tension and embarrassment result, and the painful silence, feeble joke or nervous laughter warn us that the predictable social order has broken down. Fortunately, most people learn their scripts well, and rarely act out of role. Psychologists call this skill "impression management." But we are not all equally good at presenting ourselves to advantage.

What does it take to be good at self-presentation? There are many people who seem never to lose their self-confidence, are always sociable and cheerful—but are they good impression managers? Not necessarily. In some situations, losing your temper or appearing helpless may be the most suitable strategy. Just like a skilled actor on stage, the expert impression manager must know his or her audience, be sensitive to the requirements of various social situations, and be able to judge a performance with some degree of detachment.

There are a number of psychological tests that measure these characteristics—the Self-Monitoring Scale, for example. People with high scores on this scale are better at assessing how others see their performances and are more skilled in changing their behavior to suit a particular audience or situation. For example, in one study some members of a discussion group were told that videotapes of their performances would be shown to members of the group, while others were told outsiders would see them. People who scored high on self-monitoring changed their performances to suit the expected audience, appearing friendly and likable for the in-group audience, and independent and nonconformist when expecting an outside audience. Low self-monitoring individuals failed to change their behavior to suit the situation.

Concern with effective self-presentation is by no means a recent phenomenon. In his classic work, *The Prince*, the Renaissance scholar Niccolo Machiavelli (1469–1527) offers detailed advice on how to develop strategic skills to influence people. Based on Machiavelli's ideas, modern psychologists have constructed a Machiavellianism scale to discriminate between

Brain Talk

One of the things we know about people perception is that the first impression is extremely lasting and often serves to filter later perceptions. So, if you make a good impression on first meeting, you're likely to continue to be seen in a favorable light. On the other hand, if you make a bad first impression, it will be difficult to undo. But, despite the popularity of this way of thinking, it isn't very logical. First impressions are often inaccurate and this inaccuracy will seriously distort your future perceptions of these individuals. For example, people are often nervous on a first meeting—a first date or an initial interview—and so may talk too much, fail to maintain eye contact, or laugh too much—all out of the increased anxiety accompanying initial interactions, which leads to atypical communication behavior. So, when evaluating people, ask yourself if you're being unduly influenced by first impressions. Ask yourself if your first impressions could have been in error. Ask yourself if your first meetings might have contributed to atypical behavior.

good and bad impression managers. The scale measures the extent to which a person views others and social situations with a degree of cool intellectual detachment and even skepticism.

Ethical Judgments

You're on a date with someone you really like and want to impress. Would it be ethical for you to: (1) Lie about your age? (2) Pretend to like your date's friends when you really can't stand them? (3) Dress in a way that your date would like but that really isn't you?

High scorers on this test were found to get the best deal for themselves when bargaining with others over the distribution of money, and were more successful in persuading a potential partner to go to a party with them. In one study, high and low scorers were given the task of disturbing a person allegedly taking a test, without appearing to do so. High scoring Machiavellians produced an ingenuous series of distractions, including whistling, pencil tapping, dissecting a ball-point pen, and "accidentally" knocking over a table, followed by loud and lengthy apologies. Machiavellianism can also be measured in children: for a financial reward, 10-year-old Machiavellians did far better than low scorers in convincing other children to eat several bitter-tasting cookies soaked in quinine, while appearing more innocent in doing so.

It seems that detachment, the ability to see ourselves as others will, is an important characteristic of the good impression manager. Most of the time, we are preoccupied with our environment and are not consciously aware of ourselves as others might see us.

In some situations, however, we are forced to become aware of ourselves in a different way: we come to think of ourselves as we appear to others—for example, when somebody points a camera at us, when we see ourselves on a videotape, or when we see our image in a mirror. Several studies have shown that when people are made to look at themselves in this way their thinking and actions change. They become more dependent on the "outside" view of themselves. Clearly, self-presentation should be more effective when we are consciously aware of how we appear to others.

Playing for an Audience

Generally, people tend to like people who are similar to themselves, particularly in the early stages of a relationship. A good manager can create a more positive image by adjusting self-presentation to match the characteristics of the audience. We tend to present a more modest, quiet image to a person who is an introvert, and will appear more confident and assertive to an extroverted and dominant partner. Research has shown that people will even modify deeply held political convictions to fit in with the expected attitudes of an audience.

The extent to which we match a person's opinions in our self-presentations largely depends on how much interest we have in our partner. In an interesting experiment, single, female, unattached university students matched the opinions of a male conversation partner on such issues as women's roles only if the partner was highly desirable (a tall, older, unattached student from a prestigious university). In identical conditions, no opinion matching occurred when the partner was less desirable (a younger, small student from a lesser university, with a girlfriend). Indeed, if we positively dislike a person who happens to express opinions and ideas similar to our own, we may end up changing our existing attitudes just to distance ourselves.

In general, skilled impression management involves behaving in ways that match the actions and attitudes of people we like, and esteem, but contrast with those of people we dislike. The commercial implications of this common strategy are not lost on advertisers. Images of very popular people such as sportsmen or film stars drinking a particular brand of beer or using a certain brand of shampoo are expected to create a consumer desire.

The Need for Consistency

A very important requirement for successful self-presentation is that we project a consistent image over time. Once we have established a public "face," there is a strong tendency to live up to that image. Indeed, people will often go to extraordinary lengths to remain consistent with their projected image, a need that is sometimes exploited by salesmen and advertisers.

A good example is the well-known "foot-in-the-door" technique. Once a salesman persuades you to do him a small and reasonable favor (for example, give him a glass of water or allow the use of your telephone), you have been manipulated into presenting yourself as a helpful and friendly person. It will now be much more difficult to refuse a later and less reasonable request like buying an expensive encyclopedia than it would be without the initial small favor. The deeply felt need to remain consistent with a previous self-presentation, to live up to what others expect of us is a powerful factor in impression management.

Another commercial ploy capitalizing on the need for consistency in self-presentation is the so-called "low-ball" technique much beloved by used car dealers. This involves manipulating a potential customer into a commitment to purchase—for example, by making an unrealistically good trade-in offer. Once the commitment to buy is made, the terms are renegotiated. For example, the salesman comes back with the news that the trade-in was not approved by the boss.

There will now be a powerful need to remain consistent with the initial decision, even though you would not have made a deal on the terms now offered. To be seen by others as vacillating, inconsistent, and unpredictable is perhaps the most damaging impression one can create. Few things are as threatening in social life.

Ingratiation

Although the term ingratiation is often used in a rather pejorative sense, most self-presentation and impression management strategies involve some degree of it. It simply means consciously trying to win favor, and we do it because we need to be liked and accepted, because we hope to gain something by it or as a protection against harm or danger. To avoid our motives being too transparent, complex and subtle methods of impression manage-

Communicating Skillfully

You're an attorney defending two parents against charges of murder in the second degree. Your clients face a possible sentence of 15–30 years in prison for causing the suffocation death of their two infant children by leaving them locked in a car on a hot day while they went to the movies. You decide to have your clients testify on their own behalf. What self-presentation advice would you give them?

Communicating Skillfully

You want to get a date with an attractive person who is taking some of the same classes you are. To increase your chances of success, you decide to use the four ingratiation strategies discussed here: express flattery, conform to the other person's opinion, make sure that your good points are noticed, and do favors for the person. Remembering that if you're too obvious these strategies are not going to work, what types of things would you say as you go about using ingratiation to get this date?

Cultural Analysis

What did your culture teach you about the need for esteem and approval? Are people who are in need of others' approval viewed negatively?

ment are required. For example, it may be effective to criticize someone on minor points and to praise them on major issues: this is less suspect than indiscriminately praising them and flattering them.

Four basic strategies are used in ingratiation. These are: flattery; conforming to the other person's opinion; making sure that they see your good points; doing favors. Both high- and low-status people use ingratiating strategies—often seeking no more than to be liked. Low-status people are likely to flatter another. High-status people put forward their good points and conform to the other's opinions.

The Need for Esteem and Approval

People differ greatly in how much they need and seek the approval of others. Our basic attitudes toward other people are formed in childhood and adolescence, and tend to remain with us for most of our lives. Firstborn children tend to remain more dependent on others for social support throughout their lives than do later-born children. The extent to which a person needs approval from others can be measured, using the Social Desirability Scale.

Two kinds of statement make up the scale: those about highly desirable characteristics which in fact are rarely lived up to by most people (e.g., "I never tell a lie") and those about undesirable characteristics which are nevertheless quite common ("I sometimes get angry and resentful when I don't get my way"). People who have a high need for approval tend to agree with the first kind of statement, and not with the second. In effect, they claim for themselves socially desirable characteristics even when the likelihood of this being truthful is rather low.

Is there a relationship between a person's need for approval and their ability to present themselves in a favorable light? Not necessarily. In fact, it seems that people with a high need for approval are usually also more afraid of being rejected. They tend not to initiate interaction with others, and are quiet and conformist in groups.

Public and Private Selves: Are They Linked?

By definition, self-presentation means trying to influence public perceptions. Does it also have an effect on the way we see ourselves? What exactly is the relationship between the images we present to others, and our self-image?

People often assume that their self-image is a stable, enduring entity. In reality, self-perception is intricately related to how *others* see us. Our self-image is a social creation important to the extent that it differentiates us from others, and is accepted by others.

Even other primates seem to possess a rudimentary self-image, which can only emerge as a result of intensive exposure to others.

In the course of our encounters with others, we try out various ways of presenting ourselves. The most successful presentations will eventually become part of our self-image—we slowly become what others think we are, the role turns into reality. Self-presentation thus determines not only how others will see us, but ultimately, also influences how we come to see ourselves.

Several experiments illustrate the way successful self-presentations are incorporated into our self-image. In one study, subjects were told to try to make a positive public impression of themselves on a partner, who was in fact a confederate of the experimenter.

The impressions were accepted and reinforced in half of the cases but rejected in the other half. Afterwards, subjects who were "successful" in making a good impression were much more likely than unsuccessful subjects to claim that their public presentation was consistent with their true self-image.

Other evidence suggests that people who see themselves as having a particular characteristic as part of their self-image also believe that others see them in this way, and in fact they do receive high ratings from their friends and acquaintances on precisely these traits.

Nor is self-image very stable over time. Our perceptions of ourselves can change quite rapidly, depending on the social situation we find ourselves in, and the characteristics of others we compare ourselves with. One intriguing study showed that a person's self-esteem can undergo a major change within the span of less than an hour.

Subjects in this study first completed a self-assessment questionnaire, allegedly as part of an interview for a part-time job. Soon after, a second "applicant" for the job (in fact, a confederate of the experimenter) arrived, who had either very desirable qualities (well dressed, carrying books on philosophy and science, well prepared with sharpened pencils for the test), or had very undesirable qualities (wearing worn and dirty clothes, no socks, disoriented and unprepared for the test).

After the arrival of the second applicant, the subjects' self-esteem was again assessed as part of a second questionnaire. Those who met the desirable candidate now rated their self-esteem significantly lower, while subjects who met the undesirable candidate now thought much more highly of themselves.

This study illustrates that our self-image is relatively volatile, and largely depends on the qualities of others with whom we compare ourselves. Positive self-presentation increases our standing compared with others, and thus improves our relative self-image as well.

Ethical Judgments

What types of self-presentation messages on the Internet, especially in chat groups, would you consider unethical? What specific behaviors—online or in face-to-face interaction—make self-presentation unethical?

6

How to Understand Another Person's Understanding

In this article, the authors discuss the processes behind perception and apply these to conversations you might find difficult. Their entire book is well worth reading; it will provide you with a wealth of insights into all sorts of conversations, but especially those you might find difficult.

Want to learn more? Useful works here are Chris L. Kleinke's *Meeting and Understanding People* (New York: Freeman, 1986); T. Schick, Jr. and L. Vaughn's *How to Think About Weird Things* (Mountain View, CA: Mayfield, 1995); and R. E. Ornstein, *On The Experience of Time* (Boulder, CO: Westview Press, 1998). Each of these provides a different and unique perspective on perception.

As we move away from arguing and toward trying to understand the other person's story, it helps to know why people have different stories in the first place. Our stories don't come out of nowhere. They aren't random. Our stories are built in often unconscious but systematic ways. First, we take in information. We experience the world—sights, sounds, and feelings. Second, we interpret what we see, hear, and feel; we give it all meaning. Then we draw conclusions about what's happening. And at each step, there is an opportunity for different people's stories to diverge.

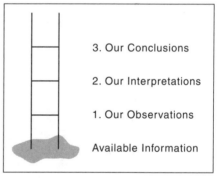

FIGURE 6.1 Where Our Stories Come From

Put simply, we all have different stories about the world because we each take in different information and then interpret this information in our own unique ways.

Douglas Stone, Bruce M. Patton, and Sheila Heen, "Different Stories: Why We Each See the World Differently," in *Difficult Conversations: How to Discuss What Matters Most* (New York: Viking, 1999), pp. 30–37. Used by permission of Viking Penguin, a division of Penguin Putnam, Inc.

In difficult conversations, too often we trade only conclusions back and forth, without stepping down to where most of the real action is: the information and interpretations that lead each of us to see the world as we do.

1. We Have Different Information

There are two reasons we all have different information about the world. First, as each of us proceeds through life—and through any difficult situation—the information available to us is overwhelming. We simply can't take in all of the sights, sounds, facts, and feelings involved in even a single encounter. Inevitably, we end up noticing some things and ignoring others. And what we each choose to notice and ignore will be different. Second, we each have access to different information.

We Notice Different Things.   Doug took his four-year-old nephew, Andrew, to watch a homecoming parade. Sitting on his uncle's shoulders, Andrew shouted with delight as football players, cheerleaders, and the school band rolled by on lavish floats. Afterward Andrew exclaimed, "That was the best truck parade I've ever seen!"

Each float, it seems was pulled by a truck. Andrew, truck obsessed as he was, saw nothing else. His Uncle Doug, truck indifferent, hadn't noticed a single truck. In a sense, Andrew and his uncle watched completely different parades.

Like Doug and Andrew, what we notice has to do with who we are and what we care about. Some of us pay more attention to feelings and relationships. Others to status and power, or to facts and logic. Some of us are artists, others are scientists, others pragmatists. Some of us want to prove we're right; others want to avoid conflict or smooth it over. Some of us tend to see ourselves as victims, others as heroes, observers, or survivors. The information we attend to varies accordingly.

Of course, neither Doug nor Andrew walked away from the parade thinking, "I enjoyed my particular perspective on the parade based on the information I paid attention to." Each walked away thinking, "I enjoyed *the* parade." Each assumes that what he paid attention to was what was significant about the experience. Each assumes he has "the facts."

In a more serious setting, Randy and Daniel, coworkers on an assembly line, experience the same dynamic. They've had a number of tense conversations about racial issues. Randy, who is white, believes that the company they work for has a generally good record on minority recruitment and promotion. He notices that of the seven people on his assembly team, two are African Americans and one is Latino, and that the head of the union is Latino. He has also learned that his supervisor is originally from the Philippines. Randy believes in the merits of a diverse workplace and has noticed approvingly that several people of color have recently been promoted.

Daniel, who is Korean American, has a different view. He has been on the receiving end of unusual questions about his qualifications. He has experienced several racial slurs from coworkers and one from a foreman. These experiences are prominent in his mind. He also knows of several minority coworkers who were overlooked for promotion, and notices that a disproportionate number of the top executives at the company are white. And Daniel has listened repeatedly to executives who talk as if the only two racial categories that mattered were white and African American.

While Randy and Daniel have some information that is shared, they have quite a bit of information that's not. Yet each assumes that the facts are plain, and his view is reality. In an important sense, it's as if Randy and Daniel work at different companies.

Often we go through an entire conversation—or indeed an entire relationship—without ever realizing that each of us is paying attention to different things, that our views are based on different information.

We Each Know Ourselves Better Than Anyone Else Can. In addition to *choosing* different information, we each have *access* to different information. For example, others have access to information about themselves that we don't. They know the constraints they are under; we don't. They know their hopes, dreams, and fears; we don't. We act as if we've got access to all the important information there is to know about them, but we don't. Their internal experience is far more complex than we imagine.

Let's return to the example of Jack and Michael. When Michael describes what happened, he doesn't mention anything about Jack's staying up all night. He might not know that Jack stayed up all night, and even if he does, his "knowledge" would be quite limited compared to what Jack knows about it. Jack was there. Jack knows what it felt like as he struggled to stay awake. He knows how uncomfortable it was when the heat was turned off at midnight. He knows how angry his wife was that he had to cancel their dinner together. He knows about the anxiety he felt putting aside other important work to do Michael's project. Jack also knows how happy he felt to be doing a favor for a friend.

And there is plenty that Jack is not aware of. Jack doesn't know that Michael's client blew up just that morning over the choice of photograph in another brochure Michael had prepared. Jack doesn't know that the revenue figures are a particularly hot topic because of questions about some of the client's recent business decisions. Jack doesn't know that Michael's graphic designer has taken an unscheduled personal leave in the midst of their busiest season, affecting not just this project but others as well. Jack doesn't know that Michael has been dissatisfied with some of Jack's work in the past. And Jack doesn't know how happy Michael felt to be doing a favor for a friend.

Of course, in advance, we don't know what we don't know. But rather than assuming we already know everything we need to, we should assume that there is important information we don't have access to. It's a good bet to be true.

Communicating Skillfully

Let's assume you see Randy and Daniel arguing about racial discrimination on the job, which, as illustrated in the article, they see very differently. If you were a third party to this discussion, what would you say to help Randy see Daniel's viewpoint? What would you say to help Daniel see Randy's viewpoint?

Explaining Ideas

How would you explain the difficulties in achieving accurate perception of another person when your communication is totally through e-mail or chat groups? How do these difficulties compare with the difficulties of achieving accurate perception in face-to-face interactions?

2. We Have Different Interpretations

"We never have sex," Alvie Singer complains in the movie *Annie Hall*. "We're constantly having sex," says his girlfriend. "How often do you have sex?" asks their therapist. "Three times a week!" they reply in unison.

A second reason we tell different stories about the world is that, even when we have the same information, we interpret it differently—we give it different meaning. I see the cup as half empty; you see it as a metaphor for the fragility of humankind. I'm thirsty; you're a poet. Two especially important factors in how we interpret what we see are (1) our past experiences and (2) the implicit rules we've learned about how things should and should not be done.

We Are Influenced by Past Experiences. The past gives meaning to the present. Often, it is only in the context of someone's past experience that we can understand why what they are saying or doing makes any kind of sense.

To celebrate the end of a long project, Bonnie and her coworkers scraped together the money to treat their supervisor, Caroline, to dinner at a nice restaurant. Throughout the meal, Caroline did little but complain: "Everything is overpriced," "How can they get away with this?" and "You've got to be kidding. Five dollars for dessert!" Bonnie went home embarrassed and frustrated, thinking, "We knew she was cheap, but this is ridiculous. We paid so she wouldn't have to worry about the money, and still she complained about the cost. She ruined the evening."

Though the story in Bonnie's head was that Caroline was simply a cheapskate or wet blanket, Bonnie eventually decided to ask Caroline why she had such a strong reaction to the expense of eating out. Upon reflection, Caroline explained:

> I suppose it has to do with growing up during the Depression. I can still hear my mother's voice from when I was little, getting ready to go off to school in the morning. "Carrie, there's a nickel on the counter for your lunch!" she'd call. She was so proud to be able to buy my lunch every day. Once I got to be eight or nine, a nickel wasn't enough to buy lunch anymore. But I never had the heart to tell her.

Years later, even a moderately priced meal can feel like an extravagance to Caroline when filtered through the images and feelings of this experience.

Every strong view you have is profoundly influenced by your past experiences. Where to vacation, whether to spank your kids, how much to budget for advertising—all are influenced by what you've observed in your own family and learned throughout your life. Often we aren't even aware of how these experiences affect our interpretation of the world. We simply believe that this is the way things are.

We Apply Different Implicit Rules. Our past experiences often develop into "rules" by which we live our lives. Whether we are aware of them or not, we all follow such rules. They tell us how the world works, how people should act, or how things are supposed to be. And they have a significant in-

Brain Talk

Because your own physiological and psychological states influence what your senses pick up and the meaning you give to your perceptions, be especially alert to how your own feelings may be influencing what you think you're seeing. The neighbor that appears to be annoying when you're busy and behind schedule may be seen as warm and friendly when you're lonely and feeling down. Similarly, your biases and stereotypes will influence your perceptions, leading you to see, for example, only the positive in people you like and only the negative in people you dislike. Beware of this self-influence when you make judgments about people; ask yourself to what extent you're influencing what you see or hear.

fluence on the story we tell about what is happening between us in a difficult conversation.

We get into trouble when our rules collide.

Ollie and Thelma, for example, are stuck in a tangle of conflicting rules. As sales representatives, they spend a lot of time together on the road. One evening, they agreed to meet at 7:00 the next morning in the hotel lobby to finish preparing a presentation. Thelma, as usual, arrived at 7:00 sharp. Ollie showed up at 7:10. This was not the first time Ollie had arrived late, and Thelma was so frustrated that she had trouble focusing for the first twenty minutes of their meeting. Ollie was frustrated that Thelma was frustrated.

It helps to clarify the implicit rules that each is unconsciously applying. Thelma's rule is "It is unprofessional and inconsiderate to be late." Ollie's rule is "It is unprofessional to obsess about small things so much that you can't focus on what's important." Because Thelma and Ollie both interpret the situation through the lens of their own implicit rule, they each see the other person as acting inappropriately.

Our implicit rules often take the form of things people "should" or "shouldn't" do: "You should spend money on education, but not on clothes." "You should never criticize a colleague in front of others." "You should never leave the toilet seat up, squeeze the toothpaste in the middle, or let the kids watch more than two hours of TV." The list is endless.

There's nothing wrong with having these rules. In fact, we need them to order our lives. But when you find yourself in conflict, it helps to make your rules explicit and to encourage the other person to do the same. This greatly reduces the chance that you will be caught in an accidental duel of conflicting rules.

3. Our Conclusions Reflect Self-Interest

Finally, when we think about why we each tell our own stories about the world, there is no getting around the fact that our conclusions are partisan, that they often reflect our self-interest. We look for information to support our view and give that information the most favorable interpretation. Then we feel even more certain that our view is right.

Professor Howard Raiffa of the Harvard Business School demonstrated this phenomenon when he gave teams of people a set of facts about a company. He told some of the teams they would be negotiating to buy the company, and others that they would be selling the company. He then asked each team to value the company as objectively as possible (not the price at which they would offer to buy or sell, but what they believed it was actually worth). Raiffa found that sellers, in their heart of hearts, believed the company to be worth on average 30 percent more than the independently assessed fair market value. Buyers, in turn, valued it at 30 percent less.

Each team developed a self-serving perception without realizing they were doing so. They focused more on things that were consistent with what

Cultural Analysis

How do your specific cultural beliefs, attitudes, and values influence how you view the following celebrations: (1) Dick and Jane, both in their late 30's, are getting married—he for the 5th time and she for the 4th time. They each have children from previous relationships, some of the children will live with Dick and Jane and some will live with previous partners. (2) Bob and Tom, an interracial gay couple, are planning a big party to celebrate being together for 40 years. The party will be held at the church recreation hall.

they wanted to believe and tended to ignore, explain away, and soon forget those that weren't. Our colleague Roger Fisher captured this phenomenon in a wry reflection on his days as a litigator: "I sometimes failed to persuade the court that I was right, but I never failed to persuade myself!"

This tendency to develop unconsciously biased perceptions is very human, and can be dangerous. It calls for a dose of humility about the "rightness" of our story, especially when we have something important at stake.

Communicating Skillfully

Using the concepts developed in this article, consider the case of Margaret and Jim who argue constantly about Jim's not doing any of the household chores, such as shopping, cooking, cleaning, and ironing. As a result, Margaret not only works full time but does all the household chores herself. Jim's response is that he does his share by making enough money to hire household help. Margaret, he argues, is too cheap and too fussy to have any one else work in the house. That, he says, is Margaret's problem, not his. If you were asked to mediate this dispute, what would you say to Margaret? To Jim?

7

How to Listen More Effectively

In this article, Morey Stettner clearly identifies several important listening distortions that can interfere with effective interpersonal communication. As you read this article, try to visualize an example from your own experience in which each of the distortions discussed occurred.

Want to learn more? Useful books for improving listening include Kevin J. Murphy, *Effective Listening* (New York: Bantam Books, 1987); Madelyn Burley-Allen, *Listening: The Forgotten Skill*, 2nd ed. (New York: Wiley, 1995); and Michael P. Nichols, *The Lost Art of Listening* (New York: Guilford Press, 1995). Also, consider visiting the International Listening Association's Web site at http://www.listen.org to learn what professionals in the field of listening do.

Ever play "Telephone"? In this popular summer-camp game, a message is whispered from player to player until it reaches the last person. Inevitably, the message gets twisted to the point where it loses all traces of its original meaning.

Same thing happens in real life. From idle gossip to talking "on the record" with journalists, conversations are rarely reported faithfully as they travel from person to person. Instead, each individual who relays the comment changes a few words or adds a new idea. This does not mean that people intentionally distort what they hear and pass along incorrect information to others. As much as we may try to summarize what we hear Norm say and express it accurately to Joe a few minutes or hours later, we are unable to function like tape recorders. We cannot reproduce Norm's exact message at will.

Even if we do not need to report a conversation to someone else at a later time, we still might distort what a speaker tells us. At any moment, whether at home or at work, our listening skills can fail us. We can end a conversation *thinking* we know what was said, but actually capturing the wrong message. We then draw conclusions and make recommendations based on faulty data.

Winning people over is hard enough without subverting what they're trying to say. I know a conspiracy theorist who thrives on twisting around

---

Morey Stettner, Listening Distortions, from *The Art of Winning Conversation* (Englewood Cliffs, NJ: Prentice-Hall, 1995), pp. 199–213. Copyright © 1995. Reprinted with permission of Prentice Hall Direct.

what he hears to fit his preconceived notions. No matter what topic you discuss with him, from American aid to a developing country to national health care, he suspects a conspiracy. Rather than taking at face value what others say, he says he tries "to find a conspiracy in everything." He distorts what he hears to match his view of the world.

Even if we resist the urge to mangle others' remarks to fit our own beliefs, we remain susceptible to distortions when we want to talk about ourselves. If we want to brag about an accomplishment, for example, we await a conversational opening to announce the big news. We may feel it is bad form to simply blurt out *I got a raise today* or *The committee accepted my proposal.* We wish that the other person would ask us about our day, but that does not happen. So we listen half-heartedly until we hear something that in some way relates to what we want to say. If a friend discusses *her* job, we jump in about *our* promotion.

Memory Jogger

When you can barely contain your excitement about something and you cannot wait to talk about it, then you are prone to distort what others say until you get your chance to speak.

Three Examples of How Distortions Block Clear Communication

Poor listening habits result in misunderstandings and lost opportunities to win people over. Distortions threaten to disrupt almost every interaction, as illustrated in these examples:

- Tammy has dated Gary for two years. Eager to get married, she frequently tells Gary about her friends who have married and how happy they are ("They both said that if they knew marriage was this great, they would've done it a year ago rather than waited"). It's her way of hinting to Gary about their wonderful future together. Gary, on the other hand, dismisses Tammy's repeated comments about marriage as part of what he thinks is her tendency to romanticize the lives of others and inflate their happiness ("You always want what you don't have"). As a result, Tammy keeps bringing up marriage, and Gary keeps ignoring her.

> **Ethical Judgments**
> Would it be ethical if Tammy was using indirectness to manipulate Gary and make him think eventually that marriage was his idea? Is Gary ethical in ignoring Tammy's underlying message that, we can assume, he fully understands?

- Tom, a vice-president at a property-management firm, works for Stan, the president of the company. Stan tells Tom to try to double the number of clients who use the firm's services. Tom, who is closer to the day-to-day operations of the organization, knows that the thin support staff is already overworked and cannot process a wave of new business. So he tries to tell his boss, albeit indirectly, that in order for the company to properly service new clients, they must first hire more staff. "I'll work with personnel to beef up our back office to get ready for the expansion of business," Tom says. Stan shoots back, "No, don't worry about hiring more people now. Do as I said and bring me more paying customers." Stan hears Tom's comment and thinks his vice-president is noncompliant. Stan does not realize that Tom intends to generate more clients as soon as he feels internal staffing needs are met.

- Denise seeks her father's approval, but she rarely gets it. After graduating from high school with honors and giving the valedictory speech, she approaches her father after the ceremony. He says, "What a special day." She replies, "Oh, Daddy, I'm so happy I could make your day special." Denise hears her father say, "You made this day special for me," but her father was making a general comment about the event.

These examples expose some of the underlying dangers of distortion. First, it becomes harder to persuade others when we falsely interpret their remarks to make ourselves feel better. Denise craves recognition from her father, so she considers his statement "What a special day" as praise for her achievements. Stan, who is used to barking out orders and having his underlings follow them, hears Tom's response as different from what he wanted to hear ("Sure, boss, I'll get right on it"). When we are overeager to hear what we want to hear, conditions are ripe for distortions to take hold.

It also becomes apparent from the preceding examples that indirect communication may lead to trouble. Tammy wants to get married, but she resists having a heart-to-heart talk with Gary about her feelings. Instead, she resorts to hinting (which he perceives not as hinting but as part of her pattern of romanticizing others). Tom feels that his boss has overlooked the need to hire more staff. Instead of expressing his opinion, however, he angers the president by not playing the "yes man" role.

Finally, Gary, Stan, and Denise remind us that we tend to listen based on our own frame of reference, not the speaker's. Distortions often result when we assume that we know why a speaker says something. We read between the lines of a conversation and conclude that we know the "real reason" that led the speaker to speak. The most astute persuaders know how to listen (free from distortions) by stepping into the speaker's world and adopting the speaker's frame of reference.

Communicating Skillfully

What would you tell Tammy if she told you of her frustration with Gary? What would you tell Gary if he told you of his frustration with Tammy?

Preventing Distortions by Listening For the True Message

So what can we do to steer clear of distortions when we listen?

If we seek to persuade with consistency, we need to accurately listen and retain what's said. A message gets distorted because we do not soak up what we hear in an unbiased, nonjudgmental frame of mind. Our fears, anxieties, and prejudices get in the way. Or we want to hear something so badly that we overlay our own preferred version of what was said on the actual words coming out of the speaker's mouth!

Most of us realize we have something to lose when we listen. Our ego and self-esteem are on the line. We might be criticized, ignored, or insulted. Some people find that the more they fish for compliments, the less they find. The more they crave approval, the more they are greeted with disapproval.

No wonder we misinterpret what we hear: We are trying to preserve our fragile sense of self.

Memory Jogger

The more you want a speaker to say something specific (from *I love you* to *Yes, I'll buy from you*), the more likely you will listen with rigidity. Keep an open mind and be prepared to accept whatever someone tells you, even if it's not exactly what you want to hear.

To combat distortions, you must take preventive steps to ensure that you listen for the true message. This means learning to absorb all types of comments, even the ones that do not immediately captivate you. A friend of mine loves to discuss baseball. No matter what you say, he'll relate it to base hits, home runs, and pitch-outs. As he readily admits, he has trouble listening to what people actually tell him *on their terms* because he's so busy trying to connect it to his favorite topic. He bores easily when the topic strays far from baseball.

Memory Jogger

When we insist on adding our own "spin" to everything we hear, we lose the capacity to fairly comprehend what others say.

We also need to identify the times when distortions arise. For example, many people find it tough to listen in a large group or during an early morning meeting. We have already noted how hard it is to hear what you do not want to hear. By knowing what situations pose the greatest difficulty, you can bring the full force of your communication skills to work for you when you need them most.

As you gain awareness of how distortions interfere with your listening, you can develop strategies to overcome them. Distortions usually occur when we let our guard down and fail to concentrate. If you do not give a speaker your undivided attention, then your chances of persuading that person plummet.

We may find ourselves trying to listen and persuade despite suffering from mood swings, nagging preoccupations, or lingering worries. If you are too distracted to listen well, then you should either postpone the conversation to another time or muster enough discipline to shove aside your distractions for the greater good of engaging in pure communication.

Whatever you do, don't lapse into sloppy habits out of laziness. Take charge of your conversations. If you are unwilling or unable to listen free from distortions, then do something to correct the problem. That's what this chapter is all about.

We will examine the three most common distortions—*exaggeration, leveling,* and *erasing*—and then present solutions that allow us to listen accurately and receptively all the time.

Brain Talk

Listening critically depends, in part, on assessing the truth and accuracy of the information and the honesty and motivation of the message sender. Ask yourself if what the speaker says is the truth as far as you understand it? Has the speaker presented the information in enough detail? Is the speaker being honest? Is the speaker's motivation self-gain?

Exaggeration: Blowing Up a Message and Missing the Point

Exaggeration falsely inflates the importance of a message by intensifying it. This usually happens when a comment strikes a chord and we dwell on it or enlarge its meaning. The result? We focus on something the speaker said even as the speaker proceeds to cover other points. Examples:

- A friend mentions a summer cabin that he has already paid for but cannot use. You home in on that cabin ("How can I get the keys?") while your friend continues to discuss other vacation plans.

- A colleague who suggests a product innovation wants your "buy in" when telling you about the plan. You respond, "Sounds good." Your colleague, suffering from a severe case of exaggeration, hears instead, "What an excellent idea. I'll help you sell it to upper management."

- A teacher opens the class by promising to "return your exams today." You are so eager to see your score that you cannot concentrate on anything else the instructor says. So when the teacher adds, "I've decided not to count your exams toward your final grade," you miss this crucial piece of information!

When someone gives us a compliment, we may exaggerate it and downplay everything else. A young woman told me, "When asking me out on a date, this guy said I looked like a beautiful model. I was so thrilled that I kept repeating what he said to myself because it made me feel so great. Of course, I accepted his invitation." It turns out that he also asked her to wear a costume because he planned to take her to a Halloween party. She missed that part, and when he picked her up she was stuck without a costume.

Aside from compliments, we invite personal trauma when we react to our own exaggerated sense of what we hear. When a supervisor discovers a work-related error and says to you, "You know, I couldn't help but notice that these files were misplaced," you might recoil in horror and think, "There I go messing up again" or "Now they must think I'm dumb." Meanwhile, you didn't bother to listen when your supervisor added, "No big deal. I'm just thankful you make so few mistakes."

If you insist on mentally scolding yourself for screwing up, then do it on your own time—not while someone is continuing to speak to you. The speaker might say something critical about you, only to brush it off moments later or even dish out a compliment. But if you exaggerate the negative comment, you will not listen for what follows. Our internal gloom-and-doom messages (*How can I be so stupid?; I'm so careless; I'm not smart enough; I can't do anything right*) can immobilize us.

A married couple shared with me how they got in a verbal brawl by distorting what each other said. The husband couched a problem (his wife's long hours at her job) in exaggerated terms. "I lost my temper and told her that her work was a waste of time, that she was throwing her life away at that corporation," he recalled, wincing at the memory. "I could tell how harsh that sounded, so I immediately brought up how much talent she had and how I felt she could maximize all her skills in another line of work that did not demand so much time."

His wife added, "The minute you said my 'work was a waste of time,' I didn't hear another word. Whatever you said after that, I wasn't listening. Those words really hit me hard. I took what you said as the ultimate insult, when you consider how hard I've worked over so many years to get where I am today."

Memory Jogger

Whether someone insults us or compliments us, we may magnify the meaning of what's said and shut off our mind to everything else.

If we're not careful, we may exaggerate a message based on hearing just one word that tees us off. When someone calls us *selfish*, for example, we may replay that word in our head and tune out the rest. Our rational side realizes that we are not always selfish, that we are being unfairly labeled, but we still have trouble listening because of the hurt or anger caused by the speaker's negative characterization.

If we assign blame while we listen, we increase the odds of exaggeration. Our minds resort to accusations or fault finding instead of remaining open and dispassionate. Distortion serves as a handy, albeit dangerous, coping mechanism. It allows us to blur what we hear in order to support our interpretation of who deserves blame.

How to Prevent Exaggeration

To prevent exaggeration from distorting messages, compartmentalize what you hear. Mentally file a speaker's remarks under certain categories. In the preceding example involving the bickering couple, the wife could have visualized a folder labeled "job criticism" and filed her husband's angry comments away. This would enable her to continue listening and engage in further conversation. Although she still might take offense at what her husband said, at least she would hear the subsequent positive statements as well.

Whenever you find yourself tempted to dwell on a word or phrase that stings, think in terms of Teach Me, Teach Me. Try to learn from what someone says even when it hurts. Ride a conversation through its ups and downs to its conclusion. The temptation to exaggerate may die down if you replace the impulse to *interpret* what people say with a determination to *understand* them.

Memory Jogger

You choose whether to inflate the significance of a particular comment. If you do, then you risk losing the entire message. You must understand the full meaning of what people try to tell you before you seek to persuade them.

Another way to guard against exaggeration is to acknowledge that there is a problem or a point of disagreement and then tell yourself that you need to solve it. This will encourage you to keep listening so that you absorb the full, accurate message. Your goal, to identify a problem and then devise a solution, will allow you to keep quiet and listen attentively. You will have little mental energy left over to dwell on how hurt or upset you feel by something the speaker said.

A middle-aged participant in my workshop told the group about a time when his marriage was on the rocks. He vividly remembered the first time his wife used the word *divorce* when discussing their future. "We were talking about our careers and how that might affect having a child, when she said that a divorce down the line would change everything," he said. "She kept talking for awhile, but I couldn't believe she had brought up divorce. So I immediately told myself 'We've got a problem, let's solve it.' And so I listened some more and finally got to the bottom of things. I'm thankful that I was able to let her continue, because she gradually opened up about what troubled her in the marriage."

Have faith in yourself to solve problems rather than allowing them to fester. This way, you can listen patiently and resist the urge to intensify a particular comment so that it crowds out everything else.

Leveling: The Opposite of Exaggeration

Leveling means we deemphasize what someone says until nothing stands out. The entire message is leveled off so that it arrives in the listener's mind without any highlighted points. Rather than exaggerate what someone tells us, we flatten the entire message to the point where it has no meaning.

We may comprehend others' comments, but we do not prioritize their importance. For a leveler, *This house is on fire* and *It's a nice day* are interchangeable. By not attributing more importance to what is clearly an important statement, we distort what is said. Examples:

- Your birthday approaches, and you express enthusiasm for a new computer. "That new model looks fantastic," you tell your spouse. Hint, hint. Your mate, who cannot afford to buy you a computer, hears your comment as, "This computer is alright, I guess. I can take it or leave it."

- A friend raves about a Vietnam War film. You don't like war movies, so even though he's effusive in his praise you hear him say, "It was so-so."

- A colleague speaks highly of a training seminar, but you don't like training programs so you hear her say, "The class was okay."

The Twin Causes of Leveling: Boredom and Biases

Leveling usually results from either our boredom or our biases. If we are uninterested in a speaker's opinion or experiences, we will discount what we hear. This makes it easy to downplay a speaker's enthusiasm.

Memory Jogger

Apathy invites distortions. If you don't care what is said, you will have less incentive to listen for the true message.

Listening requires intense concentration. If you lack the motivation to pay attention, then you will surely distort what you hear. The prevailing attitude of some levelers is, *It's all the same to me* or *I don't care.*

Our biases can prove even more troublesome when we try to listen. If we make snap judgments and jump to conclusions, we might deny a speaker's insights if they do not match how we see things. If we are inclined not to trust the government, for instance, we may not attribute much importance to a political candidate's stump speeches. As candidates blaze the campaign trail, making promises and stating positions along the way, we may dismiss their comments with a wave of the hand. Our skepticism prevents us from listening to their views and attempting to understand what they intend to accomplish. Levelers often think, *I don't need to listen to someone who has nothing to say*; they decide not to listen without giving the speaker a chance.

The Best Way to Avoid Leveling Is to Prioritize What You Hear

You can avoid leveling by prioritizing what you hear. The best persuaders can rank, in order of significance, how we feel about our jobs, our relationships, our families, our hobbies, and so on. They appeal to us by offering ways for us to achieve what we want. They seem to know what we value most in life. They persuade us by helping us fulfill our top priorities.

When you listen, try to identify the speaker's priorities. How? Look for cues that indicate how he or she feels about a particular subject. You can tell speakers care about what they say when they:

- Lean forward or move closer to you while making a point
- Raise their eyebrows
- Smile or otherwise loosen their facial muscles
- Gesture emphatically
- Remove their eyeglasses
- Give you uninterrupted eye contact
- Suddenly start talking louder and/or faster
- Emphasize or repeat certain words
- Reach out to touch you as they make a key point
- Prevent you from changing the topic

When you notice speakers exhibit any of these signs of interest in what they say, pay rapt attention. Assign degrees of importance to their comments. This takes time. You will not learn someone's priorities after a five-minute chat, but with careful listening over time you can develop an understanding of what they hold dear.

A salesperson told me that, after a series of discussions with a new client, he concluded that his client's priorities were as follows:

1. Family
2. Job
3. Golf

"He kept telling me that his family comes first, that he was always looking for ways to put his career in perspective and not get too caught up in office politics," the salesperson said. "He was also a golf fanatic who never missed a tee time. I mean, this guy would write golf into his schedule every few days and insist that nothing interfere." Armed with this information, the salesperson listened to what his client said without leveling.

Memory Jogger

It is hard to deemphasize what people say when you know how they prioritize their lives.

A young doctor complained to me of never having enough time to spend with his patients in a fast-paced managed-care environment. "What winds up happening is that I'm so rushed I don't have time to respond to the patient's concerns," he confessed. "I'm so busy asking questions and gathering information that I seem to ignore what's on their mind." After getting the answers he needed to make a quick diagnosis, he leveled off everything else that his patients told him.

I suggested that he prioritize the concerns of each patient. In order to do this, he had to look up from his notes and observe how they behaved in the examining room. Did they dwell on one worry? Did they seem ill at ease when answering certain questions (such as drug use or sexual habits)? Did they seem more interested in getting better or getting back to work? By observing his patients, the doctor was able to identify the one or two most pressing issues on their mind. Although this took a bit more time, he felt he could help patients stay healthier by understanding them better as individuals.

Another form of leveling occurs when you discount a compliment. In an effort to appear modest, you might disagree with praise that is directed your way. Examples:

- A colleague at work greets you in the morning by saying, *You got a haircut! Hey, it looks great.* You reply, *Huh. Yeah. It's okay.*

- A friend gazes out the window at the panoramic view from your new apartment and declares the place *totally fantastic.* You reply evenly, *It's a place to live.*

- A stranger notices your shoes in the elevator and says, *Hey, those look great on you.* You respond, *I don't like them.*

When someone compliments you, acknowledge the remark appreciatively before you beg to differ. Do not instantly shrug it off.

Memory Jogger

Modesty is attractive, but contradicting someone who sincerely praises you is not.

Erasing: When You Indulge In Pain Avoidance at the Speaker's Expense

If a message is threatening or harshly negative, we may block it out by erasing—or not acknowledging—what was said. Some people think that verbal threats exist only in spy movies, where extortionists possess incriminating photos of corrupt public figures engaged in sordid affairs. But in truth, threats creep into everyday conversation far more than we may realize. Distorting these nasty messages helps to soften the blow.

Phrases that begin on a threatening note may lead us to erase whatever the speaker says next. Examples:

I'd hate to …

You don't want me to …

You're forcing me to …

You better do this or else …

You're gonna be sorry if you …

When hearing these ominous openers, who wants to continue listening? It is easier just to shut out the message because we do not want to be bullied into anything.

Same goes for phrases that trigger immediate resistance. If you are the kind of person who questions authority and a speaker begins a sentence with, *You have to cooperate …* or *It is our policy to …*, you might erase whatever follows. You distort the rest of the message because you are too busy thinking, *No, I don't have to do anything!* or *I don't care about your policy!*

Other examples of phrases that may lead us to erase what we hear:

You cannot …

That's against the rules …

It's required that you …

We must insist that you …

Children learn to erase with pain avoidance. They shut their eyes at an unpleasant sight or cover their ears in a sign of defiance. This sends the message, *If I don't listen, I don't have to deal with it.* Adults are usually not as demonstrative as kids, but they also seek pain avoidance with fake smiles, canned nods, and glazed looks of feigned interest.

At least faking it is better than interruption. The moment you jump in, you harm your cause by showing impatience, disinterest, and arrogance. Speakers, their voices silenced to make room for your unwelcome interruption, feel violated and neglected. If you interrupt frequently, you will find that speakers withdraw from you and show little enthusiasm when talking with you. Rather than engage you in conversation, they will move to the other side of the room or simply keep quiet and avoid eye contact.

Memory Jogger

The ultimate form of erasing is simply refusing to listen by terminating the conversation.

When you interrupt, you create an adversarial climate where distortions run rampant. Honest communication turns into defensive maneuvering. Tempers flare. The parties talk without thinking, only to regret their remarks a moment too late. You crush any opportunity for establishing mutual trust.

This does not mean that interruption is always bad. Ted Koppel, host of *Nightline,* routinely cuts off his guests and persuades them to address the topic at hand. He explains:

> *I think it [interrupting effectively] has to do…with what I think is the key to interviewing: listening precisely to what your interviewee is saying. If you do, you come to a set of extraordinary conclusions. One, you realize when they're being repetitious. Two, you realize when they're dodging the questions. Three, you eventually realize when they've said what they basically need to say. Since people rarely have the capacity of deciding that for themselves, at least in the context of a live television interview program, I have to do that for them. In each of those instances, that constitutes interrupting, but it's not as if I'm sitting there waiting to interrupt them.[1]*

Most people equate interruption with talking over someone else. Generations of parents have scolded their youngsters for failing to "sit still and wait your turn to talk." But there are other, equally distracting forms of interruption such as gesturing in an inappropriate manner while someone speaks. Erasing, of course, represents a terrible kind of interruption because you block from your mind whatever the speaker has to say.

Explaining Ideas

How would you explain the operation of these listening distortions in Internet communication, especially in chat groups?

Physical interruptions, such as standing up to leave in the middle of a conversation or abruptly hanging up the phone, are just as bad. This harsh type of erasing often occurs in a busy workplace where "controlled chaos" rules. I know a chef at a fancy restaurant who tells me it is normal for the owner to simply walk away in the middle of a sentence if something else requires attention. "You are lucky to have ten seconds with him at any time," she says. "Normal rules of civility don't apply in the craziness of the kitchen as dinner time approaches."

---

[1]The Los Angeles Times, December 14, 1986, Part VI, p.1.

Mental Interruptions: Erasing What Someone Says Because You're Thinking of What to Say Next

Let's not forget mental interruptions. They occur when you think about what you want to say next or when you allow distortions to infiltrate the conversation. Just as erasing screens out an unpleasant message, exaggeration presents problems because it is hard to listen when you remain fixed on something the speaker said five minutes ago. Like some invisible toxic gas that has no odor and no warning signs, mental interruptions can be silent but deadly.

While I was discussing the dangers of mental interruption in one of my workshops, a tall lawyer with a clipped, staccato voice said, "What you're saying won't work for me. I *have* to think about what to say next. If I pace myself to match my clients' slow speaking, then I would be wasting their time and mine. I need to race ahead and figure out whether I've got a case. If that's what you call erasing, so be it."

An elderly woman on the opposite end of the room responded, "That's the problem with you young people nowadays." She jabbed her finger in the direction of the attorney. "You are always rushing, never taking the time to see what's really going on. You should not think about what you're going to say next while people are talking to you. You miss so much. And you start thinking you're the only one that matters."

A lively debate ensued. About half the class claimed it was acceptable to mentally interrupt at times, while others argued that all forms of interruption are destructive.

Changing Times Affect How We Communicate

This debate on interruption underscores how interpersonal communication habits are changing along with changes in the economy. As more professionals are compensated based on productivity, *time* plays a greater role in influencing how people communicate. Doctors joining managed-healthcare plans need to see more patients in less time. Attorneys racking up billable hours need to bring in more clients and somehow squeeze more lawyering into an already tight twelve-hour day. Consultants who sell their time will need to work faster to make money in an increasingly competitive marketplace.

It is easier to avoid mental interruptions when you are free of pressures. High-stress activities make listening and persuasion far more difficult. But I believe stress should not be used as an excuse to cut someone off. You have a responsibility to establish mutual understanding whenever you engage in conversation.

Two Factors that Determine Whether We Should Erase a Speaker's Remarks

We decide whether to listen to a speaker by considering two factors—competence and trust. If we judge the speaker as incompetent or untrustworthy, we may erase whatever is said. The words go in one ear and out the

Communicating Skillfully

Assume that you're an interpersonal communication expert who's been asked by a local hospital to give a talk to their entire health care staff on how to avoid listening distortions of the nature discussed in this article. What would you say to help these health professionals avoid these distortions in a health care context?

other. Even if we retain a tiny piece of the message, we distort it so much that comprehension is lost.

To assess a speaker's competence, we use scales such as experienced-inexperienced, informed-uninformed, trained-untrained, and professional-amateur. These indicators help us determine whether a speaker is in a position to know what's true or right.

Trust is associated with honest-dishonest, open-minded-closed-minded, just-unjust, and straightforward-evasive.

Memory Jogger

When we conclude that a speaker lacks competence and trust, we tend to erase what we hear.

Evaluating Ideas

How effectively did this article complement your textbook's discussion of listening?

You might think erasing makes sense when you are subjected to a less than credible speaker. I don't blame you. Listening is tough enough when you *like* the speaker, much less when you deem the speaker undeserving of your attention. But your persuasive skills soar when you discipline yourself to listen to any and all speakers.

Cut through all the distortions to unearth the accurate message, and you will position yourself to win over anyone.

8

How to Manage Feedback

In this article, Tony Alessandra and Phil Hunsaker explain the nature of feedback and describe its various types: verbal and nonverbal and fact and feeling. In addition the authors provide a number of useful suggestions for using feedback more effectively.

Want to learn more? A useful book on feedback in business is Mark R. Edwards' *360 Degree Feedback: The Powerful New Model for Employee Assessment and Performance Improvement* (New York: Amacom, 1996).

What do the following sentences mean to you?

I'll be there in a minute.

It isn't very far.

I need it quickly.

We'll provide you with a small number of these at no cost.

That will cost a lot of money.

You have probably already realized that most, if not all, of these statements are highly ambiguous. When used in normal conversation, there is a high probability that these statements will be misinterpreted—unless they are clarified. For instance, a person says: *Call me later and we'll discuss it.* Does he mean fifteen minutes from now, one hour from now, tomorrow, or next week? These statements, in addition to thousands of others not mentioned here, can have a variety of meanings. They generate misunderstandings.

Unfortunately, we frequently use these statements in everyday conversation and expect the other person to understand clearly what we mean. The same is true when other people are communicating with us. Unless statements such as these are clarified and confirmed between the two communicating parties, there is great likelihood the message received will not be the same as was intended. This is the foundation of errors, misunderstandings, and strained relationships. Through the simple use of feedback skills, these highly ambiguous statements can be transformed into specific, effective communications.

Anthony J. Alessandra and Philip L. Hunsaker, "Making Sure with Feedback," in *Communicating at Work* (New York: Simon & Schuster [Fireside], 1993), pp. 78–90. Copyright © 1993. Reprinted with the permission of Simon & Schuster.

The lack of feedback shows up in the workplace as errors, botched plans, political in-fighting, lost productivity, lost profits, and, ultimately, lost jobs. If that seems extreme, think about the errors that you see every day . . . shipping errors or delays, delivery of the wrong parts or the wrong paperwork, budget overruns, marketing plans that miss the target, new products that flop, employees who don't live up to their potential. Studies show that the lack of clear communication is a major factor in *every* organizational problem. Feedback and clarification can take the ambiguity out of promises, agreements, schedules, policies, and procedures.

The use of feedback in communication is often taken for granted. In the management process, no other communication activity is so widely used yet so misunderstood. Feedback may be the most important aspect of interpersonal communications if conversation is to continue for any length of time and still have meaning for the parties involved. Without feedback, how does each person "really" know what the other person is talking about and communicating? The effective use of feedback skills helps ensure the accurate transmission of your message.

Whenever you verbally, vocally, or visibly react to what another person says or does, or seek a reaction from another person to what you say or do, you are using feedback. Effective two-way communication depends on it. This chapter explores the feedback skills you can use to communicate effectively and clearly with your colleagues, supervisors, employees, contractors, and customers.

Types of Feedback

Feedback comes in a number of forms. There is verbal, nonverbal, fact, and feeling feedback. Each serves a specific purpose in the communications process.

Verbal Feedback.

Verbal feedback is the type we are most frequently aware of and most often use. With verbal feedback, you can accomplish a number of favorable objectives: 1) You can use verbal feedback to ask for clarification of a message. 2) You can use verbal feedback to give positive and/or negative strokes to the other person. 3) You can use verbal feedback to determine how to structure a presentation that will be meaningful and effective for the other person.

To improve the accuracy and clarity of a message during a conversation, use clarifying feedback statements such as the following:

- Let me be sure I understand what you've said.
- Let's see if I can review the key points we've discussed.
- I hear you saying . . .
- I think I hear you saying that your central concern is . . .
- As I understand it, your major objectives are . . .

Clarifying feedback statements can also end with the following:

- Did I understand you properly?
- Did I hear you correctly?
- Was I on target with what you meant?
- Were those your major concerns?
- Can you add anything to my summary?

Using feedback for clarification is probably the most critical use of feedback in the workplace. There is only one way to know if the message you're receiving is the same as the message being sent. That is by asking for clarification, or restating the message in your own words and asking for verification of your understanding. Obviously you can't clarify or verify everything that is said during the day. If your coworker says that he's going to get a cup of coffee and you ask for clarification, the results you get probably will not be positive. You need to know when to use feedback. Some typical times are: when you have any doubt about the meaning of the message or about how to proceed, when the message is highly complex, when you're dealing with an important process or project, and when the message deals with information that is new to you.

Verbal feedback should also be used to give positive and negative strokes to others. When a person does something positive, that behavior needs to be positively reinforced. Simple statements are in order, such as: "The project report you did was clear and concise—Nice job"; "You made it really easy for the committee to understand the issues"; "I really appreciate the extra effort you put in"; and "You're doing an excellent job staying within budget." Tell the person specifically what you recognize and appreciate.

Given in a timely and consistent manner, this type of feedback lets the person know what kind of performance is required. It encourages them to continue with similar performance.

On the other hand, when behavior requires negative feedback, offer it in a private, constructive environment. Ignoring inappropriate performance tends to prolong it, as silence is construed as tacit approval. No one likes to be criticized, so negative feedback should be directed only at the performance—rather than the person. Whenever possible, negative feedback should be sandwiched between positive feedback.

For example, use phrases such as: "It's obvious that you put in a lot of effort on this report. The issues are so complex that it would help if we had a one-page summary." "Your work is extremely accurate but when you come in late, it puts us all behind schedule." "I appreciate your help folding the brochures. Since they will be going to customers, it's important that they are extremely neat. Could you redo these?" Make sure you give the person enough specific information so that he can correct his performance in the future.

**Communicating
Skillfully**

Let's say you have been
asked to offer feedback on
a student teacher's performance. It was terrible!
Nothing seemed to go
right. What do you say to
the student teacher if your
feedback is to be given
face-to-face? What would
you say if you were send-
ing feedback through
e-mail?

By asking simple questions, you can determine whether a presentation is working—whether to proceed in the current direction or modify your approach. For instance, if you think you are going a bit too fast for the other person to comprehend your message, you might simply ask: "I sometimes get carried away with my enthusiasm and move along too quickly on this topic. Would it be more helpful to you if I covered these issues a bit more slowly?" The same can be done if you are getting the impression that you should speed up your presentation. Questions such as, "Shall we explore that issue some more?" allow you to determine the other person's interest and understanding of the conversation. Answers can help you avoid capriciously cutting the topic too short or dragging it on too long. You are simply asking for direction. "Would you like me to go into the details of this project, or do you have some other questions that you'd like to ask me first?" allows you to determine the person's present state of mind and level of receptivity. Without this information, you may get into the details of the project when, in fact, the other person does have a number of questions she would have liked to ask first. In this situation, the person is probably dwelling on her questions and not paying attention to what you are explaining. Through questions such as the preceding, you can determine how to tailor your delivery style and presentation to fit the needs of each individual person. Although this takes a bit more time in the short run, it saves much time in the long run, because it prevents communication problems and improves receptivity, understanding, and productivity.

Nonverbal Feedback.

Many of us can remember when the word "vibes" was in vogue. Both good and bad vibes are the result of a direct form of nonverbal feedback. By using their bodies, eyes, faces, postures, and senses, people can communicate a variety of positive or negative attitudes, feelings, and opinions. You do this consciously or unconsciously, just as others do with you. The sensitive, perceptive communicator uses the nonverbal feedback he or she is getting from the other person to structure the content and direction of the message. The outcome is a positive continuance of the interaction and increased trust and credibility in the relationship.

The amount of nonverbal feedback you receive and send is not as important as how you interpret it and react to it. Nonverbal signals help you realize when you are losing the other person's interest. With this sensitivity to and perception of the person's nonverbal feedback, you can react by changing your pace, topic, or style to recapture the person's attention, interest, or trust.

Nonverbal feedback is extremely important in the manager/employee relationship. Too often ineffective communications between managers and employees result in "mixed messages." This simply means that while one message is being verbalized, something totally different is being stated through vocal intonation and body language. These mixed messages force the receiver to choose between the verbal message and the intent signaled by the body language. Most often, they choose the nonverbal aspect of the message. When a person receives mixed messages from you, it immediately creates tension and distrust. Rightly or wrongly, the person feels that you are purposely hiding something or that you are being less than candid. Unfortunately, managers and employees often do not realize they are sending mixed messages to each other. The resulting miscommunication takes a terrible toll on work relationships. It is extremely important to keep your nonverbal feedback and your verbal feedback in sync.

In an earlier chapter on listening skills, we mentioned the process of acknowledging. This is nothing other than projecting nonverbal (and verbal) feedback to the speaker. It lets the person know that her message is getting through to you, and it also lets her know how you feel about that message. People do not like to speak to people who do not respond or show any emotion. They want and seek feedback. Make a concerted effort to give them that feedback, especially in nonverbal ways.

Fact Feedback

If the facts are worth asking for, they are certainly worth being heard accurately. This is where fact feedback comes into play. There are also times when you are relating specific information which needs to be received as accurately as possible and, again, fact feedback can help. Fact feedback is asking a specific, closed question or making a specific statement of the facts as you know them and asking for verification.

When you are depending on other people's facts and they are depending on yours, it is critical to get and give the information exactly. When you want clarification, agreement, or correction, fact feedback is called for. Fact feedback is also used in translating messages and interpreting words or phrases. The following messages contain words or phrases that are unclear. They are perfect candidates for fact feedback statements.

- Due to recent layoffs, all employees are expected to work harder.
- There will be a short wait for a table.
- Don't spend too much time on that job.
- In this company, we are liberal and democratic.
- Major credit cards are accepted.
- We will be visiting Philadelphia and New York City. We expect to open our first unit there.

Examples of requests for fact feedback would be:

- What exactly do you mean by "working harder"? Should we plan on putting in longer hours?
- How long is the wait? Will the wait be more than 15 minutes?
- How much time should I spend on the job? Is there a deadline?
- What do you mean by "liberal and democratic"?

- Which major credit cards do you honor? Do you take Visa?
- Which city will have the first unit?

If something can be misunderstood, *chances are it will be.* Use feedback to keep your messages clear and make sure you are receiving the message as it is intended.

Feeling Feedback

A firm understanding and clarification of the words, phrases, and facts of messages are obviously important. However, this increased accuracy in communications still only stays on the surface of the discussion. It is also important to know why the person is saying the things she is saying. What are the underlying causes and motivations behind her message and her facts? How much personal feeling does her message carry for her? How does she really feel about what she is saying to you? Does she know whether her message is really getting through to you—at the feeling level? Is she aware that you really care about what she is saying to you?

All these questions underscore the importance of feeling feedback in two-way communications. Feeling feedback is especially important in organizations . . . perhaps because it is so seldom requested. The old school of business etiquette believed that feelings had no place at work. Personal lives, feelings, and emotional involvements were to be taken care of outside of the workplace. Now we know that it is impossible to put our feelings in a little box as we walk into the office and to pick them up again as we leave. Research has shown that one of the most effective ways to handle organizational change is to let the people "chat" about how they feel about the change. Just the process of talking about how they feel helps them adapt to the change.

Organizations are a complex web of people working to achieve a common purpose. As organizational life becomes more complex and more demanding, it requires the full commitment of each member to achieve the organization's goals. Full commitment requires an environment of trust that allows each person to express his or her thoughts and feelings openly. Organizations that request, and provide, a high level of feeling feedback understand that the feelings of each person are a critical part of the communication process. It is as important to understand the feelings inherent in a message as it is to understand the facts of the message.

Feeling feedback should be two-directional. You need to make a concerted effort to understand the feelings, emotions, and attitudes that underlie the messages that come to you. In addition, you should clearly project feeling feedback to the other person to let her know that her message has gotten through to you—at the feeling level. The following statements are candidates for feeling feedback questions:

- I'm tired of all the politics around here.
- My last review was a joke.
- "Quality" is just another management fad.

- No one cares about my problems.
- Another reorganization . . . probably just another name for a layoff.

Examples of requests for feeling feedback would be:

- How are the "politics" here affecting you?
- What's bothering you about your last review?
- Why do you feel that management isn't committed to the quality program?
- What would make you feel like the organization cared about your problems?
- How do you feel about the reorganization?

Fact feedback is simply a meeting of the minds, whereas feeling feedback is a meeting of the hearts. Feeling feedback is nothing more than the effective use of empathy—putting yourself into the other person's shoes so that you can see things from her point of view. When you can really experience the other person's true feelings and understand where she's coming from and at the same time project this emotional awareness to her, it serves to reinforce rapport, lower interpersonal tension, and significantly increase trust. Probing questions, supportive and understanding responses, and an awareness and projection of appropriate nonverbal signals are the key tools used in sending and receiving feeling feedback. Often, until you and the other person understand how each other truly feels, the "facts" don't matter at all. Improve the accuracy of communications through the fact feedback—and improve the rapport of your relationships by practicing empathy through feeling feedback.

The Keys to Effective Feedback

If you took a few moments and really thought about it, you could probably recall numerous times you could have smoothed over problems in communications simply by using the forms of feedback that we have discussed. Effective communication between two people is not easy. You really have to practice to make it work. The proper use of questioning skills helps. Using active listening helps. Sensitivity to nonverbal behavior helps. Without feedback, however, all of these skills are for naught. Through the effective use of feedback skills, you can create a good communication climate. The following general guidelines will help you use your feedback skills more effectively.

Give and Get Definitions

The interpretation of words or phrases may vary from person to person, group to group, region to region, or society to society. When people believe or assume that words are used for one and only one meaning, they create situations in which they think they understand others but really do not. The words you use in everyday conversations almost inevitably have multiple

Ethical Judgments

Let's say you and a friend are applying for the same scholarship. Although the two of you can both win, the chances of the Foundation giving two scholarships to students from the same school are slim. Your friend, who trusts your judgment, and feels really insecure in this task, asks you to look over the application and offer feedback. You agree. Would it be ethical for you to *not* point out obvious errors, on the theory that you have no obligation to make a competing candidate look better? Would it be ethical for you to resist sharing ways in which the application could be improved? What ethical obligations do you incur when you agree to offer feedback?

Brain Talk

Each person has a some-
what different (unique, actually) meaning for each
word—at least the impor-
tant words like the nouns
and verbs. Because of this,
when trying to understand
another person, you need
to ask what does this person mean by this word
rather than simply what
does the dictionary say this
word means. Thus, expres-
sions like "I love you" or
"you really annoy me" can
only be understood by un-
derstanding the individual's
meaning system. Naturally,
you need to know the
meanings of words as pre-
sented in a dictionary, but
to appreciate the nu-
ances—the unique per-
sonal meanings—you need
to look at what the person
speaking means. Asking
questions and paraphrasing
what you think the speaker
meant are useful ways of
getting feedback on your
understanding of the
speaker's meaning.

meanings. In fact, the 500 most commonly used words in our language have
more than 14,000 dictionary definitions. For instance, according to Webster's, a person is considered "fast" when she can run rather quickly. However, when one is tied down and cannot move at all, she is also considered
"fast." "Fast" also relates to periods of not eating, a ship's mooring line, a race
track in good running condition, and a person who hangs around with the
"wrong" crowd of people. In addition, photographic film is "fast" when it is
sensitive to light. On the other hand, bacteria are "fast" when they are insensitive to antibiotics.

The abundance of meanings of even "simple" words makes it hazardous
to assume to understand the intent of a message without verifying and clarifying that message. These assumptions often lead to subsequent misunderstandings, breakdowns in the communications process, and decreased trust.
Therefore, during the process of questioning and listening, use feedback.
Give and get definitions.

Don't Assume

Making assumptions invariably gets you into trouble. During interpersonal communications, it is dangerous to make the assumption that the
other person either thinks or feels as you do at that moment. The other person may have a frame of reference that is totally different from your own.
She reacts and perceives according to what she knows and believes to be
true, and that may be different from your reactions, perceptions, and beliefs.

Do not assume anything in communications. If you do, you stand a
good chance of being incorrect. Don't assume that you and the other person are talking about the same thing. Don't assume that the words and
phrases you are both using are automatically being understood. The classic
phrase of people who make assumptions is: "I know exactly what you
mean." People who usually use that statement without ever using feedback
techniques to determine exactly what the other person means are leaping
into a communication quagmire.

Use more feedback and fewer assumptions, and you'll be happier and
more accurate in your interpersonal communications.

Ask Questions

Questions have many uses. We've discussed a number of these in the
previous chapter. Remember to use questions to test for feedback. A good
rule of thumb is: "When in doubt, check it out." One of the best ways to
check it out is through the effective use of questioning skills. Clarifying
questions, expansion questions, direction questions, fact-finding questions,
feeling-finding questions, and open questions can be used freely during
conversation to test for feedback.

Speak the Same Language

Abstain from using words that can easily be misinterpreted or mis-
translated, especially technical terms and company jargon. These terms,

which are so familiar to you, may be totally foreign to the people with whom you talk. Simplify your language and your technical terms so that everyone can understand you, even when you think the other person knows what the terms mean.

Stay Tuned In

Constantly be on the lookout for and recognize those nonverbal signals that indicate that your line of approach is causing the other person to become uncomfortable and lose interest. When this happens, change your approach and your message accordingly. This fact was stated earlier, but it is so important that it cannot be repeated too often. Observe the other person. Be sensitive to the feelings they are experiencing during your interaction; above all else, respond to those feelings appropriately.

Give Feedback on the Behavior, Not the Person

This relates to the appropriate use of positive and negative strokes. When someone does something especially well, give positive feedback, and relate it specifically to the action or behavior that was performed. When people do something especially badly, give them negative feedback specifically directed toward the action or behavior that you would like corrected. Do not under any circumstances criticize the person personally because of an inappropriate action or behavior. This is not only degrading but also counterproductive. Many ineffective managers, upon learning that one of their employees has done something wrong, criticize that employee personally: "You're an idiot"; "That was really stupid"; "You can't do anything right, can you?" These statements constitute inappropriate feedback. After a while, the employee starts believing these statements, and they become self-fulfilling prophecies. How can an employee improve performance on a particular task or behavior unless she knows specifically what behaviors or actions she must improve? So, direct your praise and punishment specifically toward your employee's behavior and actions, not toward the employee personally.

Cultural Analysis

What would you do if you were managing five assistant managers who each were supervising ten analysts. Two of your assistant managers are reluctant to voice criticism of their analysts; culturally, you understand, this type of criticism violates their rules of politeness that require them to always be positive. But, your feeling is that managerial criticism is the only way the analysts will learn their job. What would you do?

Withholding Feedback

There are times when it's best not to give feedback. Bite your tongue and restrain your body language and facial expressions in these situations. A few months ago, one of the authors was visiting a married couple. While waiting for the husband to finish getting dressed for an appointment, the author was chatting with the wife in the dining room. All of a sudden, the husband came into the dining room in what appeared to be a huff. In a loud and harsh vocal intonation he asked his wife, "Where did you get this shirt cleaned?!" While "asking" this assertion, he was shaking the collar of the shirt and seemed to be peering at his wife. The initial interpretation of this occurrence was that the husband was rather upset about the condition of his shirt. Most spouses would tend to act rather defensively, and some would even counterattack. His spouse was rather expert in withholding inappropriate feedback while at the same time asking for feedback. In a gentle voice with no disturbing body language, she simply told her husband: "I got it done at XYZ Cleaners. Why do you ask?" His reply almost floored me. He said it was the first time that any cleaner had done his shirt properly. He told his wife to take his shirts to that specific cleaner from now on. Clearly, there are times when it is best to withhold inappropriate feedback until you use effective feedback to clarify the intent of another person's message.

Feedback can reduce interpersonal tension and create a sense of trust and credibility between you and your supervisors, employees, customers, suppliers, and other coworkers, if used properly. Use feedback to help clarify messages, uncover an important need or problem, provide feedback to others, and to make sure your presentation is being clearly received. Use feedback to improve your relationships by letting the other person know what is going on in the relationship. Most of all, use feedback to improve your part of the conversation.

Feedback is an important part of communication in the workplace. As you develop these skills, you will find them an important part of every aspect of your professional life, including negotiations with bosses, employees, and customers; personnel issues; interviewing; problem-solving sessions; and building consensus to ensure efficient implementation of decisions.

Through feedback, you can determine which areas to spend more time on and which ones need less time. It is important to confirm all uncertain verbal, vocal, and observable cues through feedback. The proper and effective use of feedback skills leads to improved communication. This increased sense of mutual understanding will lead to less interpersonal tension, increased trust and credibility, and higher productivity. Everyone wins when communications are clear and open.

Evaluating Ideas

How effectively do the authors relate this material on feedback to workplace communication? What specific insights or suggestions discussed in this article would also prove useful in social situations or in family communication?

How to Ask Questions

Asking questions is one of the most difficult communication skills you'll need to master. Too often questions make other people feel defensive, as if they are being grilled and put on the spot. When they feel this way, they're more likely to become defensive and respond with the proverbial chip on their shoulder. In this brief and highly practical article, Burton Kaplan, popular author in communication, explains the ways to ask questions that actually empower the other person.

Want to learn more? Works on interviewing are especially helpful in explaining the nature and strategies of questions. See, for example, James G. Goodale, *One to One: Interviewing, Selecting, Appraising, and Counseling Employees* (Englewood Cliffs, NJ: Prentice-Hall, 1992) or Charles J. Stewart and William B. Cash, *Interviewing Principles and Practices,* 9th ed. (New York: McGraw-Hill, 2000). The publisher maintains a text-specific Web site for this book; visit it at www.mhhe.com/stewart.

Questions are laser lights. They burn through to priceless nuggets of knowledge, information we must have if we expect to get any place at all with and through others.

With that in mind, I am going to give you the tested techniques guaranteed to produce the results you want and need, right from the get go.

Read them, participate in the exercises, and I am confident you will come out a winner two ways:

First, you will pose questions that encourage your listeners to give you the information you need. And second, as your skills grow, you will start to respond to questions in ways that invite others to make your goals their goals.

Automatically, you will stop asking the disempowering questions that limit happiness in your life and career.

And just as automatically, start asking the ones that unleash your potential to take what is and make of it all that it can be.

Burton Kaplan, "A Dozen Workable Ways to Ask Empowering Questions," in *Everything You Need to Know to Talk Your Way to Success* (Englewood Cliffs, NJ: Prentice-Hall, 1995), pp. 70–78. Reprinted with permission of Prentice Hall Direct.

Think of these as a battery of ideas to jumpstart your thinking.

Apply the lessons they demonstrate, practice their techniques for the next several weeks, and see for yourself the changes they make in your life. You will be amazed at how willing people will be to share their information and points of view with you.

Technique 1: Don't Ask for Information if You're Not Prepared to Listen to Answers

When you use questions to get information, you must be prepared to listen attentively to the responses they provoke . . . or risk finding yourself worse off than ever.

"The secret around here is that to go fast you've got to work slow," reports Department of Labor interviewer Janice Onnerbee, 29, who operates out of the courthouse in Kansas City, Missouri. "Folks are uptight to begin with so if you diss them by not listening to their answers, well lookit, better it takes a little longer and gets done."

When you ask a question but don't listen to the answer, the person being questioned is certain to feel trying to talk with you is like trying to row up a waterfall.

Explaining Ideas

How would you describe the questioning style of some popular television hosts? For example, how would you characterize the questioning style of a late night talk show host such as Jay Leno or David Letterman? Of daytime hosts such as Rosie O'Donnell, Montel Williams, or Sally Jesse Raphael? Of morning show hosts such as Regis Philbin, Diane Sawyer, or Matt Lauer? What television personality would you consider the most effective questioner? Why?

Technique 2: Make the Q & A Process Enjoyable

Your questions should convey a sense of appreciation for the information the other person makes available to you. Even though you may be impatient to get to the heart of things, give the other person's response the time and attention it deserves.

Here are four ways to show your interest:

- Comment on what he says. "I wish I had known about that before. I could've saved a lot of trouble."

- Express sympathy with his point of view. "In times like these, it's not easy to put aside a few dollars."

- Share a similar experience of your own. "My kids, too—it seems they all want to grow up faster than we did."

- Give him some information in return. "Oh, really? I'm in advertising too. I've spent most of my career in an agency—Byrd, Seed & Fieder."

Technique 3: Make Questions Easy to Understand

Phrase questions in language everybody understands. Use them to cover one point at a time. Avoid asking two questions when one will do.

"It's a least-common-denominator kind of thing—the people in my department aren't dumb. They speak five different languages perfectly. It's just that none of those five happens to be English," reports Sam Anastas, 28, a south Florida production supervisor. "When I need to ask them something I try to use simple words and terms they know."

Technique 4: Start with Questions That Are Easy to Answer

Everybody enjoys giving answers they know are right. That's why your first question must be one you are confident he can answer effortlessly, e.g., "What time did the accident occur?"

Make your second question easy, too. The idea is to build his trust in you, e.g., "Where were you standing when it took place?"

Technique 5: Follow with Questions That Can't Be Answered with a Fact

Once answers are flowing easily, frame your succeeding questions to get the other person to talk at length about the topic at hand rather than provide a simple "yes" or "no."

For instance,

"Why do you suppose things turned out as they did?"

"Can you tell me how you see it?"

"What do you suppose went on?"

Technique 6: Let the Other Person Know What You Are Hearing

As the conversation develops, feedback to the other person your understanding of what he is saying. Structure the feedback in question form. For example, "Am I right in saying that you think the root cause was worn tires?" If he agrees, move on to the next topic. If he disagrees, allow and encourage him to give you more information by prefacing his key thought with the words, "What about," as in "What about the weather?"

Six Ways Questions Make A Difference In Your Life

1. They trigger positive emotions when you are feeling down, put you in a better frame of mind instantly.

2. They keep people focused on your priorities.

3. They uncover people's hidden needs and motives.

4. They help you cultivate the one personality trait common to successful people.

5. They make you a hero when you are only half right.

6. They keep people from ignoring or interrupting you.

Technique 7: How to Use Questions to Trigger Positive Emotions When You Are Feeling Down and Put Yourself in a Better Frame of Mind Instantly

We usually don't give much thought to the need to know how to explore issues with others. We give even less to the idea of exploring issues within ourselves.

Yet, like it or not, the information we need to get the most out of living is almost always contained in our own minds. Sometimes, we are forthcoming about what we think.

More often, it is a seam of emotional pay dirt deep in the geology of our lives: We need the help of questions to haul it up to the surface.

Questions define us to us. They shape our view of ourselves and what we believe our capabilities to be. They control everything about us, including our moods.

Simply by learning to control the questions you ask yourself, you can trigger positive emotions when you are feeling down, and put yourself in a better mood instantly.

Ethical Judgments

What ethical considerations, if any, should govern the ways in which an elementary school teacher asks students questions? What types of questions would you consider unethical in the elementary school classroom?

"I came back from work to find my kids complaining about the baby sitter, my husband bellyaching about a note we had gotten asking us to help raise church funds, and a list of phone messages," reports Nancy Hulce, 34, mother of three and a New York retail services manager. "The first question that came to me was, Why don't they leave me alone? Then I realized my frustration was going to make things harder on me. So I said to myself, What could be good about coming home to this? It made me stop and think. Ten years ago, all I dreamed about was having a career and a family. Right away I began to feel better. There were so many people who wanted my attention, it was nice to feel wanted. So I started to think about how I could make time for everyone by making some changes in the way I schedule things."

Because Nancy asked a question guaranteed to empower her in the situation, she had an instant reason to feel better about life. The question led her to think in more positive terms about what she really wanted, and make her a happier person, a better wife, a more giving mother.

Technique 8: The Best Way to Keep People Focused on Your Priorities

In Chapter 2, I gave you my needs/benefits formula, $N = B \rightarrow C$. To refresh your thinking, let me sum it up: When the benefits you offer match the other person's needs, minds meet.

I left it up to you to discover the best way to deliver those benefits, to use them to persuade others to share your enthusiasms and priorities. There's no end to the possible routes of delivery you might try. You can make a speech. You can tell a funny story with a point. You can even make an announcement.

But by far the best way to deliver the benefits they want most is in the form of a question that promises to reward them just for sharing your priorities.

It works every time without fail—and that is not a matter of opinion, it is a matter of evidence. Even the brattiest child is unlikely to be immune to a question that asks, "How would you like a raise in your allowance?"

Here are some other examples:

- How would you like to get a promotion?
- If I could show you a way to cut labor costs in half while increasing output 10 percent, would you be interested?
- Wouldn't you feel more secure if you were the low-cost producer in the marketplace?
- How would the congregation feel if we could get the extra classroom we need and still save money?
- If I could show you how to clean up your room in ten minutes flat, that would give you time to get to the ball park, wouldn't it?

No matter who you are, whether you are at home, on the job, or out in the community, use questions to deliver benefits and others will tune in instantly.

"When interest rates drop, my bank puts on a campaign to refinance existing mortgages, but some people don't like the idea of fluctuating interest rates," reports Dubuque telemarketer Ed Pierson, 30. "So I worked up a way to get them involved. I ask them, "How would you like to lower your cost of living for the next year, guaranteed, without having to change where you are living? That gets me in the door because they always answer, Yes!"

Here's why Ed's question worked.

First, because it promised a relevant benefit, the question immediately pointed the other person in the direction of Ed's top priority. Second, it established the basis for a meeting of the minds because it identified the common ground between them: the customer wants lower costs, the bank wants to sell more mortgages. Third, it put the other person in a "yes" frame of mind. This sets up a positive mood that makes agreement with your priorities easier to obtain.

Technique 9: The Best Way to Uncover People's Hidden Needs

Like most people I am something of a creature of habit. Every morning I head to the bakery for a cup of coffee. And every morning, when the clerk rings up my order, he asks, "Is that all?"

Invariably, I answer, "Yes, thanks."

As I left home today, it occurred to me that I needed a loaf of bread. But when the clerk asked, "Is that all?" I simply answered out of habit, "Yes, thank you," and went on my way, breadless. Here's my point. Most people take other people's needs for granted. Then, they build these assumptions into their questions. The clerk assumed all I needed was coffee. That prevented him from discovering my need for bread.

Imagine the impact on yearly sales if he asked every customer, "Is there anything else I can get for you?"

Here are some other examples of questions that uncover people's hidden needs:

Cultural Analysis

You're a teacher and a few of your students never ask questions. When they're confused, they usually say nothing, but on occasion may ask another student (who unfortunately may be just as confused). You suspect that asking questions is avoided in some cultures because it may be taken to mean that the teacher was not clear and thus to ask questions would insult the instructor's teaching abilities. What would you say to your students?

- Do you feel you have been treated fairly?
- Why do you suppose most people would disagree?
- May I show you our policy on that?
- Do you think it might be a good idea if I drove on the way home?

Remember, a question is supposed to bring you news. You use it to find out what somebody really wants.

The whole idea is to uncover hidden needs so that you can satisfy them on a timely basis using the $N = B \to C$ formula.

"At an alumni function, I was talking with one of our most loyal givers, an African American who had come up the hard way," reports Dick Durfee, 35, a fund raiser for Hobart College, Geneva, New York. "He was saying that his education gave him everything he got in life, so, sure, he would make his regular donation. But then he said that, even after all the years since he graduated, the place still looked lily white. So I asked him, If you were to make an additional gift to the school, how would you set it up to be certain we attracted more minorities? Not only did he give me answer, he called several of his friends and they chipped in to set up a grant for inner-city kids."

Dick's question succeeded because it focused immediately on the alumni's hidden need to run the show. It offered the donor an opportunity to express a hidden desire for control in a proud and useful way.

Technique 10: The One Trait Common to Successful People—and How to Cultivate It in Yourself

Ever notice how people on the automobile showroom floor never start a conversation by asking which specific model you are interested in? Or how insurance salespeople, no matter how rushed, never start by asking how big an estate you intend to leave to your heirs? Or how college and business recruiters who have just 10 minutes to make up their minds never open an interview with a specific question about your background?

Before they get down to the nitty gritty, people who ask questions for a living take you through a warmup. Their apparently aimless questions cover family, sports—everything but the topic you are meeting on.

Don't be deceived by appearances. People who make their living through persuasion always have a mental plan of attack. First, they talk about things that will make you feel comfortable.

Then, when they sense you are at ease, they build questions on the information you reveal about your needs. These turn your mind to the thing they want to get across.

"My daughter left her soccer gear in my office," reports Roanoke broker Lesley Joplin, 39. "This customer notices it and says his sons are soccer crazy. Tells me all about where they play, how many goals they average. I listen, make a comment here and there, and when he is done talking I say, Are you in the market for good value in a family house with a big enough yard for a

Communicating Skillfully

Visit one of the Web sites devoted to interviewing. Perform a few different searches for *interviewing, interview questions, employment interviews,* or similar terms. Do they offer any suggestions on asking or answering questions? How might you improve your interviewing and responding skills?

soccer field? Oh yes, he says. He ended up with the Horganwiller place—great buy!"

Use the secret of successful people: use your questions to bring hidden needs to the surface and you cannot fail to get what you want from others.

Technique 11: How to be a Hero When You Are Only Half Right

"For crying out loud, Danny, how many times do I have to ask you not to leave your jacket on the front hall railing?"

"Me? Who do you think you are, Mr. Clean? What about the cassettes you leave all over the coffee table every night?"

It happens to all of us. Oh, sure, the words are different. And the times, places, and subjects, too. But can't you see yourself in the sort of situation bedeviling Danny Orten, 26, and his companion, Rick Seelig, both Los Angelinos?

The natural impulse is to fight or flight. Let me save you a lot of time. Ignore your natural impulse. Neither choice works.

For one thing, it is certain to be one of the few sparring matches to produce two losers. And as for heading for the nearest border, it makes a repeat performance an eventual certainty.

You are better off to do three things:

- Stay put
- Stay calm
- And, difficult as it may seem at first, focus more on solutions than on problems.

The whole idea in these situations is to understand people better than they seem to want to be understood!

Here's Rick's approach:

"Gee, Danny, you're right. I do leave tapes lying around," Rick said. "I am sure that bothers you as much as your jacket bothers me. I'll tell you what, I'll do a better job picking up the tapes, and if I come across your jacket I'll just hang it up. Can I count on you to do the same for me?"

"Well . . . what the hell, why not?"

Rick recognized that the way to be a hero when you are only half right is to ask a question in an understanding way . . . a way that attracts cooperation.

Technique 12: How to Keep People from Ignoring or Interrupting You

About the only thing more toxic to conversation than being interrupted every 10 or 15 words is the dead silence of being ignored. The antidote for both is to keep people involved in what you have to say. So involved, in fact, they become part of it.

Here, questions can be show-stoppers. They break the patterns of either neglect or interruption so that you can get things back into focus. In these

Communicating Skillfully

Using the twelve suggestions offered by Kaplan as a basis, how skillfully do your instructors ask questions? What specific suggestions would you offer them for making their questions more empowering?

Evaluating Ideas

Can you think of question and answer situations where these twelve suggestions would actually be counter productive? That is, can you identify situations where following Kaplan's advice would prevent the questioner from realizing his or her communication goals?

situations, you want your questions to appeal immediately to whatever need drives people to behave as they do.

"I was presenting the bimonthly figures but I couldn't seem to complete a sentence. One manager kept interrupting," reports Phoenicia Drell, 26, an account manager in a Chicago public-opinion polling company. "I was at my wits end and I just had to break the chain so I asked him, Bob, this next slide's right up your alley. Since it's in your field, would you mind giving us your comments? He did, and those were the last things he said for the rest of the meeting."

Phoenicia's question instantly broke the pattern of interruption. It appealed instantly to Bob's need to express his personal power, leaving Phoenicia in complete charge.

As you approach the end of this chapter, let's take a minute to review the major points.

1. We use questions to change minds, confirm suspicions, open purse strings, pluck heartstrings, reveal emotions, recover initiatives. Most important, we use them to get information.

2. How we manage questions makes a powerful difference not just in our ability to communicate but in our lives.

3. The secret of controlling our encounters is through questions that make your thoughts their thoughts.

10

How to Communicate with Other Cultures

In this article Farid Elashmawi and Philip Harris discuss cultural competence, what it is and how it influences managerial success, though—as you'll see—the insights are clearly applicable to any form of intercultural communication, whether in the classroom or at a social gathering. Elashmawi and Harris focus on differences among Americans, Japanese, and Arabs and consider nonverbal communication, language, and space-time differences (an area most interpersonal communication texts would include under nonverbal communication).

Want to learn more? Here are some useful sources: Stella Ting-Toomey, *Communicating Across Cultures* (New York: Guilford Publications, 1999); Larry A. Samovar and Richard E. Porter, *Intercultural Communication: A reader*, 9th ed. (Belmont, CA: Wadsworth, 2000); and Geert Hofstede, *Cultures and Organizations: Software of the Mind* (New York: McGraw-Hill, 1997). Another way to learn about culture is to log on to some international chat groups and to visit some of the international Web sites concerned with topics in which you're already interested.

From the outside, a tree grown in California would probably look just like a tree grown in Japan. However, the growth of each tree is largely dependent on the soil that the roots of the trees have to "interact" with in order to grow. The strength of the roots is also dependent on the environment the tree is exposed to, from sunshine to thunderstorms. Imagine the values of a particular culture represented as the roots of a tree. These roots (values) are the source of strength needed by the tree to survive in the surrounding environment (society). Of course, we don't really see the roots, but we are constantly exposed to the tree nevertheless. The type of fertilizer and water fed to the tree contributes significantly to the growth of it (reward). In addition, you cannot transplant a tree into other soil unless you prepare the roots for the new soil.

The roots of each tree may have a different form, much like the cultures they represent. The Japanese roots are twisted together because they may have rockier soil and need the combined strength of the roots to support the tree during rough weather. The American roots, however, are individual, separate, straight, and deep, responding to their soil condition.

Using this model, we see that these roots present the sets of individual, company, or country values, which produce a certain type of society (branches, leaves, and flowers). In that sense you cannot ask a Swede or Russian used to being rewarded/punished by a specific set of values to immediately comply with a new set. In the same way, an American executive cannot ask a Malaysian company worker to comply fully with his American set of values while dealing with him.

A successful culturally competent person must be aware of his or her own priorities, as well as those of his or her country or society, and reorganize them properly to achieve group success. That person must also make an attempt, in initial dealings with the other culture, to adhere to and respect the other system. When they are accepted by the group, then they can slowly introduce their own set of values to the other group. If both sides recognize the new values as necessary for coexistence, then they will be accepted, and cultural synergy will naturally occur.

Figure 10.1 proposes that all of our behaviors in business or social life are influenced by both our belief systems, such as life, death, religion, and nature, plus our rewarded values. These beliefs are taken by human beings as accepted norms, and it takes a major crisis to change them.

However, our set of values change according to the group or societal system of rewards and punishment. In the American system, for example, the values of independence, competition, and risk-taking are rewarded, enhanced, and encouraged by the group. If an executive working in the United States tries to introduce group harmony, seniority, and status as prime values for his business success, he will probably be discouraged and be forced to comply with the more valued system of American independence, openness, directness, and risk-taking.

By contrast, many of the Japanese reward systems are based on group harmony, group consensus, and group achievement. If a Japanese executive were to attempt to introduce self-reliance, individual competition, and risk-taking into the Japanese work environment, he would more than likely be disparaged within his culture.

Building one's cultural sensitivity requires that we enhance three important input sensors of the human being. As shown in Figure 10.2, these are listening, watching and feelings, or Phase I. During our interactions, most of us filter the messages coming to us, either verbal or nonverbal. We usually like to hear what we want and filter out what we don't like. As discussed, the use of language and nonverbal communication plays an important factor in our crosscultural encounters and understanding.

In addition to listening, we must expand our vision to see beyond what is directly in front of us. However, the most important feature in building cultural competence is to stimulate our feelings when we interact with other

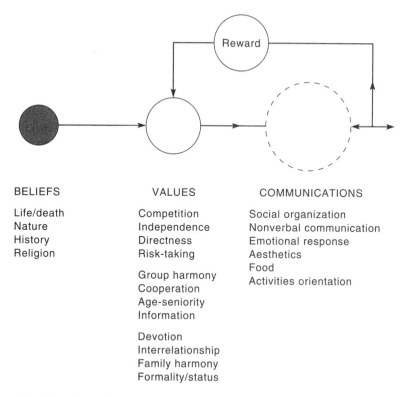

Brain Talk

Seeing an issue from the viewpoint of someone of the opposite sex, different affectional orientation, or different age, religion, or culture can often provide extraordinary insights. Because of this, it's useful to expand your circle of interpersonal contacts to include those who are different from you and from whom you'll be able to gain different perspectives, points of view, attitudes, and beliefs. An effective and efficient way to do this is to visit some international Web sites, chat groups, or newsgroups. Even travel Web sites have information that is useful in mastering intercultural communication.

BELIEFS

Life/death
Nature
History
Religion

VALUES

Competition
Independence
Directness
Risk-taking

Group harmony
Cooperation
Age-seniority
Information

Devotion
Interrelationship
Family harmony
Formality/status

COMMUNICATIONS

Social organization
Nonverbal communication
Emotional response
Aesthetics
Food
Activities orientation

FIGURE 10.1 The Belief, Values, and Communications Model.

people, even within our own cultural group. These three elements represent a dynamic process that we must use to expand our understanding of other cultures. If this input is sufficient then it must be followed by Phase II, in which we react and participate with other persons or groups.

A good analogy is the food and water that our physical body requires: If it is the proper food, our body takes the time to digest it and this results in physical growth. If Phases I and II are successful, then in Phase III a person should be able to adapt and, most importantly, to share the experience with others in a more enjoyable way, demonstrated by the output of the dynamic cross-cultural joy model.

In some cultures, such as the Japanese, the elements of Phase I—listening, watching, and feeling—are highly valued and practiced. In business meetings, for example, most Japanese would listen, watch, and sense the thoughts of their foreign partner more than they would respond directly. Within the Japanese culture, in Phase II, they will participate, react to new ideas, and come up with agreed-upon decisions adapted to their own values. However, the last two phases may not be adequate when interacting with other cultures.

Building Cultural Sensitivity

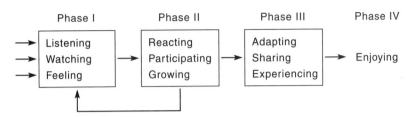

FIGURE 10.2 The Joy Model.

Cultural Analysis

What one person—someone you know or someone from the media—best exemplifies cultural competence? Cultural incompetence? What specific interpersonal communication behaviors distinguish the competent from the incompetent?

On the other hand, American cultural values may put less emphasis on listening and watching, and instead put more on Phase II, fast reaction and participation, which again would not necessarily result in a true cultural synergy due to an inability to adapt adequately to other cultures, most often due to the wrong input. The proposed process is, in fact, an ideal way to achieve cultural synergy and requires extensive awareness and skill development.

Nonverbal Communication

- *Why does she keep raising her voice? I can hear her perfectly.*
- *This is just a working meeting. Why is he wearing a suit?*
- *He keeps staring at me. What's wrong?*
- *Every time I meet him, he wants to shake my hand.*

Nonverbal communication represents an important element of our cultural dimension. Each culture has its own unique system of nonverbal messages, whether it is the use of hand gestures, tone of voice, or even physical contact such as a pat on the back or a handshake. Let us now discover some elements of cross-cultural nonverbal messages.

Shaking hands is a form of nonverbal communication that nearly every businessperson uses. When, and in what context, the handshake is used shows the difference between cultures. For example:

Most Americans expect to shake hands

(a) When they meet for the first time.

(b) Before they leave for work.

(c) In the morning.

(d) Only if you extend your hand first.

In American culture, first-time greetings are almost always accompanied by a firm handshake. This is used to show a sense of equality and sincerity between the two people involved in the greeting.

Americans use hand and arm gestures sparingly to add emphasis, but in most gestures the elbow does not go above shoulder level, as it may in other cultures. Americans tend to make eye contact when beginning and ending their speech. This factor establishes their directness, sincerity, and equality, which are important values in American culture.

Within the Japanese culture, the proper form of nonverbal expression during a greeting is not a handshake, but a bow. The depth, duration, and repetition of the bow reflect the communicator's social status. Physical distance between those involved is maintained, and contact is avoided.

In Arab culture, a greeting between close friends often consists of the two people hugging each other. A greeting between strangers, however, is usually just a handshake.

Other forms of nonverbal communication in American culture that demonstrate the value of equality can be measured in many different ways. Consider this situation:

You are visiting the United States for the first time. You notice that most Americans stand in line at theaters, supermarkets, bus stations, etc. This indicates that they

(a) Are formal and believe in one status.

(b) Like to maintain harmony with everyone.

(c) Do not believe in competition.

(d) Believe in equality.

Americans wait in line with others because one of their top cultural values is equality. Standing in line demonstrates a value that Americans learn in childhood—that every person has the same chance at something. They wait for their turn when others before them are waiting for the same thing. The line scenario would probably not happen in Arabic cultures, where status is a top value. Someone who has higher status than another would not wait in line with the other person because he would feel uncomfortable.

Japanese culture also has many forms of nonverbal communication that are also unique to their way of life and are used as values to guide them through every situation. What role does smiling play in Japanese culture, for example?

In a meeting with a Japanese team, you notice that one of the managers has a continuous smile on his face. This means

(a) He likes what you are saying.

(b) He feels sorry for you.

(c) You should smile back.

(d) He is reacting to what you are saying.

The Japanese tend to communicate with little eye contact, few facial expressions, and almost no hand gestures. Especially in negative situations, an expressionless face is considered highly desirable. A smile, however, is often used to mask embarrassment or discomfort in certain situations.

On the other hand, an Arab smiles to show hospitality and a desire for friendship. Americans have essentially the same use for smiling.

Nonverbal messages do not always have to be visual, as this situation demonstrates:

You are discussing a subject with a Japanese team. Suddenly everyone is quiet. You should

(a) Tell a joke to wake them up.

(b) Give your discount now.

(c) Be quiet too.

(d) Ask them what the problem is.

In Japan, silence is a virtue, and most conversations contain periods of silence during which each participant tries to sense the thoughts and feelings of the other. Therefore, the answer is to be quiet too. Such use of silence would probably not work in American culture, however, because Americans, with their directness and openness, feel uncomfortable with prolonged periods of silence.

Arabs, on the other hand, value hospitality, family, friendship, and religion, and use these values when making decisions. The Arab culture has many nonverbal messages as well, such as the use of hand gestures and tone of voice. For example, consider this scenario:

You are discussing a business proposal with two Arabs in their office. You notice that their tone of voice changes depending on the subject matter. Should you

(a) Keep your tone of voice quiet?

(b) Go along with their high/low tone?

(c) Use a higher tone to impress them further?

(d) Tell them they are speaking too loudly?

In Arab culture, increased pitch or volume while speaking indicates heightened emotional involvement or interest in the subject. Therefore, to interact successfully with them, it would be a good idea to follow their high-low speech style.

Another Arab nonverbal message involves the important Arab value of hospitality, as in the following case:

After finishing your visit to an Arab company, the president offers to escort you to your car. He is offering this gesture in order to

(a) Discuss privately the final commissions.

(b) Further express his hospitality.

(c) Show his competitors next door that he has a contract with you.

(d) Give you a last chance to offer that discount he has been seeking.

Hospitality is a top Arab value and is shown in this example by the president of the company offering to walk you to your car. The president wishes to establish a relationship with you and, therefore, is friendly and hospitable in order to achieve his goal. An American company president, using his cultural value of privacy, may make the offer, but is most likely to discuss the deal with you out of earshot of the other staff members.

Use of Language

- *Hi, how are you?*
- *Drop by my house for a visit sometime.*
- *Yes, yes.*
- *What can I do for you?*
- *Please, have a cup of coffee.*

Use of language is perhaps one of the most obvious barriers in cross-cultural communication—the problems of communicating in a language different than your own go beyond learning to translate a set of words. Language defines culture and structures our patterns of thinking, our perceptions, and our very concepts of reality. Ideally, each of us should know at least something about our intercultural partners' language. Of course, it is impossible to speak every language, but being aware of the differences is the first step to increasing the effectiveness of that communication.

Let us consider the following:

This is your first week in an American office. Your American co-worker says to you, "Let's get together sometime this week." You should

(a) Accept it as a friendly comment.

(b) Invite him to your house to meet your family.

(c) Tell your spouse to prepare to have dinner with your co-worker.

(d) Expect the American to invite you to play tennis this weekend.

Americans often say things just to be friendly, sometimes without actually intending to follow through. When they say, "Let's get together," it could mean they want to do something with you, but it is generally used to indicate their desire to keep in touch with you or as a polite ending to a conversation, so you should accept the statement as a friendly comment.

In contrast, if an American said, "Let's get together" to a Japanese acquaintance, the Japanese person would probably plan to have dinner or do some other activity with the American soon. The formal way the Japanese use language is quite the opposite of the casual American style.

You are calling an American businesswoman on the telephone. She immediately says, "Yes, what can I do for you?" You should respond by saying

(a) "Thank you, I don't need your help."

(b) "Where is the order you promised me?"

(c) "You are too impersonal."

(d) "How was your weekend?"

Because American culture places a high value on directness, your answer should be geared toward finding out where your order is, if that is the reason for your call. A response to the point would be the expected procedure for dealing in American business, and would not be considered rude. In Arab culture, a person might begin the conversation by asking how your weekend was, but in American culture that is not related to the task at hand and would be considered irrelevant. Let's explore the way the Japanese might approach the following:

On your visit to Japan, you noticed that most Japanese people say "Excuse me" when they approach you or begin a conversation. This is common because

(a) Japanese value independence.

(b) They are always in a rush.

(c) They try to maintain harmony.

(d) Japanese do not like surprises.

Many Japanese may say "Excuse me" when beginning conversations because they do not like surprises, and prefacing a comment with "Excuse me" helps to maintain group harmony.

In a discussion with a Japanese businessman, if he nods his head and says, "Yes, yes," he

(a) Understands what you are saying.

(b) Agrees with what you are saying.

(c) Is listening.

(d) Is bored.

When a Japanese person says "yes, yes," he is usually indicating that he is listening to what you are saying or follows along with your train of thought. It doesn't necessarily mean, as in American culture, that he agrees with your statement.

You are calling your Arab business contact on the telephone. He says "When will I see you?" You answer,

(a) "God willing we will meet again soon."

(b) "Any time you wish."

(c) "I will call you when I am ready."

(d) "Give me an order and I will come to deliver it myself."

Arab culture values religion and hospitality, therefore your response should be along those lines of "God willing we will meet again soon." An American, who values directness, might say something like, "I will call you when I've got the information." This would be insulting to the Arab person, though, because he was showing his hospitality to the caller, and to not reciprocate the same sentiment would be rude.

In discussing commissions with your Arab partner, he will probably

(a) Tell you straightforwardly that he wants a 25 percent commission.

(b) Talk about the expense of distribution systems in Saudi Arabia.

(c) Tell his assistant to inform you how much he is willing to accept.

(d) Give you his requested commission in writing.

Arab business values the indirect approach when conducting business. Therefore, when discussing commissions, instead of saying straight out what he feels, he will often discuss the general market value of the product, and then indirectly come to an agreement. How would the answer differ between two Americans?

Space and Time Orientation

- *Our meeting was at ten o'clock but it's ten forty-five, and he's still talking with the previous visitor. Should I wait or leave?*
- *The invitation was for dinner at seven o'clock. What time should I show up?*
- *Time is money. Does that mean save it or spend it?*
- *When she said, "I'll get back to you," does that mean in an hour, a day, a week? When?*

How space is used and what that use signifies, vary from culture to culture. Some cultures require a larger "comfort zone" of interpersonal space than others. Most people are unaware of how their own culture structures spatial relationships, and therefore do not take this factor into account when interacting with other cultures in business. Cross-cultural violations of spatial requirements can produce discomfort, anxiety, hostility, and even conflict, often without the participants understanding why they feel their territory has been invaded.

Like space, time has different meanings in each culture. How the culture defines time, and what value it gives to the past, present, and future, communicates just as surely as words. The vocabulary, grammar, and meaning of time vary widely around the world.

In this section, we discuss both space and time orientation by offering different scenarios using the American, Arab, and Japanese cultures.

You are visiting your American partner's office, and have seated yourself in the conference room. When he joins you he will probably

(a) Sit on your right side.

(b) Sit on your left side.

(c) Sit in front of you.

(d) Wait for your invitation to sit.

Evaluating Ideas

How effectively do this season's prime-time television shows represent the various cultural groups throughout the country? Are certain groups portrayed more often or more favorably than others? Which groups do you think benefit from this year's prime-time television lineup? Which groups do you think suffer?

The seating in American business meetings is usually set up in a face-to-face manner, placing the participants directly across from each other, exhibiting equality and competition. In Arab culture, your business contact, depending on his status, will probably sit next to you.

You have received a fax from an American company asking for a price quotation. They are expecting your reply

(a) By return fax.

(b) By phone.

(c) By regular mail.

(d) In about one week.

Most Americans, as you know by now, value directness and often use the phrase "time is money." This means that when dealing in business, any time not spent directly on solving the task at hand is considered wasted. Therefore, the Americans probably expect you to fax or even call back as soon as possible. In dealing with Japanese or Arabs, it will take a longer time to respond, and will probably be by mail.

Japanese culture values modesty, group achievement, and group harmony, which can be seen in their use of open space in the business environment. It is different than workplaces in other cultures, and has the potential to cause a cultural clash as seen from the following example:

You are on a training assignment in a Japanese company in Tokyo. They offer you a desk in the middle of a big hall with fifteen other staff members. Will you

(a) Ask for a special room because you are used to working in a quiet office?

(b) Ask for a portable wall to keep others from looking at you?

(c) Accept the offer?

(d) Ask for a corner location away from traffic?

The Japanese workplace is usually a large hall with many desks in it. The open space plan in most Japanese companies reflects their inner harmony, and promotes sharing and group discussion. To ask for your own office would be interpreted as antisocial and would be considered nonproductive for the company.

This is your second visit to your Arab business contact's office. He asks you to come from ten o'clock to eleven o'clock in the morning to continue your discussion. You should arrive at:

(a) Nine-thirty.

(b) Ten o'clock.

(c) Eleven o'clock.

(d) Ten-thirty.

Evaluating Ideas

How accurately do the authors represent the American organization as you understand it? Would you disagree with anything the authors say? Would you add anything to their discussion?

An Arab's time frame is generally much longer than most other cultures'. In Arab culture, the present is an extension of the past, and the future depends very much on the will of God. Regular clock time is not as highly valued as in the American culture, and in the above situation, ten o'clock to eleven o'clock means your discussion will continue sometime within that hour. The Arab businessman will most likely have a few other people in his office during the same time period you are there, so the loose time structure fits within the cultural value of time.

part two

Messages in Interpersonal Communication

It is not only true that the language we use puts words in our mouths; it also puts notions in our heads.

—Wendell Johnson

11

How to Communicate with Men and Women

In this article Judith Tingley, a corporate consultant, reviews some of the research findings on female-male communication and offers suggestions on how to make such communication more effective.

Want to learn more? If you find this article interesting, you might want to continue your study by reading one of the books Tingley discusses. Or, if you'd like something more academic take a look at Diana K. Ivy and Phil Backlund's *Exploring GenderSpeak: Personal Effectiveness in Gender Communication*, 2nd ed. (New York: McGraw-Hill, 2000).

Evaluating Ideas

Often articles on female-male communication blame one sex for failing to communicate fairly, openly or honestly. As you read this article, ask yourself if the author is fair to both men and women. If not, in what ways is the article slanted? What would you add or amend to balance the ledger as you see it?

Evaluating Ideas

Does your own experience support the idea that men aren't good listeners? Is it necessary to listen with your eyes as well as your ears?

Men's and women's communication styles are startlingly dissimilar. Besides the obvious physical factors, communication is the most glaring of the differences between the sexes. Men and women both recognize, talk and joke about the distinctions between them. When men are off talking in a group together, women will groan, roll their eyes and say, "Football!" When women gather together to talk, men often joke, "Who are they gossiping about now?"

Many jokes, cartoons and comic strips elicit humor by playing on people's conscious and subconscious knowledge of gender communication differences. Bill Keane shows a child talking to his father who is reading the paper: "You hafta listen to me with your eyes Dad, not just your ears." Why is that funny? Because men and women both recognize that men aren't good listeners. The cartoon wouldn't be funny if it portrayed a child talking to a woman. Another cartoon in *The New Yorker,* and a bit more subtle, shows a woman and man talking in a business setting. She says to him, "Actually, what I'm selling is my own intensity." Why is this funny? Because many people recognize the prevalence of seriousness and career absorption in businesswomen of the '90s. Again, the cartoon wouldn't be funny if a man were making the comment. Yes, the communication differences are noticeable—even glaring!

For the purpose of clarity in this chapter, female-male communication differences are discussed under the categories of content, style and structure—major areas of difference that research has elucidated. "Content"

Judith C. Tingley, "The Big Three—Content, Style and Structure." From *Genderflex: Men & Women Speaking Each Other's Language at Work* (New York: American Management Association, 1993): 21–38. Copyright © 1993 Judith C. Tingley, Ph.D. Published by AMACOM, a division of American Management Association International. Used with the permission of the publisher. All rights reserved. http://www.amacombooks.org

refers to the topics that men and women generally prefer to talk about. The "style" of communication pertains to the manner of expression rather than to what is being expressed. Finally, the "structure" of communication concerns ways of using words, phrases, statements and questions in verbal communication.

Using the content, style and structure format provides a means for you as a learner of genderflexing to start the adaptive process. If you're going to move out of the "attack and defend" mode and into the "adapt" mode, you have to know what to adapt to. Are you adapting to the *content* of women's communication? Or perhaps to the male *style* of communication? Or making changes in the *structure* of your communication in order to come across as more accessible to the opposite sex?

If you're going to make some changes in communication, adopt some characteristics of the other person's communication in order to seem more accessible, and be a more effective influencer, it is essential to know exactly what you're being similar to. It's time to develop some new strategies that work effectively with an age-old adversary . . . the opposite sex.

Content

Differences in the preferred topics or content of communication between men and women are usually apparent to everyone, at work and at home. There are exceptions, but men generally talk about money, sports and business, while women generally talk about people, feelings and relationships. My male workshop participants all attest to the fact that men also talk frequently about sex, although research has yet to quantify this finding. And not to be outdone, female workshop participants think that women are beginning to talk much more openly about sex. Men jokingly comment that sex fits under the "sports" category for them, whereas women see sex under the "relationship" category.

Certainly, men sometimes talk about people and relationships, and women can talk about sports or politics, but most studies demonstrate that there is a major gender content difference. Some researchers say that men like to talk about things and women like to talk about people. Others say that women talk about feelings and men talk about facts, women talk about the abstract and men talk about the concrete, or women talk about emotional issues and men talk about intellectual issues. But all agree on one thing—there is a big difference!

Men and women can sometimes appear to be talking about the same topic but, because their focus is somewhat different, it may not seem to them or even to observers that they're really communicating. For example, a man and a woman may be talking about an impending organizational restructuring which would result in huge layoffs. The man might be talking about it from a business needs point of view and the woman may be talking about it from a people's needs point of view. She may conclude he's hard-nosed, hard-hearted. He may conclude she's too emotional. And they may both conclude they're on different wavelengths.

I was confronted with a vivid example of the female-male content difference when I took a sailing lesson with four male students and a male instructor. We were together from 7 a.m. to 7 p.m. All of us were intermediate level sailors and no one knew each other. I decided to take a more passive role, at least in conversation. I wanted to use this opportunity to gather more information about male-female conversation as well as about sailing! From dawn till dusk, the conversation whirled around participant sports— sailing, of course, but also dirt-bike riding and javelin throwing. Then there was conversation about spectator sports—baseball, basketball and football—focusing on what happened last season and what was going to happen next season.

The majority of the conversation, however, was centered on business and money. There was, to my ears, a competitive quality to this topic, with the men one-upping each other with knowledge and experience related to business and the accumulation of money. They boasted about who had made more money, who was going to make more money, and who had more leadership, management or entrepreneurial experience. One man even brought up his participation in World War II as a bid to one-up in the leadership realm.

There was no discussion of people, feelings or relationships. No one mentioned a wife, a child, a brother or sister, a mother or father. The conversation was almost totally about each individual man and what he had done or seen or been relative to sports, business or money.

Toward midafternoon, I was tiring of my chosen passive role and decided to make a stab at a "female" topic. My comment was business related, but somewhat of a non sequitur, as was most of the men's conversation with each other. I commented that I was a psychologist and, just prior to leaving Phoenix to come to California for this sailing lesson, I had been called about the possibility of being a host on a TV call-in talk show. I mentioned my enthusiasm and interest in getting the job. The quick response from one of the men was that he knew a video shrink in California and she and her whole family were the most screwed up people he had ever met! End of conversation related to me and my topic! Back to more sports stories . . .

Evaluating Ideas

Is the male conversation characterized here typical of what you've observed? If not, in what ways does it differ?

Given turnabout circumstances, for example if the ratio had been five females to one male, the male would have probably felt and been equally isolated from the women's conversation. What went on was certainly a consequence of the fact that the group consisted of five men and one woman who were taking a sailing lesson together. Context is always an essential component of the differences in communication between the sexes. In another situation, with a different male-female ratio, the conversation would have been different.

Carol Tavris, in her 1992 book *The Mismeasure of Woman*, points out that the culture gap between men and women results in their use of very different sets of influence strategies. She says, "Just as when in Rome most people do as Romans do, the behavior of women and men depends as much on the gender they are interacting with than on anything intrinsic about the gender they are." Since I was a minority of one, the men were interacting with men in a "manly" way. I chose not to attempt to markedly alter the conversation in this particular circumstance. If I had taken a more active role, the conversation might have turned out differently.

There are hundreds of examples of the female-male difference in content of communication, and you can see and hear them every day. I recently heard an ad for a Mercedes dealer. A husband and wife, recent buyers of the car, spoke separately in the ad. He told of the speed, the slick lines, the power. She talked of the comfortable feeling she had driving the car, and how the whole process of buying the car had been so easy, with no pushiness from the helpful, friendly salesman.

A clear written example of content difference appeared in an article about consulting in *Training and Development,* July 1992. Four experts had been asked to respond to the question, "What are the necessary 'street smarts' for international consultants?" Peter Koestenbaum, one of the three men interviewed, began his recommendations with this comment: "One way in which every leader must make a commitment to greatness is through what I call the vision factor—the seer or the genius in all of us. That means we have to show intellectual brilliance."

Nancy Adler, the sole female expert interviewed, began her recommendations with this thought: "Know that you don't know. Be humble. Ask questions and listen. And on your very best days, you will feel as if you are the one who has learned the most."

Neither approach is right. Neither is wrong. Just an obvious difference in preferred focus of content of communication. As the examples given illustrate, differences in content may result in men and women feeling isolated from each other at times, and certainly as if they're on different frequencies, but rarely does the content difference cause tremendous conflict between people at work.

Certainly, men have been heard to complain that women talk too much at work about non-work-related topics, or that women are too emotionally wrapped up in their own and other people's problems and aren't concerned enough with productivity. Meanwhile, women may complain that joining the men for lunch is a drag because all they're talking about is sports or business, or that people's problems never seem to take precedence over bottom-line concerns for men. But these differences are usually only a cause of annoyance rather than of downright hostility. Consequently, making adaptations for content difference is relatively simple for both men and women. These adaptations are discussed in detail in the following two chapters.

> **Explaining Ideas**
>
> How would you explain male-female differences in the content of their conversations based on your own interactions and those you've listened to?

Style

The disparity in style of communication is the difference that generally causes the most conflict between men and women in the workplace. In the Thomas-Hill hearings, the all-male senators' questioning of Anita Hill's statement about alleged harassment demonstrated this difference. They assumed she would have and should have handled the problem very directly—the male style of communication. Because she didn't handle the situation directly, but in a more indirect and what appeared to be conciliatory female manner, she was viewed as less credible by many men.

Because the senators were direct and bluntly questioned witnesses in a competitive manner—coming from their own perspective about what was right and wrong, and how they assumed women should be—women viewed them as completely without understanding of what work life was like for women. Women generally sensed that men's communication style was different, but the hearings demonstrated that men were completely unaware that women's style was so markedly different from theirs. The difference was viewed as cause for open conflict.

Joe Tannenbaum, in his book *Male and Female Realities,* describes women as "expressers" and men as "resolvers." Women express to express, men express to fix. Dale Spender's book *Man Made Language* quotes anthropologist Edwin Ardener, who used the terms "dominant" and "muted" to describe the relative communication styles of the sexes.

The terms "subjective" and "objective", "passive" and "active", "restricting" and "enabling", "powerless" and "powerful" have also been used to describe women's and men's relative styles of communication. Philip Smith, who authored *Language, the Sexes and Society,* saw the communication differences between men and women as clearly regulated by a difference which is not a bipolar variable. He saw men as concerned about managing and monitoring interactions in order to control, and women as managing interaction in the pursuit of affiliation. Their goals are different, so their styles are different.

Competitive Versus Facilitative

Evaluating Ideas

Are these descriptions accurate? How would you go about testing the validity of the claim that the male communication style is "competitive" and the female style is "facilitative"?

I prefer the term "competitive" to describe the male style, and "facilitative" to describe the female style. For men, communication is somewhat like a sporting event. You win it, lose it or reach a tie. The conversation has a clear beginning, middle and end, and it has a definite purpose—to solve a problem or fix a situation. Like a football game, once the conversation is over, it's over. Going back to rehash or redo is as useless as trying to reschedule a completed football game. You can have a new game, but not redo the old one. You can have a new conversation, but not reschedule the old one.

For women, conversation is a means of further understanding others and being understood themselves. Their goal is to facilitate or enable others to be understood and to express themselves in order to provide an opportunity for others to truly understand them. Consequently, the same conversation can go on forever and be restarted and rehashed with different nuances, because deeper and broader understanding is always possible.

Men Talk More

What are some characteristics of these gender-specific styles of communication? Probably the most surprising research finding, in the sense of violating long-held stereotypes, is that men actually talk more than women! Dale Spender notes, "There has not been one study which provides evidence that women talk more than men, and there have been numerous studies which indicate that men talk more than women." He further speculates that the stereotype of women as more talkative than men evolved from men's historical belief that women shouldn't really talk at all. Like children, women should be seen and not heard. So when men compare the actual situation (that women do talk) with their desire (that women should keep quiet), they conclude that women are too talkative.

I have a different explanation for the stereotype, based on the differing content of male-female communication as well as the differing style. Women do prefer to talk about relationships, feelings and people rather than the male-preferred topics of business, money and sports. From a male point of view, women do talk much more than men *on the subjects of people, feelings and relationships,* just as men talk much more than women on *their* preferred content. Support for this viewpoint comes from a study quoted in *Gender Voices* by David Graddol and Joan Swann. Gender and expertise were the two variables studied in relation to amount of talk. In this study, both male gender and expertise were associated with an increase in output of talk.

My conclusion then, is that if one views men as experts in business, money and sports, and women as experts in people, feelings and relationships, one would expect the workplace standoffs I hypothesize. Men do talk more about their preferred topics, and women about theirs. But, because men's style is more competitive, they dominate and interrupt women in conversation more frequently than women dominate and control men in communication.

A humorous article in the January/February 1992 *The Utne Reader,* "The Male Answer Syndrome," discusses men's talkativeness about information. The author, Jane Campbell, says: "They (men) take a broad view of questions, treating them less as requests for specific pieces of information than as invitations to expand on some theories, air a few prejudices, and tell a couple of jokes. Some men seem to regard life as a talk show on which they are the star guest."

Eavesdropping at the airport recently—an occupational hazard of communication buffs—I heard a great example of differences in content, style and structure put together. First, two men were talking about the state of the economy and the state of their own businesses. The theme was persistence. They conducted a somewhat parallel conversation, trading stories about athletes' or historical figures' or nations' or their own successes through determination and persistence. Their conversation was short, specific and to the point. Few words were used.

Shortly thereafter, two women were discussing the same topics—the state of the economy and their individual businesses—and the talk went in an entirely different direction. One woman, the more highly facilitative person, used questions and very active, attentive listening to turn the focus almost entirely to the successes of the other woman for being innovative, creative and persistent in staying afloat during tough times. Their conversation was lengthy and occasionally seemed off target and rambling.

Both pairs—the two men and the two women—seemed quite satisfied at the end of their respective conversations. The men would not have enjoyed the women's conversation, or vice versa, mainly because of the style difference. The men were satisfied because they had solved the problem using their competitive style. The problem . . . tough times. The solution . . . persistence. In contrast, the women had not been trying to solve any problems with their facilitative style—they had been trying to acquire a better understanding of each other, and they seemed to have accomplished that goal.

A second component of men's competitive style is the frequency with which they interrupt female communicators. A study described by Dale Spender in *Man Made Language* found that in conversations between men and women, men make 98 percent of all interruptions. Men's interruptions are generally followed by silence on the women's parts. Whether you watch TV political analysis shows or just observe at meetings or cocktail parties, you will find an amazing sample of the interruption pattern between men and women. In the rare instance that a woman interrupts a man, the man's nonverbal behavior clearly indicates that her behavior is not acceptable.

Carol Tavris, in her book *The Mismeasure of Woman*, views the style difference in male-female communication as one that has primarily to do with power, rather than to do with cultural difference. Other observers view the style difference similarly. Dale Spender quotes Dana Densmore who says that refusing to talk on someone else's topic, interrupting and withholding personal information are all ways of winning the power game. Men's desire to be in and maintain the dominant role may be the basis for their communication style.

Women Listen Longer

Women's style of communication is facilitative or geared to enabling conversation to continue, expand and elaborate. Their goal is to be understood and to understand. Facilitative conversation is characterized by asking questions of the other person, restating their comments, reflecting their feelings, nodding and encouraging with "Mmm-hmms" or "How interesting" to encourage further elaboration on the part of the other person.

Women are so good at facilitating other people's conversations, particularly men's, that they don't even realize they're doing it. Consequently they will often complain that all men ever talk about is themselves, or their ideas, work and plans, and that they never ask about the woman. But generally speaking, the woman is not only allowing and encouraging this pattern, she is almost forcing it by her constant facilitation of the man's conversation. She is seeking first to understand, and then expecting later to be understood. She may wait for the man to turn the tables and ask her about herself, but she's wasting her time, because the man's style is to keep on talking about what he's interested in, not to reciprocate by asking about her and listening.

Evaluating Ideas

There is conflicting evidence on interruptions. Visit some of the databases containing research on interruptions and gender; Psychlit, Sociofile, and ERIC would be excellent starting places. On the basis of this evidence, how would you describe the gender differences in conversational interruptions?

I recently found myself in this exact situation while attending a seminar on "The White Male in the Corporation." The presenter, a man, mentioned that he was in the process of writing a book about male-female relationships in the corporation. Since I was in the midst of writing this book on male-female communication in the workplace, I thought we might have some common thoughts, concerns and questions. Perhaps we could be helpful to each other. Rather than being direct and asking for what I wanted and needed, I began a facilitative conversation with this man about his book, his experience, his writing and publishing experience. At the end of 10 minutes I knew more than I needed to know about him, he knew nothing about me, and time was up for me to ask him what I really wanted to know. Meanwhile, I was ticked off and felt discounted because he never asked one question about me. Is this unusual? No. Should I have expected him to be different? No . . . unless he reads my book and applies the techniques I suggest. Or I change to a more direct approach.

Eleanor Maccoby, whose article on gender differences and influence was published in *American Psychologist*, quotes researchers who use the term "enabling" to describe the female style of communication. "Enabling or facilitative styles are those, such as acknowledging another's comment or expressing agreement, that support whatever the partner is doing and tend to keep the interaction going." The authors of *Gender Voices* describe women's communication style as "supportive." They point out that, in any conversational endeavor, someone must "manage" or support the process—and that task is generally assumed by women.

Many men will say they prefer talking to women rather than men because women are better at conversation. What women are actually better at is listening and the art of supporting the other person's conversational efforts, encouraging them to go on, enabling them to explain fully, and reinforcing their conversational efforts with smiles, head nods, good eye contact and other indications of attentiveness. Women, in all female groups, have a tendency to use a collaborative or cooperative form of communication. They build on each others' points, tell stories to illustrate, and then build on each others' stories.

The consequence of having two quite different styles of communication is that men and women often view the other gender's style as wrong. They assume that the other gender is trying to accomplish the same goal as their own gender, but assume the other gender is going about it the wrong way. For example, women think men do a lousy job of managing conversation, of being facilitative when women are trying to talk. And men think that women are poor at resolving issues and getting to the bottom line conversationally. Both men and women often become critical and angry at the other gender for not using the correct means to the desired end. They battle about who's right and who's wrong, but the reality is that *both* are using the correct means for their gender's desired end. Men aren't trying to facilitate conversation, and women aren't trying to get to the bottom line. Men are trying to fix it and women are trying to understand.

Brain Talk

One of the most often observed obstacles to accurate perception of others is overattribution, the tendency to attribute everything a person does to one particular characteristic such as gender. *Alice is that way because that's the way women are. He says that because that's the way men talk.* Physical condition, race, and affectional orientation are also frequently singled out as being the reason people do just about everything they do. *She acts that way because she's blind, or he acts that way because he's from the South.* Most things people do and believe are the result of a variety of factors and very rarely just one. When you attribute a great deal of what a person says or does to one factor, ask yourself if you may be guilty of overattribution.

Structure

The difference in structure of men's and women's communication can also be a source of controversy. The structure of women's communication tends to be polite, contain many adjectives, use fillers such as "you know" or "I mean" or "well," and be detailed in description. Men's communication tends to be brief and concise, using description more sparingly than women.

Women may view men's normal way of speaking as being impolite, brusque and without adequate detail. For example, in answer to the question, "How did the meeting go?" a man will often answer, "Fine." Women generally would prefer more information about what went on and often think that men are keeping information from them.

Answering the same question, a woman might say, "Well, it was sort of tedious at times, but I would say altogether that we covered pretty much of what needed to be discussed." Men may view that type of answer and the way in which women speak as imprecise and filled with too many details. They would prefer, "Fine," unless something unusual happened!

The structure of women's communication has generally been measured against the male standard. For example, one characteristic identified as typical of the structure of women's communication is the "tag question." A tag question is an added-on question at the end of a statement. "It's a great day, isn't it?" But, argue feminists, why is it not equally valid to comment that men *don't* use tag questions? Why not use the female model as the standard instead?

The male as model is the standard because, in the workplace, the male has been the dominant culture. The dominant culture always sets the standards by which others abide, until the culture is no longer dominant. In essence, the change from white male dominance to diversity as dominant is now going on in the workplace. The female standard is emerging as a model for certain kinds of interactions, particularly teambuilding, collaboration and adapting to individual differences. The direction is toward using different standards of different cultures to accomplish particular outcomes.

Although the male as model has been used in research on the structure of female communication, there is little research about the male structure per se. What the male actually does in terms of structure of communication can only be assumed to be the opposite of what females do. Men make more statements than they ask questions. Men use fewer adjectives, fluffy or otherwise. Men don't use as many disclaimers and apologies and qualifiers and fillers. But I've not seen any research that necessarily validates these assumptions. There have certainly been opinions expressed and assumptions made. Dale Spender says, "English speakers believe—and linguists appear to be no exception—that men's speech is forceful, efficient, blunt, authoritative, serious, effective, sparing and masterful." In her book *Women and Men Speaking,* Chris Kramarae says men use forceful, persuasive, demanding and blunt language.

Pioneering research on the differences in structure of gender communication has been led by Robin Lakoff. She determined that women tend to use more questions than statements, particularly tag questions, excessive apologies and disclaimers, and trivial or "fluffy" adjectives. An example would be, "I could be wrong but, my goodness, I think that's really just a super way to do it . . . don't you think?"

Lakoff followed up her early research by formulating what she called the "Rules of Rapport," and the fact that they were for women was unstated but implied: Don't Impose, Give Options, and Be Friendly. In *Constructing and Reconstructing Gender*, Lakoff's sample instructions for the "Don't Impose" rule are quoted by Nancy Hoar:

- *Be sure to soften your assertions with hedges, qualifiers and tag questions; better yet, phrase your assertions as questions.*

- *Dissipate the force of opinions and feelings by expressing them with weak expletives and vague adjectives.*

- *Be sure you sprinkle your conversation with self-depreciation and apologies from time to time in case you might have unknowingly offended someone.*

Clearly, these rules are not for men and were formulated somewhat tongue in cheek. But they point to the idea that the difference in structure as well as in style of communication has to do as much or more with power differences than gender differences. Carol Tavris points out that both men and women who are in a one-down position resort to the hesitations and uncertainties of what is referred to as women's structure of communication.

Psychologist Linda Carli adds an interesting viewpoint in her 1990 study related to gender and influence. Same-sex and mixed-sex twosomes were discussing a topic on which they disagreed. Carli found that women were hesitant in conversation only when they were talking to men, and not with each other. Their tentativeness was demonstrated by the old familiar tag questions and disclaimers. But Carli noted that, when women talked tentatively to men, they were more influential than when they were assertive. Conversely, when they were tentative with women, they were less influential.

Carli formulated a different explanation for the tentative structure other than the traditionally held belief that it was caused by no power. She saw it as an indication of women's pragmatism. Women *chose* to use the approach that was going to work for them with men.

Carli's interpretation belies one of the principles underlying genderflex, which states that people are more easily influenced by people they see as similar to themselves. Men may view assertive women as similar to themselves, but so alien from men's view of how women are or should be that they see them as alien creatures! Perhaps more time is needed for men to view assertive, direct, concise women communicators as normal females.

Cultural Analysis

What positive or negative consequences do women experience when they "communicate like men" in the workplace? What consequences do men experience when they "communicate like women" in the workplace?

What Are You Adapting To?

When men and women begin to think about adapting to each other in terms of communication, they can review the differences in the content, style and structure as a way to recall *what* they're trying to adapt to. The content of

Ethical Judgments

What ethical obligations, if any, do you feel a college communication instructor has in preparing a woman entering a traditionally male-dominated field or a man entering a traditionally female-dominated field?

Communicating Skillfully

John and Maria argue constantly. John says that Maria just rattles on about nothing—talking about insignificant things that occurred during the day, a television program, or what's going on with the neighbor's children. Maria, on the other hand, says that John only wants to talk about work or money or politics. If you were asked to mediate this problem, what would you say to John and Maria?

men's speech tends to be about money, business and sports. The content of women's speech tends to center on people, feelings and relationships.

In terms of style of communication, women tend to use a supportive or facilitative style which encourages the other person to expand and expound. They work at managing and encouraging a two-way conversation where each is understood. Men often use a competitive conversational style where they provide answers and solutions to problems and offer advice or suggestions about what to do and how to do it.

Finally, the structure of women's communication tends to be vague and apologetic, with inclusion of many adjectives and extra words. Men's structure tends to be crisp and concise, with specific words and points. In the next chapter, you will learn a step-by-step systematic approach to genderflexing, adapting effectively to these differences in communication.

Important Points to Remember

1. Neither men nor women have the RIGHT or the WRONG way of communicating.

2. Recognizing the content, style and structure differences in conversation between the sexes is essential to flexible communication.

3. To be an effective, adaptive communicator, you need to know what you're adapting to.

4. Male-female differences in style cause much of the communication conflict between the genders.

5. Once you understand gender communication differences, you can begin to use a systematic approach that better adapts to the opposite sex.

12

How to Say "I'm Sorry"

Here psychiatrist Aaron Lazare explains the apology and discusses the motives underlying the apology, the characteristics of an effective apology, and some of the causes of ineffective apologies.

Want to learn more? If you'd like to read more about the apology, take a look at William L. Benoit's *Accounts, Excuses, and Apologies: A Theory of Image Restoration Strategies* (Albany, New York: State University Press of New York, 1995). You might find this book a bit difficult to read but it will be worth it. A popular and practical approach to language and communication is General Semantics, the study of the relationships among language, thought, and behavior. Visit the Web site for the International Society for General Semantics at www.crl.com/~isgs/isgshome.html to explore what this approach to language has to offer.

A genuine apology offered and accepted is one of the most profound interactions of civilized people. It has the power to restore damaged relationships, be they on a small scale, between two people, such as intimates, or on a grand scale, between groups of people, even nations. If done correctly, an apology can heal humiliation and generate forgiveness.

Yet, even though it's such a powerful social skill, we give precious little thought to teaching our children how to apologize. Most of us never learned very well ourselves.

Despite its importance, apologizing is antithetical to the ever-pervasive values of winning, success, and perfection. The successful apology requires empathy and the security and strength to admit fault, failure, and weakness. But we are so busy winning that we can't concede our own mistakes.

The botched apology—the apology intended but not delivered, or delivered but not accepted—has serious social consequences. Failed apologies can strain relationships beyond repair or, worse, create life-long grudges and bitter vengeance.

As a psychiatrist who has studied shame and humiliation for eight years, I became interested in apology for its healing nature. I am perpetually amazed by how many of my friends and patients—regardless of ethnicity or

Aaron Lazare, "Go Ahead, Say You're Sorry," *Psychology Today* (January/February, 1995), 40–43, 76, 78. Reprinted with permission from *Psychology Today* Magazine. Copyright © 1995 Sussex Publishers, Inc.

social class—have long-standing grudges that have cut a destructive swath through their own lives and the lives of family and friends. So many of their grudges could have been avoided altogether or been reconciled with a genuine apology.

In my search to learn more about apologies, I have found surprisingly little in the professional literature. The scant research I've unearthed is mostly in linguistics and sociology, but little or nothing touches on the expectations or need for apologies, their meaning to the offender and offended, and the implications of their failure.

Religious writings, however, in both Christian and Jewish traditions, are a rich source of wisdom on the subject, under such headings as absolution, atonement, forgiveness, penance, and repentance. The *Talmud*, in fact, declares that God created repentance before he created the universe. He wisely knew humans would make a lot of mistakes and have a lot of apologizing to do along the way. What makes apologies work is an exchange of shame and power between offender and offended.

No doubt the most compelling and common reason to apologize is over a personal offense. Whether we've ignored, belittled, betrayed, or publicly humiliated someone, the common denominator of any personal offense is that we've diminished or injured a person's self-concept. The self-concept is our story about ourselves. It's our thoughts and feelings about who we are, how we would like to be, and how we would like to be perceived by others.

If you think of yourself first and foremost as a competent, highly valued professional and are asked tomorrow by your boss to move into a cramped windowless office, you would likely be personally offended. You might be insulted and feel hurt or humiliated. No matter whether the interpersonal wound is delivered in a professional, family, or social setting, its depth is determined by the meaning the event carries to the offended party, the relationship between offender and offended, and the vulnerability of the offended to take things personally.

No-shows at family funerals, disputes over wills, betrayals of trust—whether in love or friendship—are situations ripe for wounds to the self-concept. Events of that magnitude put our self-worth on the line, more so for the thin-skinned. Other events people experience as personal offenses include being ignored, treated unfairly, embarrassed by someone else's behavior, publicly humiliated, and having one's cherished beliefs denigrated.

So the personal offense has been made, the blow to the self-concept landed, and an apology is demanded or expected. Why bother? **I count four basic motives for apologizing:**

- The first is to salvage or restore the relationship. Whether you've hurt someone you love, enjoy, or just plain need as your ally in an office situation, an apology may well rekindle the troubled relationship.

- You may have purely empathic reasons for apologizing. You regret that you have caused someone to suffer and you apologize to diminish or end their pain.

The last two motives are not so lofty:

- Some people apologize simply to escape punishment, such as the criminal who apologizes to his victim in exchange for a lesser plea.

- Others apologize simply to relieve themselves of a guilty conscience. They feel so ashamed of what they did that, even though it may not have bothered you that much, they apologize profusely. A long letter explaining why the offender was a half hour late to dinner would be such an occasion. And in so doing, they are trying to maintain some self-respect, because they are nurturing an image of themselves in which the offense, lack of promptness, violates some basic self-concept.

Whatever the motive, what makes an apology work is the exchange of shame and power between the offender and the offended. By apologizing, you take the shame of your offense and redirect it to yourself. You admit to hurting or diminishing someone and, in effect, say that you are really the one who is diminished—I'm the one who was wrong, mistaken, insensitive, or stupid. In acknowledging your shame you give the offended the power to forgive. The exchange is at the heart of the healing process.

Anatomy of an Apology

But in practice, it's not as easy as it sounds. There's a right way and a wrong way to apologize. **There are several integral elements of an apology** and unless they are accounted for, an apology is likely to fail.

First, you have to acknowledge that a moral norm or an understanding of a relationship was violated, and you have to accept responsibility for it. You must name the offense—no glossing over in generalities like, "I'm sorry for what I have done." To be a success, the apology has to be specific—"I betrayed you by talking behind your back" or "I missed your daughter's wedding."

You also have to show you understand the nature of your wrongdoing and the impact it had on the person—"I know I hurt you and I am so very sorry."

This is one of the most unifying elements of the apology. By acknowledging that a moral norm was violated, both parties affirm a similar set of values. The apology reestablishes a common moral ground.

The second ingredient to a successful apology is an explanation for why you committed the offense in the first place. An effective explanation makes the point that what you did isn't representative of who you are. You may offer that you were tired, sick, drunk, distracted, or in love—and that it will not happen again. Such an explanation protects your self-concept.

A recent incident widely reported in the news provides an excellent, if painful, illustration of the role of an apology in protecting the offender's self-concept. An American sailor apologized at his court-martial for brutally beating to death a homosexual shipmate: "I can't apologize enough for my actions. I am not trying to make any excuses for what happened that night. It was horrible, but I am not a horrible person."

Communicating Skillfully

Consider the last few times you apologized to someone else or were apologized to in light of the four motives discussed in this article. Which of these motives, if any, influenced you to apologize to others? Which of these motives, if any, do you think influenced another person to apologize to you?

Explaining Ideas

How would you explain the qualities that make apologies effective and ineffective?

Another vital part of the explanation is to communicate that your behavior wasn't intended as a personal affront. This lets the offended person know that he should feel safe with you now and in the future.

A good apology also has to make you suffer. You have to express genuine, soul-searching regret for your apology to be taken as sincere. Unless you communicate guilt, anxiety, and shame, people are going to question the depth of your remorse. The anxiety and sadness demonstrate that the potential loss of the relationship matters to you. Guilt tells the offended person that you're distressed over hurting him. And shame communicates your disappointment with yourself over the incident.

You Owe Me an Apology

Then there's the matter of settling debt. The apology is a reparation of emotional, physical, or financial debt. The admission of guilt, explanation, and regret are meant, in part, to repair the damage you did to the person's self-concept. A well-executed apology may even the score, but sometimes words are just not enough. An open offer of, "Please let me know if there is anything I can do?" might be necessary. Some sort of financial compensation, such as replacing an object you broke, or reimbursing a friend for a show you couldn't make it to, could be vital to restoring the relationship. Or, in long-term close relationships, an unsolicited gift or favor may completely supplant the verbal apology—every other dimension of the apology may be implicit.

Reparations are largely symbolic. They are a way of saying, "I know who you are, what you value, and am thoughtful about your needs. I owe you." But they don't always have to be genuine to be meaningful. Say your boss wrongfully accused you in front of the whole office. A fair reparation would require an apology—in front of the whole office. His questionable sincerity might be of secondary importance.

Ultimately, the success of an apology rests on the dynamics between the two parties, not on a pat recipe. The apology is an interactive negotiation process in which a deal has to be struck that is emotionally satisfactory to both involved parties.

Nor is the need for an apology confined to intimates. Used strategically, it has great social value within the public domain. The apology is, after all, a social contract of sorts. It secures a common moral ground, whether between two people or within a nation. Present in all societies, the apology is a statement that the harmony of the group is more important than the victory of the individual. Take a look at what will certainly go down in history as one of the world's greatest apologies, F. W. de Klerk's apology to all South Africans for his party's imposition of apartheid.

On April 29, 1993, during a press conference, de Klerk *acknowledged* that apartheid led to forced removals of people from their homes, restrictions on their freedom and jobs, and attacks on their dignity.

He *explained* that the former leaders of the party were *not vicious people* and, at the time, it seemed that the policy of separate nations was better than the colonial policies. "It was not our intention to deprive people of their rights and to cause misery, but eventually apartheid led to just that. Insofar as that occurred, we deeply regret it."

"*Deep regret,*" de Klerk continued, "goes further than just saying you are sorry. Deep regret says that if I could turn the clock back, and if I could do anything about it, I would have liked to have avoided it."

In going on to describe a new National Party logo, he said: "It is a statement that we have broken with that which was wrong in the past and are not afraid to say we are deeply sorry that our past policies were wrong." He promised that the National Party had scrapped apartheid and opened its doors to all South Africans.

De Klerk expressed all the same ingredients and sentiments essential in interpersonal apologies. He enumerated his offenses and explained why they were made. He assured himself and others that the party members are not vicious people. Then he expressed deep regret and offered symbolic reparations in the form of his public apology itself and the new party logo.

In fact, as the world becomes a global village, apologies are growing increasingly important on both national and international levels. Communications, the media, and travel have drawn the world ever closer together. Ultimately we all share the same air, oceans, and world economy. We are all upwind, downstream, over the mountains, or through the woods from one another. We can't help but be concerned with Russia's failing economy, Eastern Block toxic waste, Middle Eastern conflicts, and the rain forest, whether it be for reasons of peace, fuel, or just plain oxygen.

In this international community, apologies will be vital to peaceful resolution of conflicts. Within the last several years alone Nelson Mandela apologized for atrocities committed by the African National Congress in fighting against apartheid; Exxon for the *Valdez* spill; Pope John Paul II "for abuses committed by Christian colonizers against Indian peoples"; former Japanese Prime Minister Morihiro Hosokawa for Japanese aggression during World War II; and Russian President Boris Yeltsin apologized for the massacre of 15,000 Polish army officers by Soviet forces during World War II. And that's only the start of it.

But apologies are useful only if done right. There are in the public arena ample examples of what not to do—stunning portraits of failed apologies. They typically take the form of what I call "the pseudoapology"—the offender fails to admit or take responsibility for what he has done. Recent history furnishes two classics of the genre.

Reel back to August 8, 1974—President Richard Nixon's resignation speech. "I regret deeply any injuries that may have been done in the course of events that have led to this decision. I would say only that if some of my judgments were wrong, and some were wrong, they were made in what I believed at the time to be in the best interest of the nation." Unlike de Klerk, Nixon never acknowledges or specifies his actual offense, nor does he describe its impact. By glossing over his wrongdoing he never takes responsibility for it.

Cultural Analysis

Do you think apologies are used and responded to differently in individualist cultures (cultures that give primary importance to the individual) and in collectivist cultures (cultures that give primary importance to the group)?

Consider, too, the words of Senator Bob Packwood, who was accused of sexually harassing at least a dozen women during his tenure in Congress. His 1994 apology outfails even Nixon's: "I'm apologizing for the conduct that it was alleged that I did." No acceptance of responsibility or accounting for his alleged offense to be found. An *alleged* apology, not even named.

The most common cause of failure in an apology—or an apology altogether avoided—is the offender's pride. It's a fear of shame. To apologize, you have to acknowledge that you made a mistake. You have to admit that you failed to live up to values like sensitivity, thoughtfulness, faithfulness, fairness, and honesty. This is an admission that our own self-concept, our story about ourself, is flawed. To honestly admit what you did and show regret may stir a profound experience of shame, a public exposure of weakness. Such an admission is especially difficult to bear when there was some degree of intention behind the wrongdoing.

Egocentricity also factors into failed or avoided apologies. The egocentric is unable to appreciate the suffering of another person; his regret is that he is no longer liked by the person he offended, not that he inflicted harm. That sort of apology takes the form of "I am sorry that you are upset with me" rather than "I am sorry I hurt you." This offender simply says he is bereft—not guilty, ashamed, or empathic.

Another reason for failure is that the apology may trivialize the damage incurred by the wrongdoing—in which case the apology itself seems offensive. A Japanese-American who was interned during World War II was offended by the U.S. government's reparation of $20,000. He said that the government stole four years of his childhood and now has set the price at $5,000 per year.

Timing can also doom an apology. For a minor offense such as interrupting someone during a presentation or accidentally spilling a drink all over a friend's suit, if you don't apologize right away, the offense becomes personal and grows in magnitude. For a serious offense, such as a betrayal of trust or public humiliation, an immediate apology misses the mark. It demeans the event. Hours, days, weeks, or even months may go by before both parties can integrate the meaning of the event and its impact on the relationship. The care and thought that goes into such apologies dignifies the exchange.

For offenses whose impact is calamitous to individuals, groups, or nations, the apology may be delayed by decades and offered by another generation. Case in point: The apologies now being offered and accepted for apartheid and for events that happened in WWII, such as the Japanese Imperial Army's apology for kidnapping Asian women and forcing them into a network of brothels.

Far and away the biggest stumbling block to apologizing is our belief that apologizing is a sign of weakness and an admission of guilt. We have the misguided notion we are better off ignoring or denying our offenses and hope that no one notices.

Cultural Analysis

In general, do you find that men and women use apologies in the same way? For example, do they apologize for the same things? Do they express their apologies in the same way? Are they equally sincere when they apologize?

In fact the apology is a show of strength. It is an act of honesty because we admit we did wrong; an act of generosity, because it restores the self-concept of those we offended. It offers hope for a renewed relationship and, who knows, possibly even a strengthened one. The apology is an act of commitment because it consigns us to working at the relationship and at our self-development. Finally, the apology is an act of courage because it subjects us to the emotional distress of shame and the risk of humiliation, rejection, and retaliation at the hands of the person we offended.

All dimensions of the apology require strength of character, including the conviction that, while we expose vulnerable parts of ourselves, we are still good people.

13

How to Gossip for Fun and Profit

In this article, Robin Westen discusses gossip, something everyone does but few like to admit to doing. Here Westen discusses the social and psychological functions that gossip serves and its positive and negative aspects.

Want to learn more? An interesting perspective on gossip is offered by Robin Dunbar in *Grooming, Gossip, and the Evolution of Language* (Cambridge, MA: Harvard University Press, 1998) who argues that people gossip because they don't groom each other.

Communicating Skillfully

How effective are you in telling gossip? In listening to gossip? How might you improve your effectiveness in gossiping in face-to-face situations? In gossiping online?

During the past week, I learned that rock singer Rod Stewart prepared for his upcoming world tour with a nip and tuck, O. J. Simpson's co-prosecutors Christopher Darden and Marcia Clark were romantically involved, Mel Gibson faxes dirty jokes to Jody Foster, and an old college pal of mine is leaving her husband for a man twenty years her junior.

This is quite a bounty of eclectic information, but for the average American of the nineties, it's probably not a big haul at all. Gossip, for those millions of us who are interested, is everywhere. At last count, over 40 newspaper columns, dozens of magazines, 50 television talk shows, and three major tabloids are spreading the word. In addition, there's gossip via cyberspace and, of course, good old-fashioned word of mouth.

Although most of us enjoy and engage in it, gossip is a slippery subject with a sullied reputation. The idea of gossip originated with the Old English word "godsibb," meaning "a person related to one in God," or a godparent. Until about the 1800's "gossip" denoted a man who drank with friends and the fellowship they shared, or a woman who was a family friend and helped during childbirth.

Today, gossip is a national growth industry and the dictionary defines it simply as "chatty talk; the reporting of sensational or intimate information." Despite its banal definition, gossip is often perceived as a dangerous weapon, one that can ruin reputations, poison relationships, and halt careers. A gossip can be referred to eruditely as a quidpune (from the Latin) or colloquially—and disdainfully—as a yenta (from the Yiddish). But social scientists who have researched the subject insist that gossip is more closely related to its seventeenth-century meaning. In the vast majority of cases,

Robin Westen, "The Real Slant on Gossip," *Psychology Today* (July/August 1996), 44–48, 80–81. Reprinted with permission from *Psychology Today* Magazine. Copyright © 1996 Sussex Publishers, Inc.

they contend, it's beneficial. Gossip serves important social and psycholog-ical functions: it's a unifying force that communicates a group's moral code. It's the social glue that holds us all together.

Gossip Is Golden

"If people aren't talking about other people, it's a signal that something is wrong—that we feel socially alienated or indifferent," says Ralph Rosnow, Ph.D., a professor of psychology at Temple University and coauthor of *Rumor and Gossip: The Social Psychology of Hearsay.*

"For a real understanding of our social environment, gossip is essential," agrees Jack Levin, Ph.D., professor of sociology and criminology at Boston's Northeastern University and coauthor of *Gossip: The Inside Scoop.* "Its pri-mary function is to help us make social comparisons. For example, if we read bad news about celebrities in the tabloids, or get into the gruesome de-tails of our neighbor's misery over a cup of coffee, our own problems begin to pale in comparison."

You may have to bring the car in for an oil change, get through a stack of laundry, mow the lawn, and pay your taxes, but don't think for one minute that Princess Di has it any better. She suffers bouts of bulimia, is be-ing divorced by a prince, has an ex-paramour who called her Squidgy and a mother-in-law who cringes in her presence.

Not that a little dirt has to hurt a reputation if, like Diana's, it's a good one to begin with. In fact, when someone who's reputable and in a position of power is the target of gossip, he or she may actually *gain* from being gabbed about. Gossiping about someone humanizes them. They become flesh-and-blood people with whom we can identify.

It's also a way for folks to let you know what the limits on personal behavior are without confrontation, says Rosnow. "If you move into a community and your neighbor tells you how the previous homeowner never disposed of his garbage properly, his gossip is letting you in on something else."

"There is only one thing worse than being gossiped about, and that is not being gossiped about," quipped Oscar Wilde. But there's a fine line be-tween a little dirt and a mudslide. This may be especially true for politicians. "Gossip is the primary reason Bill Clinton is the president of the United States today," Levin asserts. "If he wasn't a womanizer who owned up to his marital problems and claimed he failed to inhale, he wouldn't have won. We understood, forgave, and voted for him. Judging by history and Bush's de-feat, Senator Dole could probably use a little gossip to 'taint' his campaign."

However, Levin adds this kibitzing caveat: "There is a point beyond which reporters will not permit public officials to go with impunity." He dates this change in attitude to Ted Kennedy's infamous car accident at Chappaquidick.

"You couldn't find a reporter in Washington who didn't want to go for the jugular," syndicated columnist Liz Smith recalls. "They had all been

Explaining Ideas

The examples of Princess Di and Bill Clinton are, of course, dated. If you were writing this article today what examples would you use?

observing Teddy Kennedy for a long time; both *Time* and *Newsweek* had re-
porters on that trip to Alaska in 1969 where he got drunk on the plane and
misbehaved quite badly. Nobody reported it because they didn't want to
hurt him. But Chappaquidick was the end." From then on, the volume on
tattling was turned up full blast and the nature of gossip was never the same.

"In a sense, it's right out of Nietzsche," says Rosnow. "Gossip shepherds
the herd. It says: these are the boundaries and you're crossing them. You're
not abiding by the rules and you'd better get back in step." This type of chatter control, Rosnow reports, is especially effective in managing the morality
and affairs of small groups, especially in an office.

"If you want to know about the kind of insurance coverage your em-
ployer offers, look in the company handbook," says Levin. "But if you want
to know who to avoid, who the boss loves or loathes, who to go to when you
need help, what it really takes to get a promotion or raise, and how much
you can safely slack off, you're better off paying attention to the company
grapevine."

Gossip also defines who's in and who's out in a group. If you're considered worthy enough to be buzzed about on the grapevine, you're in. If you've
got "valuable" information to share, you're also in. But, if you don't fit into
either group, consider yourself out of the loop, and out to lunch—alone.

The High-Tech Grapevine

With giant computer networks linking up millions of personal computers
across the planet, the grapevine has gone high-tech. Seth Godin, author of
E-Mail Addresses of the Rich and Famous, says gossip is easier to spread,
reaches wider audiences, and travels at a faster rate thanks to e-mail. "It's the
first new form of communication that combines the weight and measured
thought of something written with the speed and instant tenacity of a telephone call."

But Godin says there's no such thing as a carefree ride on the superhighway. Cybergossip is often misinterpreted because it's so flat: no voice in-
flection, no room for subtleties of language. In other words, it may be more
difficult to tell whether someone is making a joke, being sarcastic, or passing on the gospel.

That's not the only cyberhassle. It's also extremely easy to copy e-mail
and pass it on. "In our office, I'm often around the twentieth person to see
a piece of cybergossip," says Godin, "and many times it was intended for one
set of eyes. Basically, you're dealing with the world's greatest gossip engine.
Someone can start with something that's a fact or a misstatement, and suddenly thousands of people are potentially privy to it."

That's exactly why cybergossip gets top grades from Prashant Bordia,
Ph.D., an assistant professor of psychology at the University of Queensland
in Australia, who has studied rumors on-line and off. Computer communication, he says, lets social scientists and psychologists study gossip as never
before: in its natural state. "With the Internet, you get public, informal, and
often juicy stuff in an unobtrusive way."

In the more than two dozen on-line rumors Bordia looked at for a study of how rumors are transmitted via computer, he found that "conversations" have a typical pattern: First, they're tentatively introduced, generating a flurry of requests for information. Next, facts and personal experiences get shared and the group tries to verify the rumor's veracity. Finally, the group breaks up or moves on to another topic.

C. Lee Harrington, a professor of sociology at Miami University in Ohio, who's conducted her own cybergossip survey, concurs. She says chat room enthusiasts, like ordinary gossipers, "attempt to establish the veracity of the information they're sharing through references to outside sources. They rely on secondary sources, refer to personal knowledge and relationships, or, as is the case with entertainment gossip, claim to have direct connections to it, accounting for their 'inside information.'"

While many tabloid items are planted and meant to be spread—especially when they benefit their subject—in cyberspace some celebrities have handled their own PR, responding to fans and critics. Others patrol message boards anonymously gauging response to their work. Even ex-Vice-President Gore, who popularized the phrase "information superhighway," has answered some unsolicited messages via e-mail.

Lips on the Loose

According to researchers, everyone gossips, and we begin almost as soon as we learn to speak. But kids' gossip is decidedly different from adults'; it's more innocent and often more cruel. First, children will gossip in front of the kid they're talking about, using such common bon mots as: "You pick your nose" or "You're a cheater."

"Cruel comments, but effective ones," says Levin, "because the target learns some important information. Namely, that he is not invisible to the rest of the world. The result? This vital piece of information helps him see he needs to change his offensive behavior."

Second, unlike adults, who often gossip to bring someone with power down a notch or two (like celebrities, politicians, bosses, etc.), children, psychologists have found, usually gossip about their marginal peers—the kid who can't hit the ball, or the one in the special class. Rather than bring someone down, they feel more powerful by elevating themselves from the less fortunate and siding with the kids on top.

In his study of gossip among preteens, University of Michigan assistant psychology professor Jeffrey G. Parker, Ph.D., found that adolescents blabbed an average of 18 times an hour, with gossip sometimes taking up as much as 50 percent of their time. "Surprisingly," says Parker, "they were three times more likely to gossip about someone of their own sex as they were about someone of the opposite sex, and they were just as likely to talk about other people's relationships as they were about their own."

Although girls and boys traded inside info about the same amount of time each day, Parker says their subjects differed. "Girls were more apt to talk about boys they 'liked'—and the more popular the boys were, the more likely the girls were to talk about them." But even the most popular boys rarely talked about the girls they 'liked.' Perhaps an indication that early on, men are loath to express their emotions.

Similarly, Parker's research also concluded that pairs of boys who were best friends were less likely to spend time gossiping, while pairs of girl-friends disclosed more. Much of the young women's scuttlebutt was filled with character admiration; conversations were sprinkled with comments like "She's a great dresser" or "She's so cool around boys."

By college, gender differences in gabbing are even more striking. Levin asked his graduate students to sit in the Northeastern cafeteria and tape conversations. They found that women do indeed gossip more than men and that the nature of their gossip is different. The women gossiped about people in their lives who were close to them: family, friends, roommates, people they knew very well. Men usually engaged in "shop talk," which primarily revolved around sports figures, politicians, and people in their class who they hardly knew. "Gossip is similar to a Rorschach test," says Levin. "If you look at the nature of someone's gossip, you can find out what concerns them."

Age continues to play a role in the dynamics of gossip. Older women who have lived in their community longer gossip less than younger women who are relatively new residents, according to research conducted by Lynette Gochenaue, Ph.D., at the University of Pennsylvania. Her study concluded that one way for neophytes to become part of an established group is to know the gossip and spread it. "Another reason newcomers are more inclined to gossip," Gochenaue says, "is anxiety—perhaps caused by unfamiliarity with a new environment."

Other studies support the idea that worry warts are prattle prone. "We found that people who gossip the most rank highest on the anxiety scale," says Rosnow. "Not only do they disclose more, but the anxious are on the receiving end of gossip more often and are more likely than those less anxious to consider information crucial."

Susan Anthony, Ph.D., a professor of psychology at Gallaudet University in Washington, D.C., who has worked with Rosnow and conducted her own gossip research with the deaf population, concurs. "Anxious people are not only more susceptible to gossip, but they're the ones who will transmit information to a larger number of people. What's even more interesting is the speed with which gossip travels within the deaf community. It can start on the East Coast and within hours have landed in California. This is much faster than the hearing population, even if you take cyberspace into account."

The reason, Anthony says, is that in any closed culture—as in a small town or office—"news" travels more quickly because there's a small pool of communicators and communicatees to go around.

But contrary to what most of us might think, when a circle of friends gossips about members of its inner sanctum, it's usually a compliment. "It's a way of saying that others are important," says Gary Allen Fine, Ph.D., a

Evaluating Ideas

Does your own experience support the research findings reported by Westen on gender differences in gossiping? For example, do you find that women gossip more than men and that women gossip more about people close to them, whereas men gossip more about sports figures or people they don't know well?

Explaining Ideas

Of all the gossip you hear on campus what percentage is positive? Neutral? Negative? Are these percentages similar to those you'd find in the workplace or in the neighborhood or in your Internet chat groups?

professor of sociology at the University of Georgia. "We gossip about people we care about. We don't bother talking about people who don't matter to us."

But Fine admits this is a shadowy area. "Most of the time, the gossip spread between two people about a third absent friend is neutral news: a pregnancy, a promotion. But gabbing about buddies can also be a breach of the social structure." Often prefaced with the plea, "Swear you won't tell anyone," these are negative tidbits, like someone's being cheated on by a spouse. Obviously, this kind of betrayal is difficult to overlook and many a friendship has ended because of a broken confidence. When it comes to talking about friends, it's probably best to follow the adage: If you don't have anything nice to say, don't say anything at all.

While there's also wisdom in the old Irish proverb, "Who brings a tale, takes two away," Rosnow and colleagues say there's more to it. When Rosnow asked subjects who they "liked," he found gossipees—the people being talked about—were usually not the most popular, essentially because they're different and don't conform. But the people engaging in gossip weren't particularly popular either because of their untrustworthiness. Highest rated were those who could keep a balance between their roles as gossiper and gossipee.

Gossiping also seems to lead to lying, if only because most people want to appear as if they have the inside track. When Levin and other researchers posted notices inviting college students to a wedding that never took place, a surprising 12 percent of the students later questioned claimed to have attended. Some even described the bride's wedding dress.

Psychologists are not immune to the gossip mill, either. Ofra Nevo and Anat Derech, professors at the University of Haifa, Israel, decided to study gossip because during long hours of case conferences it sometimes seemed that colleagues discussing clients were actually gossiping. "We were impressed by the similarity between what takes place in clinical conferences when professionals analyze patients' personal problems and what takes place in social settings when friends gossip about acquaintances," Nevo reports.

After administering a newly developed test called the Tendency to Gossip Questionnaire, Nevo and Derech concluded that there is a correlation between the inclination to gossip and the job you chose. People who are gossip junkies tend to work in people-oriented professions—including psychology. Further, they suggest, therapy can actually be regarded as a sublimated form of gossip. After all, in both cases, people talk and exchange intimate information about other people.

Communicating Skillfully

Let's say that you're in a small group around the proverbial water cooler and someone begins gossiping about an office colleague. The gossip is especially negative and, what's more, you're pretty sure it's false. What do you say, if anything?

The Big Blur

Although the average yenta doesn't distinguish between gossip and rumor, people who study the subject do. Rosnow says gossip is always about people and can involve either fact or supposition. Rumors, on the other hand, may or may not involve people but are always speculative. "It's a collective hypothesis," says Rosnow. "Let's say there's a rumor that a company's going to be bought. When an employee of that company discusses the rumor with another employee who knows the facts, for that person it's not a rumor. For one individual it's speculative and a rumor, but for the person in command of the facts, it's not." If the employee with information confirms the rumor for the other employee, then it becomes gossip.

Rumors basically deal with people's anxieties and uncertainties, Rosnow says, and he divides them into two types: wish rumors that we hope are true, and dread rumors that we pray are false. Your company is giving a year-end bonus, property taxes are going down, there's not going to be a final exam. These are examples of wish rumors. Dread rumors are on the darker side: there are going to be layoffs at work, a fare increase is on the way, your company is going to be moving.

Frederick Koenig, Ph.D., a professor of social psychology at Tulane University and author of *Rumor in the Marketplace,* says commercial rumors can also be divided into two categories: conspiracy and contamination. In the former, speculation is that some group or movement is thought to have infiltrated a commercial operation. For example, recent conspiracy rumors erroneously alleged that Genesee Beer, Entenmann's Bakery, and Celestial Seasonings Tea were owned by the Unification Church (the Moonies) and that the Church of Satan controlled Proctor and Gamble and Mobil Oil. Contamination rumors run the gamut from worms in McDonald's hamburgers to urine in Corona Beer and spider eggs in Bubble Yum bubble gum.

In 1984, Jean-Hoel Kapferer, a dedicated rumor maven and French academic, created the Foundation for the Study of Rumors based in Paris. Kapferer contends that rumors are not just idle speculation. They are based on xenophobic tendencies or our society's fears. He believes farfetched rumors that refuse to die—like the ones about snakes slithering out of bananas and children's teddy bears—indicate a fear of Africa or South America, where bananas grow, and of Asia, where the teddy bears are manufactured. The rumor that McDonald's burgers were infested with worms coincided with the rising concern in the United States about the deleterious effects of junk food on health. "Rumors," says Kapferer, "are an echo of ourselves. They reveal the desires, fears, and obsessions of a society."

Although Koenig often consults with corporations about how to put a stop to specific rumors, he insists that like jokes, nobody knows who starts them in the first place. "I have no illusions about the free enterprise system. Corporations will do anything to make money. But savvy companies know that a rumor can easily be transferred from a competitor's product to their own." Case in point: Koenig was originally hired to dispel the rumor that Wendy's hamburgers were contaminated with worms. Weeks later, the worms must have had a Big Mac attack because they'd supposedly moved on to McDonald's.

Directing positive corporate rumors—also known as creating buzz— appears to be easier. When Chrysler wanted to create word of mouth about

Ethical Judgments

What kinds of gossip do you find unethical? One example that ethicist Sissela Bok offers in her *Secrets* is that gossip is unethical when you know it to be false but still pass it on. Can you think of other kinds of gossip that would be unethical?

a new line of cars, it lent them to about 6,000 community leaders as well as top executives for weekend use. Chrysler's strategy succeeded; 98 percent of those who'd been lent the cars said they would recommend them to friends.

Gossip Crazed?

There's no arguing that the media are ablaze with gossip. From *A Current Affair* and the *National Enquirer* to *Nightline* with Ted Koppel and even the venerable *New York Times,* we're inundated with dirt. Scooping has become a national pastime. But Rosnow insists the media's obsession with gossip doesn't necessarily reflect our insatiable craving for it. "You know, one year it's medical shows, the next it's comedies, and now it's talk shows and gossip."

But journalist Nicholas Lemann disagrees. He believes there's a national longing for gossip and it's something we need and can be proud of. In an article for the *New Republic,* Lemann said, "Gossip is an appurtenance of a striving, socially unified society. It's worth watching as a barometer of our aspirations. As the middle classes obtain for themselves the glamorous, turbulent lives of the rich and famous, there is real danger that gossip as we know it could whither away. We could return to the status quo, ante-Society in which nobody's personal life was considered to be nationally riveting.

"The truth is, the proper time to become alarmed about the role of gossip in American Society is when there starts to be less of it."

Levin believes we have nothing to worry about. He says gossip will never go out of style. Rosnow agrees gossip's not going anywhere because it's "part of human nature." It may sometimes look as if it's reached a fever pitch, he says, but it's cyclical. "At a particular point in the cycle, it seems like it's reached its nadir and is disappearing. But then it starts back up again and ultimately reaches a pinnacle." Because we're coming up on the Olympics and an election season, Rosnow says, plan on lots of chatter; the same thing happens around World Series time.

But is there a point where the dirt we dig up is, well, just too personal? There seems to be only one area where even the most callous columnist won't tread: 'outing' a public figure. But Rosnow suspects that won't continue for long. "As soon as one person breaks a taboo and profits either financially or through notoriety, then other people will jump on the bandwagon."

For those insatiable gossip fiends with a tough case of dependency, that's good news. Spread the word.

Brain Talk

When listening in general, but in listening to gossip in particular, perceptual accentuation can lead to serious message distortion. Perceptual accentuation leads you to accent certain things you think you hear, you want to hear, or expect to hear instead of what is actually said. Beware of this tendency; it can seriously distort your ability to listen critically. Ask yourself, for example, if you're interpreting messages as favorable because they concern people you like and as unfavorable because they concern people you dislike. Are you seeing the motivation in a friend's charity as help and seeing the same behavior from someone you dislike as tax avoidance?

Cultural Analysis

Office gossip is part of the culture of many organizations. Focusing on your own place of employment, what topics do people gossip about? What's the single favorite topic of gossip? Do they focus more on office issues or on personal issues? Are they more positive than negative? Are they generally kind or unkind?

14

How to Use Your Face

The face is clearly one of the most communicative channels you have. With your face you can communicate a wide variety of emotions and can often read the thoughts and feelings of others from facial expressions. In this article Deborah Blum reviews what we know about the communicating face.

Want to learn more? Terry Landau's *About Faces* (New York: Doubleday, 1989) is a fascinating and detailed account of the evolution of the human face and how it communicates thoughts and feelings as well as deceives others by helping to hide these thoughts and feelings. Any of the many nonverbal communication textbooks provide useful reviews of research and theories on facial communication. Search one of the on-line bookstores for *nonverbal communication.* *Psychlit, Sociofile,* and *ERIC* all contain abstracts of useful research studies on nonverbal communication. Search the Web for *nonverbal communication + syllabus* to find syllabi for courses in nonverbal communication; they'll effectively illustrate the breadth and depth of this area of communication.

Who hasn't waited for an old friend at an airport and scanned faces impatiently as passengers come hurrying through the gate? You can recognize instantly the travelers with no one to meet them, their gaze unfocused, their expressions carefully neutral; the people expecting to be met, their eyes narrowed, their lips poised on the edge of a smile; the children returning home to their parents, their small laughing faces turned up in greeting. Finally, your own friend appears, face lighting up as you come into view. If a mirror suddenly dropped down before you, there'd be that same goofy smile on your face, the same look of uncomplicated pleasure.

Poets may celebrate its mystery and artists its beauty, but they miss the essential truth of the human countenance. As scientists now are discovering, the power of the face resides in the fleeting split-second expressions that slip across it thousands of times each day. They guide our lives, governing the way we relate to each other as individuals and the way we connect together as a society. Indeed, scientists assert, the ability to make faces—and read them—is vital both to our personal health and to our survival as a species.

Deborah Blum, "Face it!" *Psychology Today* (September/October, 1998), 32–39, 66–70. Reprinted with permission from *Psychology Today* Magazine. Copyright © 1998 Sussex Publishers, Inc.

Growing out of resurging interest in the emotions, psychologists have been poring over the human visage with the intensity of cryptographers scrutinizing a hidden code. In fact, the pursuits are strikingly similar. The face is the most extraordinary communicator, capable of accurately signaling emotion in a bare blink of a second, capable of concealing emotion equally well. "In a sense, the face is equipped to lie the most and leak the most, and thus can be a very confusing source of information," observes Paul Ekman, Ph.D., professor of psychology at the University of California in San Francisco and a pioneer in studying the human countenance.

"The face is both ultimate truth and fata morgana," declares Daniel Mc-Neill, author of the new book *The Face* (Little Brown & Company), a vivid survey of face-related lore from the history of the nose to the merits of plastic surgery. "It is a magnificent surface, and in the last 20 years, we've learned more about it than in the previous 20 millennia."

Today, scientists are starting to comprehend the face's contradiction, to decipher the importance of both the lie and leak, and to puzzle out a basic mystery. Why would an intensely social species like ours, reliant on communication, be apparently designed to give mixed messages? By connecting expression to brain activity with extraordinary precision, researchers are now literally going beyond "skin deep" in understanding how the face connects us, when it pulls us apart. "The face is a probe, a way of helping us see what's behind people's interactions," explains psychology professor Dacher Keltner, Ph.D., of the University of California-Berkeley. Among the new findings:

- With just 44 muscles, nerves, and blood vessels threaded through a scaffolding of bone and cartilage, all layered over by supple skin, the face can twist and pull into 5,000 expressions, all the way from an outright grin to the faintest sneer.

- There's a distinct anatomical difference between real and feigned expressions—and in the biological effect they produce in the creators of those expressions.

- We send and read signals with lightning-like speed and over great distances. A browflash—the lift of the eyebrow common when greeting a friend—lasts only a sixth of a second. We can tell in a blink of a second if a stranger's face is registering surprise or pleasure—even if he or she is 150 feet away.

- Smiles are such an important part of communication that we see them far more clearly than any other expression. We can pick up a smile at 300 feet—the length of a football field.

- Facial expressions are largely universal, products of biological imperatives. We are programmed to make and read faces. "The abilities to express and recognize emotion are inborn, genetic, evolutionary," declares George Rotter, Ph.D., professor of psychology at Montclair University in New Jersey.

- Culture, parenting, and experience can temper our ability to display and interpret emotions. Abused children may be prone to trouble because they cannot correctly gauge the meaning and intent of others' facial expressions.

Making Faces

Deciphering facial expressions first entails understanding how they are created. Since the 1980s, Ekman and Wallace Friesen, Ph.D., of the University of California in San Francisco, have been painstakingly inventorying the muscle movements that pull our features into frowns, smiles, and glares. Under their Facial Action Coding System (FACS), a wink is Action Unit 46, involving a twitch of a single muscle, the *obicularis oculi,* which wraps around the eye. Wrinkle your nose (Action Unit 09), that's a production of two muscles, the *levator labii superioris* and the *alaeque nasi.*

The smile, the most recognizable signal in the world, is a much more complex endeavor. Ekman and colleagues have so far identified 19 versions, each engaging slightly different combinations of muscles. Consider two: the beam shared by lovers reunited after a long absence and the smile given by a teller passing back the deposit slip to a bank patron.

The old phrase "smiling eyes" is exactly on target. When we are genuinely happy, as in the two lovers' reunion, we produce what Ekman and Richard Davidson of the University of Wisconsin-Madison call a "felt" smile. The *zygomatic major* muscles, which run from cheekbone to the corner of the mouth, pull the lips upward, while the *obicularis oculi* crinkle the outer corner of the eyes. In contrast, the polite smile offered by the bank teller (or by someone hearing a traveling salesman joke for the hundredth time) pulls up the lips but, literally, doesn't reach the eyes.

It doesn't reach the brain either. Felt smiles, it seems trigger a sort of pleasurable little hum, a scientifically measurable activity in their creators' left frontal cortex, the region of the brain where happiness is registered. Agreeable smiles simply don't produce that buzz.

Are we taught to smile and behave nicely in social situations? Well, certainly someone instructs us to say, "Have a nice day." But we seem to be born with the ability to offer both felt and social smiles. According to studies by Davidson and Nathan Fox of the University of Maryland, ten-month-old infants will curve their lips in response to the coo of friendly strangers, but they produce happy, felt smiles only at the approach of their mother. The babies' brains light with a smile, it appears, only for those they love.

Evolution's Imperative

Why are we keyed in so early to making faces? Charles Darwin argued in his 1872 book, *The Expression of the Emotions in Man and Animals,* that the ability to signal feelings, needs, and desires is critical to human survival and thus evolutionarily based. What if infants could not screw up their faces to communicate distress or hunger? Or if foes couldn't bare their teeth in angry snarls as a warning and threat? And what if we couldn't grasp the meaning of those signals in an instant but had to wait minutes for them to be decoded?

Everything known about early hominid life suggests that it was a highly social existence," observes Ekman, who has edited a just-published new edition of Darwin's classic work. "We had to deal with prey and predators; we had a very long period of child rearing. All of that would mean that survival would depend on our being able to respond quickly to each other's emotional states."

Today, the need is just as great. As Ekman points out, "Imagine the trouble we'd be in, if when an aunt came to visit, she had to be taught what a newborn baby's expression meant—let alone if she was going to be a caretaker." Or if, in our world of non-stop far-flung travel, an expression of intense pain was understood in one society but not in another. "And yet," says Ekman, "we can move people from one culture to another and they just know."

Researchers have identified six basic or universal expressions that appear to be hardwired in our brains, both to make and to read: anger, fear, sadness, disgust, surprise, and happiness. Show photos of an infuriated New Yorker to a high-mountain Tibetan or of a miserable New Guinea tribeswoman to a Japanese worker, and there's no translation problem. Everyone makes the same face—and everyone gets the message.

One of the expressions that hasn't made the universal list but probably should is embarrassment. It reflects one of our least favorite emotions: who doesn't loathe that red-faced feeling of looking like a fool? Yet such displays are far less self-centered than has been assumed. Rather than marking a personal humiliation, contends Keltner, embarrassment seems designed to prompt social conciliation.

Think about it. If we accidentally spill a drink on a colleague, stumble into a stranger in the hall, what's the best way to defuse the tension and avoid an escalation into battle? Often, notes Keltner, even before offering a verbal apology, we appease the injured party by showing embarrassment.

When we're embarrassed, our hands tend to come up, partly covering the face. We rub the side of the nose. We cast our eyes downward. We also try to appear smaller, to shrink into ourselves. These behaviors aren't uniquely ours. In awkward social situations, chimpanzees and monkeys do the same thing—and accomplish the same end. The actions defuse hostility, offer a tacit apology, even elicit sympathy in viewers. (When Keltner first tentatively introduced his chosen topic at research meetings, even jaded scientists let out immediate empathetic "oohs" at the slides of people with red faces.)

"There are physiological changes associated with this," notes Keltner. "If people see an angry face staring at them, they have a heightened autonomic response—rising stress hormones, speeding pulse—all the signs of fear. When they see an embarrassment response, fear is reduced."

A reddened face and downward glance typically start a rapid de-escalation of hostility among children involved in playground quarrels, says Keltner. Parents go easier on youngsters who show visible embarrassment after breaking a household rule, such as playing handball on the living room wall or chasing the dog up and downstairs throughout the house. Adults also go easier on adults. In one of Keltner's studies, jurors in a hypothetical trial meted out much lighter sentences when convicted drug dealers displayed the classic signs of embarrassment.

Cultural Rules

Expressions aren't dictated by biology alone, however; they are deeply influenced by cultural attitudes. De Paul University psychologist Linda Camras, Ph.D., has been exploring why European-American adults seem so much more willing than Asians to express emotion in public. In one experiment, she studied the reactions of European-American and Asian infants, age 11 months, to being restrained by having one arm lightly grasped by a researcher.

European-American and Japanese babies were remarkably similar in their visible dislike of being held still by a stranger's grip. (The scientists let go if the babies cried for seven seconds straight.) Since infants show no apparent inborn difference in the willingness to publicly express dismay, it stands to reason that they must eventually learn the "appropriate" way to express themselves from their families and the society in which they are reared.

Ekman's work clearly shows how culture teaches us to subdue our instinctive emotional reactions. In one set of studies, he asked American and Japanese college students to watch nature films of streams tumbling down mountainsides and trees rustling in the wind, and also graphic tapes of gory surgeries, including limb amputations. Everyone grimaced at the spurting blood at first. But when a note-taking scientist clad in a white coat—the ultimate authority figure—sat in on watching the films, the Japanese students' behavior altered radically. Instead of showing revulsion, they greeted the bloody films with smiles.

"No wonder that foreigners who visit or live among the Japanese think that their expressions are different from Americans," says Ekman. "They see the results of the cultural display rules, masking and modifying the underlying universal expressions of emotion."

Blank Looks

Mental or physical illness, too, can interfere with the ability to make faces—with profound consequences for relationships, researchers are learning. Neurophysiologist Jonathan Cole, of Poole Hospital at the University of Southampton, Great Britain, and author of the new book *About Face* (MIT Press), points out that people with Parkinson's disease are often perceived as boring or dull because their faces are rigid and immobile.

Consider also depression. As everyone knows, it shuts down communication. But that doesn't mean only that depressed people withdraw and talk less. The normal expressiveness of the face shuts down as well.

In one experiment, psychologist Jeffrey Cohn, Ph.D., of the University of Pittsburgh had healthy mothers mimic a depressed face while holding their infants. The women were told no to smile. Their babies responded with almost instant dismay. At first they tried desperately to recruit a response

Cultural Analysis

How would you explain the cultural influences on your own facial expressions? For example, has your culture taught you to reveal certain emotions and to conceal others? Has it taught you that in certain situations some facial expressions are appropriate and that in other situations the very same expressions would be inappropriate? How did it teach you these "rules"?

from their mother, smiling more, gurgling, reaching out. "The fact that the babies were trying to elicit their mother's response shows that at an early age, we do have the beginnings of a social skill for resolving interpersonal failures," Cohn notes.

But equally important, the infants simply could not continue to interact without receiving a response. They stopped their efforts. The experiment lasted only three minutes, but by that time, the babies were themselves withdrawn. "When mothers again resumed normal behavior, babies remained distant and distressed for up to a minute," says Cohn. "You can see that maternal depression, were it chronic, could have developmental consequences.

In fact, children of depressed parents tend to become very detached in their relationships with others. They often fail to connect with other people throughout their life and experience difficulties in romantic relationships and marriage, in large part, researchers suspect, because they have trouble producing and picking up on emotional signals. "We think that the lack of facial animal interferes with forming relationships," says Keltner.

Reading Faces

Displays of emotion are only half the equation, of course. How viewers interpret those signals is equally important. "We evolved a system to communicate and a capacity to interpret," observes Keltner. "But much less is known about the interpreting capacity."

What scientists do know for certain is that we are surprisingly bad at discerning the real emotions or intentions behind others' facial expressions. "One of the problems that people don't realize is how complicated face reading is," notes Pollak. "At first glance, it seems very straightforward. But if you break it down—think of all the information in the face, how quickly the brain has to comprehend and analyze it, memories come in, emotions, context, judgments—then you realize that we really can't do it all."

Or can't do it all well. What we seem to have done during our evolution is to learn shortcuts to face reading. In other words, we make snap judgments. "It's not actually a conscious decision," Pollak explains. "But decisions are being made in the brain—What am I going to pay attention to? What am I going to clue into?"

Most of us are pretty good at the strong signals—sobbing, a big grin—but we stumble on the subtleties. Some people are better than others. There's some evidence that women are more adept than men at picking up the weaker signals, especially in women's faces.

In an experiment conducted by University of Pennsylvania neuroscientists Ruben and Raquel Gur, men and women were shown photos of faces. Both genders did well at reading men's expressions. Men also were good at picking up happiness in female faces; they got it right about 90% of the time. But when it came to recognizing distress signals in women's faces, their accuracy fell to 70%.

"A woman's face had to be really sad for men to see it," says Ruben Gur. The explanation may lie in early human history. Charged with protecting

Explaining Ideas

How would you explain the gender differences that you observe in encoding and decoding facial expressions? For example, do men and women use facial expressions to reveal the same negative and positive emotions? Do men and women express facially the same intensity of emotions? Are men and women equally adept at reading the facial expressions of others?

their tribes, men had to be able to quickly read threats from other males, suggests Gur. Women, in contrast, entrusted with child-rearing, became more finely-tuned to interpreting emotions.

We may be biologically primed to grasp certain expressions, but our individual experiences and abilities also filter the meaning. Mental disorders, apparently, can swamp the biology of facial recognition. People with schizophrenia, for instance, are notoriously bad at face reading; when asked to look at photographs, they struggle to separate a happy face from a neutral one.

Mistaking Cues

Seth Pollak, Ph.D., a psychologist at the University of Wisconsin-Madison, has been exploring how children who have suffered extreme parental abuse—broken bones, burn scarring—read faces. In his studies, he asks these youngsters and those from normal homes to look at three photographs of faces which display classic expressions of fear, anger, and happiness. Meanwhile, electrodes attached to their heads measure their brain activity.

Battered children seem to sustain a damaging one-two punch, Pollak is finding. Overall, they have a subdued level of electrical activity in the brain. (So, in fact, do people suffering from schizophrenia or alcoholism. It seems to be a sign of trouble within.) However, when abused youngsters look at the photo of an angry face, they rapidly generate a rising wave of electrical energy, sharper and stronger than anything measured in children who live in less threatening homes.

When Pollak further analyzed the brain activity readings, he found that abused children generate that panicky reaction even when there's no reason to, misreading as angry some of the other pictured faces. They are so primed to see anger, so poised for it, that when making split-second judgments, they tilt toward detection of rage.

This falls in line with findings from DePaul's Camras and other psychologists, which show that abused children struggle significantly more in deciphering expression. "Overall, there's a relationship between the expressive behavior of the mother and the child's recognition ability," Camras says. "And it's an interesting kind of a difference."

Identifying negative expressions seems to be essential in human interaction; four of the six universal expressions are negative. In most homes, notes Camras, mothers use "mild negative expressions, little frowns, tightening of the mouth." Children from such families ar every good at detecting early signs of anger. But youngsters from homes with raging furious moms have trouble recognizing anger. "If the mom gets really angry, it's so frightening, it's so disorganizing for children that it seems they can't learn anything from it."

Explaining Ideas

How would you explain your own ability to distinguish between real and feigned facial expressions of happiness or sadness, for example? Have you ever misjudged a feigned expression as genuine or a genuine expression as feigned? What happened?

The Best Defense

So, out of sheer self-protection, if the children from abusive homes are uncertain about what a face says—as they often are—they'll fall back on anger as the meaning and prepare to defend themselves. "They overdetect rage," says Pollak. Does this create problems in their relationships outside the home? It's a logical, if as yet unproven, conclusion.

"What Darwin tells us is that emotions are adaptations," Pollak explains. "If a child is physically abused, I'd put my money on an adaptation toward assuming hostile intent. Look at the cost for these kids of missing a threat. So what happens is, they do better in the short run—they're very acute at detecting anger and threat because unfortunately they have to be. But take them out of those maltreating families and put them with other people and their reactions don't fit."

One of Pollak's long-terms goals is to find out if such harmful effects can be reversed, if abused children can regain or reconstruct the social skills—that is, reading faces—that are evidently so critical to our design.

Failure to read signals accurately may also figure in juvenile delinquency. "There are studies that have found that juvenile delinquents who are prone to aggression have trouble deciphering certain expressions," says Keltner. "They're not as good as other kids at it. Is that because they're particularly bad at reading appeasement signals like embarrassment? That's something we'd really like to know."

Truth or Lies?

One area where *everyone* seems to have trouble in reading faces is in detecting deception. We average between 45% and 65% accuracy in picking up lies—pretty dismal when one considers that chance is 50%. Secret Service agents can notch that up a bit to about 64%; scientists suspect that improvement comes only after years of scanning crowds, looking for the faces of potential assassins.

Con artists, too, seem to be especially adept at reading expressions. The latter are also skilled at faking emotions, a trait they share with actors. Not surprising, since success in both careers depends on fooling people.

We seem to be duped particularly easily by a smile. In fact, we tend to implicitly trust a smiling face, just as we do a baby-faced one. In one experiment, Rotter cut out yearbook photos of college students and then asked people to rate the individuals pictured for trustworthiness. In almost every instance, people chose the students with smiling faces as the most honest. Women with the biggest grins scored the best; men needed only a slight curve of the lips to be considered truthful. "Smiles are an enormous controller of how people perceive you," says Rotter. "It's an extremely powerful communicator, much more so than the eyes."

Incidentally, we aren't suckered only by human faces. We can be equally and easily tricked by our fellow primates. In one classic story, a young lowland gorilla gently approached a keeper, stared affectionately into his face, gave him a hug—and stole his watch. Chimpanzees, too, are famous for their friendly-faced success in luring lab workers to approach, and then triumphantly spraying them with a mouthful of water.

Ethical Judgments

At what point, if any, do you feel facial management techniques—the kinds of strategies you might use to hide your true feelings or to substitute a socially acceptable expression for the one you're really feeling—are unethical? Under what conditions, if any, would you feel it would be unethical to *not* use such facial management techniques?

There *are* clues to insincerity. We tend to hold a simulated expression longer than a real one. If we look carefully, a phony smile may have the slightly fixed expression that a child's face gets when setting a smile for a photograph. As we've discussed, we also use different muscles for felt and fake expressions. And we are apt to blink more when we're lying. But not al-ways—and that's the problem. When Canadian researchers Susan Hyde, Kenneth Craig, and Christopher Patrick asked people to simulate an ex-pression of pain, they found that the fakers used the same facial muscles—lowering their brows, tightening their lips—as did those in genuine pain. In fact, the only way to detect the fakers was that the expressions were slightly exaggerated and "blinking occurred less often, perhaps because of the cog-nitive demands to act as if they were in pain," the scientists explain.

We do a better job of finding a falsehood by listening to the tone of a voice or examining the stance of a body than by reading the face, maintains Ekman, who has served as a consultant for police departments, intelligence agencies, and antiterrorist groups. He's even been approached by a national television network—"I can't tell you which one"—eager to train its re-porters to better recognize when sources are lying.

Which brings us to perhaps the most provocative mystery of the face: why are we so willing to trust in what the face tells us, to put our faith in a steady gaze, a smiling look? With so much apparently at stake in reading fa-cial cues correctly, why are we so prone to mistakes?

Living Smoothly

Most of us don't pick up lies and, actually, most of us don't care to," declares Ekman. "Part of the way politeness works is that we expect people to mis-lead us sometimes—say, on a bad hair day. What we care about is that the person goes through the proper role."

Modern existence, it seems, is predicated to some extent on ignoring the true meaning of faces: our lives run more smoothly if we don't know whether people really find our jokes funny. It runs more smoothly if we don't know when people are lying to us. And perhaps it runs more smoothly if men can't read women's expressions of distress.

Darwin himself told of sitting across from an elderly woman on a rail-way carriage and observing that her mouth was pulled down at the corners. A proper British Victorian, he assumed that no one would display grief while traveling on public transportation. He began musing on what else might cause her frown.

While he sat there, analyzing, the woman's eyes suddenly overflowed with tears. Then she blinked them away, and there was nothing but the quiet distance between two passengers. Darwin never knew what she was think-ing. Hers was a private grief, not to be shared with a stranger.

There's a lesson in that still, for all of us airport face-watchers today. That we may always see only part of the story, that what the face keeps secret may be as valuable as what it shares.

15

How to Use Eye Contact

In this article Gordon R. Wainwright discusses eye contact and offers some interesting exercises to heighten your awareness of how eye contact works and how it can be used more effectively.

Want to learn more? Peter Marsh's *Eye to Eye: How People Interact* (Topside, MA: Salem House, 1988) and Evan Marshall's *Eye Language: Understanding the Eloquent Eye* (New York: New Trend, 1983) provide readable and thorough reviews of how the eye communicates. If you want to look at the recent research consult the *Psychlit, Sociofile,* and *ERIC* databases for such terms as *eye contact, eye avoidance, pupil dilation,* and *eye communication.*

We begin improving our mastery of body language by looking at the eyes and at how they are used in the process of everyday face-to-face communication. We begin with the eyes because they are the most powerful means of communication we possess, after words (although sometimes, a single glance can speak volumes, as they say). This power of the eyes is at its greatest, of course, when two people are looking at each other (which usually means looking at each others' eyes). This is usually called mutual gaze or, as we shall call it here, *eye contact.*

Why eye contact should be so powerful is not clear. Several writers on nonverbal communication (an alternative term for body language) have speculated on the possible reasons. Some have suggested that, from the cradle, we find other people's eyes of compelling interest and will even respond to sets of circles that look like eyes because it is through the eyes that we first have contact with others. Some have suggested our response to eye contact is instinctive and connected with basic survival patterns, in that youngsters who could secure and retain eye contact, and therefore attention, stood the best chance of being fed and of having their other needs satisfied. Others have suggested that the significance of eye contact is learned and that, as we grow up, we quickly learn not to misbehave if an adult is watching us or we learn that certain kinds of look tell us that people like us (or dislike us).

Whatever the reasons, the power of eye contact in communication is clear and we shall give most of our attention here to considering the forms it takes, the uses it can be put to, and how we can use it more effectively.

Cultural Analysis

How would you explain your own cultural teachings—from say your parents or teachers—about appropriate and inappropriate eye contact? How were these teachings communicated to you? For example, were you explicitly taught the rules of eye contact or did you learn them from observing the adults around you?

Gordon R. Wainwright, "Eye Contact," *Body Language* (Chicago, IL: NTC Publishing Group, 1993), pp. 5–16. Used with permission of NTC/Contemporary Publishing Group, Inc.

First of all, though, let us begin our study of eye contact with an exercise. It will be helpful, as you read through this book, if you can find the time to carry out the simple exercises and experiments described. In this way, you will learn better body language in the same way you would learn to improve any other language. Here is an exercise in eye contact for you to try as soon as a suitable opportunity presents itself. After it, we shall discuss the kind of results you might have expected. We shall do this in each chapter so that you will have plenty of opportunities to put the instruction offered into practice.

Exercise: What Are They Looking At?

Next time you are in a public place, like a bar or a restaurant, observe the other people present as discreetly as you can. Note how they look at each other when they are talking. Note how long each period of eye contact is (no need to time it—just note whether the mutual glances are short or long). Do they spend all their time looking at each other or do they look around at the other people present? Do they spend much time looking at objects in the room? How do they react when someone enters or leaves? What kinds of people look at each other the most (and least) when they are talking? How do the patterns of eye contact of people sitting side by side differ from those of people sitting opposite each other? What else do you notice about patterns of eye contact?

Explaining Ideas

As the author notes, staring at a stranger can often be interpreted as aggressive behavior and can easily provoke an argument. How would you explain why this can very easily occur?

If your discreet observations are noticed by others, it will be advisable to abandon them for a while. The reason for this is that people can react in unpredictable ways to being watched. Some become embarrassed, some will consider you some sort of eccentric, and yet others may become irritable and even aggressive. You might like to speculate on why this should be so. What is it about being watched that should be so disturbing? Some of the possible reasons will be suggested in the next section, but you will find it useful to consider the problem first yourself before you read them.

You will find it helpful if, as you work through this book, you record your responses to the exercises in a notebook. Alternatively, if you have a cassette recorder, you may prefer to record them on tape. In this way, you will have something to refer to when you read through the Exercise Review which follows each major chapter exercise. You will find that this increases the benefit you derive from your study of body language.

Exercise review

So, what did you find out? If the observations you made were anything like typical (as indicated by the research studies on which this book is based), you will probably have noticed some of the following points:

1. When people are talking, they do not look at each other the whole time, but only in a series of glances.

2. In places like bars and restaurants, some time will be spent in looking at other people present, especially those who are attractive or who may be behaving oddly (e.g., drunks and those engaged in disputes with a waiter).

3. Unless the above criteria apply, little attention will be paid to staff members of the establishment and even confidential conversations will probably continue uninterrupted when staff are within earshot (the same usually happens in places like taxis and chauffeur-driven cars).

4. When people pay more attention to objects in the room and even to the decoration, it may signify that they are bored with the conversation, are newcomers to the place, or are so familiar with each other (e.g., those who have been married a long time) that little conversation is necessary (or possible).

5. Leaving or entering tends to attract attention. Many people who are a little embarrassed about walking alone into a bar or a restaurant tend to forget that this initial curiosity is typical and that it will cease as soon as someone else enters.

6. Those who are having an intimate, personal conversation may look at each other more and for longer than those who are not.

7. People sitting opposite each other will display more eye contact than those sitting side by side. If those sitting side by side desire more eye contact they will turn to face each other.

8. You will probably not have been conducting this exercise for many minutes before someone has noticed what you are doing or is at least aware that you are not behaving normally.

Some of the possible reasons why people find it disturbing to be watched by someone else are:

1. The watcher may have an intention of harming them in some way.

2. Being watched makes you ask yourself *why* you are being watched, which makes you self-conscious and therefore undermines your self-confidence.

3. They may feel they ought to recognize the watcher and if they cannot this may disturb the pattern of their interaction with others.

4. They may think the watcher is sexually attracted to them and may not find him or her attractive, which would make them want to avoid eye contact. They would find this difficult, and therefore embarrassing or irritating, if the watcher continued watching.

5. They may be being rather silly, as people often are when with loved ones or friends, and may feel that the watching stranger will assume they are always like that. This might be a blow to their images of themselves as intelligent and sophisticated people.

6. They may take the watching as a sign that the watcher wants to join their group and group members often do not welcome newcomers as this affects the structure of the group. The smaller the group, the stronger this feeling may be (witness the popular proverb, 'Two's company, three's a crowd').

Eye Grammar

Now that we have completed our first exercise, let us examine some of the forms eye contact can take and some of the rules which govern its use. Eye contact can be long-lasting (as when two lovers gaze into each other's eyes) or it can be short (as when looking at someone we know does not like being stared at). It can be direct (a bold, full-frontal gaze) or indirect. It can be intermittent (the kind we use in conversation simply to check that the other person has understood us) or continuous (as in a stare).

There are rules about where we can look at each other and for how long. Try looking at someone's genital region or down a girl's low-cut dress and you will soon realise that you have broken a rule. Many people will find it embarrassing just to read that last sentence, let alone try it out, so rigid is the rule under all but the most exceptional circumstances.

Too much eye contact can be very unsettling for most people. Staring is usually considered impolite, at the very least. The only people who seem to be able to use a frank, open stare are young children, in whom it may even be regarded favourably as a sign of a healthy curiosity about the world.

It is nearly always tolerated in children, but some mothers (especially of middle-class backgrounds) may tell children of school age that it's rude to stare. It is almost never tolerated in adults and those who stare are often regarded as mentally deficient or socially dangerous and threatening in some way. A continuous stare is an easy way to unsettle or provoke someone.

Most of the rules of eye grammar (as is the case with all other forms of body language) are dependent on the context in which eye contact occurs. Some, however, are universal. That is to say they have similar applicability in any context, at any time, anywhere in the world (or almost anywhere). The main ones, according to Michael Argyle and other researchers, are:

Communicating Skillfully

How would you use eye contact to signal that you're paying attention and are interested in what the speaker is saying? To signal that you agree or disagree with what the other person is saying? To signal that you like and are perhaps romantically interested in another person? How do you compensate for the lack of eye contact when you communicate online, in e-mail, or in chat groups especially, but also in newsgroup postings?

1. Too much eye contact (as in staring or frequent glances at another person) is generally regarded as communicating superiority (or at least the sense of it), lack of respect, a threat or threatening attitude, and a wish to insult.

2. Too little eye contact is interpreted as not paying attention, being impolite, being insincere, showing dishonesty, or being shy.

3. Withdrawing eye contact by lowering the eyes is usually taken as a signal of submission.

4. A person will look at another a lot: when they are placed far apart; when they are discussing impersonal or easy topics; he is interested in the other and his/her reactions; he likes or loves the other person; he is trying to dominate or influence the other; he is an extrovert; or he is dependent on the other and the other has been unresponsive.

5. A person will look at another very little: when they are placed close together; they are discussing intimate or difficult topics; he is not interested in the other's reactions; he doesn't like the other person; he is of higher status; he is an introvert; or he is suffering from one of certain forms of mental illness.

6. People will communicate with each other more effectively if their interaction contains the amount of eye contact they both find appropriate to the situation.

Uses of Eye Contact

A number of the uses which we make of eye contact have already been mentioned, but there are others. Broadly speaking, most of the uses can be grouped into six categories. In other words, we establish eye contact when we are:

1. Seeking information.
2. Showing attention and interest.
3. Inviting and controlling interaction.
4. Dominating, threatening and influencing others.
5. Providing feedback during speech.
6. Revealing attitudes.

Let us examine each of these categories a little more closely. The kind of information we acquire through eye contact consists of such things as clues about whether or not someone is telling the truth (liars tend to avoid eye contact unless they are very brazen); whether someone likes us or not; whether the other person is paying attention to or understanding what we say; what a person's state of mind is (people who are depressed or introverted, for instance, tend to avoid eye contact); and whether a person recognises us or not (here, eye contact will be used together with facial expression to arrive at a decision).

As soon as we look at someone, they know they have our attention. If we look at them for longer than a few seconds, they will infer that they also have our interest. Eye contact plays a vital role in one aspect of showing attention and interest and that is in sexual attraction. Consider the problem of indicating to a stranger that you were sexually attracted to her (or him) if you were unable (or too shy) to look at her.

When we look at someone, we invite them to interact with us. If this interaction takes place, eye contact is then used in a number of ways to control the nature and duration of the interaction. It plays a major role in synchronising what happens between two people.

There is not only more looking at the other when listening than when speaking, but eye contact also signals the end of an utterance when one speaker is, as it were, handing the floor over to the other. When we greet people we not only look at them but our eyebrows also move up and down quickly once. This 'eyebrow flash' as it is called occurs worldwide in a variety of cultures as an indication of recognition and greeting. When eye contact is broken, another pattern is seen. Individuals habitually break gaze to left or to right, that is, when they look away, they look to something else to the right or the left of the speaker. There is some evidence to suggest that left

Communicating Skillfully

While walking down the street, you see two friends who have been dating for the last few years and they are embroiled in a heated argument. They see you coming and they notice that you see them arguing. You really like these people and don't want them to feel embarrassed. What messages—especially those from your eyes—would you try to communicate to them?

breakers tend to be arts rather than science-trained and to be visualisers with strong imagination. Right breakers tend to be science-trained and to have less visual imagination. Further, if people are posed verbal questions they will tend to break gaze to the right and downwards; if they are asked spatial questions they will tend to break to the left and upwards, though this tendency is not so marked. Winking can also be used to control interaction to indicate that something is not to be taken seriously or to show a friendly attitude toward the other.

Long, unflickering looks are used by those who seek to dominate, threaten, intimidate or otherwise influence others. Many people do not like to feel dominated or threatened so that, if this kind of behaviour occurs in situations like negotiations or interviews, it can have an adverse effect on the outcome.

Feedback is important when people are speaking to each other. Speakers need to be reassured that others are listening and listeners need to feel that their attentiveness is appreciated and that speakers are talking *to* them rather than *at* them. Both sets of requirements can be met by the appropriate use of eye contact. The effects of eye contact in interpersonal communication are explored in the exercises at the end of this chapter.

Attitudes are often revealed by the willingness, or otherwise, of one person to provide another with opportunities for eye contact. People who like each other engage in more eye contact than those who do not. Aggression, an extreme form of dominance, may be signalled by prolonged eye contact—the phrase 'eyeball to eyeball confrontation' conveys what is involved here. Shame, embarrassment and sorrow are usually characterised by the deliberate avoidance of eye contact. Other emotions, too, have typical eye behaviour. When people are excited, their eyes tend to make rapid scanning movements. When they are afraid, their eyes appear to be frozen open, as if not to miss the slightest movement that may bring danger nearer. When people are angry, their eyes narrow, often into little more than slits. Sadness is expressed by looking downwards as well as by reducing eye contact and this seems to happen almost universally.

> **Ethical Judgments**
>
> Can you identify instances where eye contact would be considered unethical?

Research into Eye Contact

It is not part of the purpose here to discuss research methods, and those who are interested in exploring the subject of eye contact in more detail should read *Gaze and Mutual Gaze* by Michael Argyle and Mark Cook (Cambridge University Press, 1976). But it is interesting to note that experiments have shown that people, especially children, will respond even to very simple drawings of eyes in much the same way as they respond to eyes themselves. Eye movements when perceiving stationary objects, or when reading, follow similar patterns to those used in the perception of people. A good deal of evidence has accumulated to indicate that greater eye contact leads to greater liking—you can actually come to like someone more by engaging in more eye contact with them.

There are considerable individual differences in the amounts and types of eye contact employed (as, for instance, between introverts and extroverts, or men and women) and there is the consequent need to note the context carefully before attempting too free an interpretation of the precise meaning of a particular pattern of eye contact. Patterns of eye contact change with certain kinds of mental illness and this may become a diagnostic tool in the future. Even when people are talking on the telephone, and therefore cannot see each other, eye movement patterns have many similarities with those in face-to-face communication.

In these and other areas, research into eye contact and eye movement behaviour is revealing that the communicative uses of the eyes are many and varied. They are coming to be seen as much more than 'windows to the soul' and it will be useful at this point to consider some of the secrets of the eyes that we are only now beginning to learn.

What Our Pupils Can Teach Us

Two intriguing facts about eye behaviour have been discovered in recent years. One is that when we see something interesting our pupils dilate. The other is that we like people with dilated pupils better than those with contracted pupils.

The first fact was the result of research carried out by Eckard Hess and reported in his book *The Tell-Tale Eye* (Van Nostrand Reinhold, 1975). In his experiments he showed people a set of five pictures: a baby, a mother and baby, a nude male, a nude female, and a landscape. He measured pupil responses to these pictures and found that men's pupils dilated most to the nude female (except for homosexuals whose pupils dilated most to the male nude). Women's eyes dilated to the male nude, but dilated most to the mother and baby. His researches established that these pupil changes equated to people's interest in the various pictures.

Hess also showed people two pictures of the face of an attractive girl. The pictures were identical, but in one the pupils had been retouched to make them appear larger. Almost everyone asked thought the picture with the enlarged pupils was more attractive, but very few were able to say why. It seems, therefore, that while we respond to pupil changes, we are not aware of their effect on our responses at the conscious level (Fig. 15.1).

Pupil responses have also been used to measure attitudes towards various things, such as products advertised or political candidates. The more favourable the attitude, the more dilated the pupils. It is also possible to measure changes in attitude by measuring changes in pupil responses over time. Because pupil changes are not within our conscious control, they provide a very reliable indication of interest, attraction and a number of different attitudes.

Cultural Analysis

What rules do most members of your culture observe in eye contact? For example, does your culture have different rules for men and for women? For adults and for children? For friends and for strangers? What types of eye contact are typical for a male student at your college? For a female student? What is the single major difference?

FIGURE 15.1   Both faces are smiling, but to most people the one on the left appears cold and insincere. What do you think?

Making Better Use of Your Eyes

How can we use the kind of information given in the last few pages to improve our use of this aspect of body language?

First, we can become more observant. We can, without making it too obvious, pay a little more attention to where other people are looking and for how long. We can be particularly observant about any changes in pupil size. This can clearly only be done with people we are physically close to. We can note the amounts of eye contact that the different individuals we meet seem to prefer. And we can remember that we can often tell things about others' real thoughts and feelings from how and where they look that they would never think (or dare) to put into words.

Secondly, we can engage in more eye contact in order to promote greater liking of ourselves by others and to produce other positive responses.

Thirdly, we can remember that, on most occasions, a direct, open gaze is preferable to any hint of avoidance of eye contact or a tendency to look quickly from one thing to another (which may be interpreted by others as shiftiness on our part).

Next, we can use all the information given above to increase our sensitivity to the kinds and amounts of eye contact appropriate in different contexts and avoid the extremes of staring or a total refusal to meet someone else's gaze.

We can develop positive attitudes towards other people, since this will, quite unconsciously and without any effort, promote a more effective use of eye contact on our part.

We can develop a more outgoing approach to other people for the same reason. If you like people and go out of your way to mix with them, this does seem, quite naturally, to produce a better use of eye contact.

Finally, we can use the information given in later chapters about other aspects of body language to enable us to integrate a better use of eye contact into a much more effective deployment of all our nonverbal and verbal communication skills.

What you should do now is to set some time aside over the next few days for practising the various uses of eye contact explored in the exercises which follow.

Exercises and Experiments

1   Look at me when I'm talking to you

With a person you know well, in an encounter, provide them with as much eye contact as you can without embarrassing them. Do they appear to take this as a signal that you want to carry on talking and prolong the encounter? You should find that they do.

2   Staring down

Stare at someone until they look away. Select someone you know well enough to conduct this experiment with but do not tell them about it in advance. *Do not select a stranger as staring can easily be interpreted as aggressive behaviour and may well provoke aggression in return.* Consider how you feel as you perform this experiment. Ask your subject how he or she felt during your staring. How long, approximately, was it before your subject looked away? If you are able to try this experiment with a number of people you should not only be able to explore in more detail your own feelings about staring but should be able to collect quite a lot of useful information about the nature and effects of staring generally.

3   Look into my eyes

Select someone you know well and like very much. Persuade them to sit down with you and look into your eyes for about a minute. Then discuss what you both experienced during the experiment.

4   Does she/he like me?

Select an attractive stranger at a party, dance hall or other place where it is socially acceptable for strangers to approach and talk to each other. Try to decide from their eyes alone, as you chat casually, whether or not they like you. How does their willingness or otherwise to engage in eye contact affect your estimate of how much they like or dislike you? Observe other couples and try to assess the nature of their relationship from the amount and type of eye contact they engage in. How easy or difficult is it to select just one aspect of body language for observation in this way?

16

How to Express Criticism

In this article, the author discusses a unique approach to criticism: the TACTful approach: Tell, Affect, Change, Tradeoff. As you read this article, consider your own approach to criticism as well as your own tendencies in responding to criticism.

Want to learn more? The entire book from which this section was taken will prove helpful in learning how to deal with the criticism of others. Another approach offers advice on giving criticism: Hendrie Weisinger, *The Critical Edge: How to Criticize Up and Down Your Organization and Make It Pay Off* (New York: HarperCollins, 1990).

According to Confucius, "*Not to enlighten one who can be enlightened is to waste a man; to endeavor to enlighten one who cannot be enlightened is to waste words. The intelligent man wastes neither his man nor his words.*"

Most people believe giving criticism is tough. Why is that? Actually, there are a number of reasons why we procrastinate or avoid giving criticism.

1. *We don't like to rock the boat.* We see criticism as an invitation to conflict, and we tend to avoid conflict. So even when there are gnawing problems that negatively affect relationships, job performance, or the ability to grow, we do not address them. We prefer to ignore these problems and hope they'll go away by themselves.

2. *We feel uncomfortable when we give criticism.* Since we feel uncomfortable when we get criticism, we project those feelings of discomfort onto the person we want or need to confront. Our assumption that the other person will react badly keeps us from giving criticism.

3. *Giving criticism takes time.* We think that giving careful, constructive criticism is so time-consuming that we would rather avoid it and take up the slack ourselves. This problem is prevalent among managers who believe that keeping after employees to do their jobs properly is more time-consuming and difficult than doing it themselves

4. *We believe that giving criticism does not work.* Because we procrastinate about giving criticism, when we finally do give it our uncomfortable feel-

---

Mary Lynne Heldmann, "The TACTful Message: How to Give Criticism," *When Words Hurt: How to Keep Criticism from Undermining Your Self-Esteem* (New York: Ballantine Books, 1988), pp. 183–188. Reprinted by permission of the author.

ings have grown so strong that we have to let off steam. The criticism is given in the heat of the moment, thoughtlessly and badly. The response to a poorly delivered criticism is often negative. Therefore, the experience tells us that giving criticism doesn't work very well.

Giving criticism is easier when we recognize its worth.

1. *Criticism uncovers problems.* It does not create them. It is far better to bring problems out in the open than to let them accumulate and harm a relationship, a job performance, or an individual's effectiveness. Calling attention to problems is the first step in solving them.

2. *Criticism saves time in the long run, especially on the job.* A manager may invest time in observing and talking to his or her staff, but the alternative is allowing problems to go unsolved. Then the manager sacrifices efficiency and is not doing the job properly.

3. *Careful, thoughtful criticism stops the build-up of uncomfortable, unhealthy feelings.* Consistent, ongoing criticism is far better than an accumulation of destructive feelings that eventually will have to be vented.

4. *Criticism encourages learning and growth.* Without feedback and criticism, our efforts in many areas could be less effective and less successful.

Ethical Judgments

What one ethical guideline for using criticism would you suggest for the "Ethical Criticism Bill of Rights"? Would this guideline apply equally to teacher-to-student, manager-to-assistant, General-to-Sergeant, friend-to-friend, and lover-to-lover?

The Tactful Message

Preparing your criticisms according to this model will give you an excellent chance of getting your message across. There are four elements in the tactful message:

Tell	Talk about the other person's behavior
Affect	Describe how the behavior affects you, the relationship, or the organization
Change	Request a change in the behavior
Tradeoff	State the positive consequences of a change in behavior.

Tell

Before you can tell the other person what the unwanted behavior is, you must observe both the action and the spoken word carefully. Then describe the specific action and/or statement to the person. Do not describe what the person does not do; stick to what he or she does do. Be sure to address behavior, not attitudes. Behavior is objective; attitude is subjective. Also, include the frequency of the action. Do not use words like "always" and "never" when describing the behavior. If you do, the other person is likely to become defensive and tell you about the one time he or she did not behave in the way you have just described. Be sure to remain calm and non-judgmental. Address only one unwanted behavior at a time.

Brain Talk

One of the ways in which your perceptions may be distorted is by the self-serving bias—the tendency to take credit for the positive ("I'm just naturally generous") and to disclaim responsibility for the negative ("The instructions weren't clear, no wonder I got a low score"). This type of thinking helps to preserve self-esteem, but at the same time distorts perceptual accuracy and may prevent you from hearing criticism that may help you. In listening to criticism, it often helps to ask yourself if you're blocking out potentially useful insights.

Poor	Good
You are constantly leaving priority work to help Grace. That's ridiculous because you're falling behind in your own work.	I've seen you at Grace's desk three times today and twice yesterday.
I find that you have a nonchalant and bored attitude when I talk to you about this Project.	When I talk to you about this Project you stare into space and sometimes yawn.
You never listen to me.	Frequently when we have discussions, such as yesterday and this morning, you interrupt me or look around as I am speaking.

Affect

Let the person you are criticizing know how the behavior affects you, the relationship, or the organization. Express how you feel about the troublesome behavior, not what you think about the behavior or the person. Take responsibility for your own feelings. Do not say, "That makes me feel …" Remember, no one makes you feel anything.

Cultural Analysis

What has your culture taught you about the relationship between gender and criticism? Do the sexes have equal rights when it comes to criticism or are men and women expected to focus their criticism on different things or to express criticism differently?

Poor	Good
You make me worry. I feel that you are pampering Grace too much.	I'm concerned because your work seems to be suffering. Your last report was late and incomplete.
You put me off and degrade me because you are ignoring me.	I feel put down and ignored when you won't focus on me. Also, I'm concerned about your interest in this important Project because the department is working as a team. One person's enthusiasm will affect another's.
I feel that you are not interested in anything I have to say. You want your way, period. You're spoiled.	I feel ignored and hurt and I'm afraid this does not lead to an open give-and-take relationship, which is what I am looking for and hope that you are, too.

Don't say "I feel that …" when you mean "I think that …" Just because you use the word "feel" does not mean you are talking about feelings. When you describe your feelings, use words like, for example, hurt, angry, frustrated.

If it is inadvisable to express your own feelings, then refer to the adverse effects on the relationship or organization. Be clear, not dramatic. You are negotiating a change in behavior, not trying to make the other person feel bad.

Change

Tell the other person what you want him or her to do instead of continuing the troublesome behavior. Limit your request to one or two specific actions. Don't be overbearing or dictatorial. Be responsive to the other person. Ask for feedback or agreement. Perhaps you will need to change your behavior in this situation, too.

When you are specific about the change you want, you can monitor the other person's progress. If Carl does homework for only half an hour, instead of the hour you agreed on, tell him. If Lynn interrupts, tell her right on the spot. Simply give the information; don't get emotional or lecture.

Tradeoff

State what the other person is apt to gain by changing his or her behavior. Think carefully about what the other person wants, what will truly motivate him or her, keeping in mind that people are more apt to be motivated by reward than by punishment.

Poor	Good
Stay out of Grace's office. She'll figure out her own work if you leave her alone.	I think you'd do better to stay at your own desk and help Grace once or twice a day at most. What do you think?
Stop ignoring me! Hold still and pay attention. This is important.	I would like you to establish eye contact with me so that I know you are listening. If this Project doesn't interest you, let's talk about that.
I want you to pay attention to me for a change!	Please make eye contact when I am talking, and wait until I finish my thought before you speak. You might try taking a moment to think before you respond. Does that make sense to you?

Ethical Judgments

Would it be unethical to negatively criticize: (1) A friend's success because you feel jealous? Because you honestly believe it will bring your friend unhappiness later on? (2) A colleague's proposal to make your own proposal look better? Because you honestly believe it's weak and needs improvement? (3) Another person who is dating the same person you are and to whom you seem to be losing out? Because you honestly believe that this person is basically an unsavory character?

Communicating Skillfully

Your romantic partner repeatedly dresses in the most inappropriate ways imaginable. Sometimes— like at formal business functions—it's embarrassing and potentially damaging to your career. You'd really like your partner to develop more appropriate dressing habits. How would you confront this problem using the TACTful approach to criticism?

Evaluating Ideas

How effective do you think this TACTful approach to giving criticism would be in online communication? What additional guidelines to giving criticism online would you offer?

If you have spoken about this problem before and you think it is necessary to mention negative consequences, then do so, but try a TACTful message with positive consequences first. In all cases, avoid threats; they only lead to counterthreats and arguments.

Be very careful to avoid judgments and labels when stating your trade-off (and, for that matter, in the other parts of a TACTful message). The more aware you are of those words and phrases, the less you will use them. Here are some commonly used ones: that's wrong, bad, boring, disrespectful, dumb, terrible, awful. Or, you are irresponsible, stupid, clumsy, disorganized, lazy, too sensitive, slow, conceited, loud, crazy.

Judgment words reflect opinions; when giving a TACTful message, stick to the facts.

17

How to Deal with Lying

In this article Charles Ford discusses the nature of lying, the levels or sophistication of the lie, the types of lies, and nonverbal communication of deceit.

Want to learn more? A lively and practical look at lying is offered by Gini Grahman Scott, *The Truth about Lying* (Petaluma, CA: Smart Publications, 1994). A great deal of research has been done on lying and especially the communication signals that reveal whether someone is telling the truth or lying. Search *ERIC, Sociofile,* and *Psychlit* for up-to-date studies.

Man was given a tongue with which to speak and words to hide his thoughts.

—Hungarian proverb

The full genius of language is inseparable from the impulse to concealment and fiction.

—Steiner

The language of lying is often complex and confusing, reflecting the nature of the subject itself. Deception occurs by a variety of means, some with conscious intent and others without. To lie is, by definition, to be deceptive, but not all forms of deception are lying. In this chapter, I consider the various definitions of lying and its associated permutations, the use of nonverbal communication to deceive, and some of the language used to describe the phenomenon of self-deception.

Lying: Deceiving Others

Webster's Seventh New Collegiate Dictionary (1971) defines "to lie" as 1) to assert something known or believed by the speaker to be untrue with intent to deceive, or 2) to create a false or misleading impression. This commonly accepted definition contains two major components. The first is the statement of something believed to be untrue by the liar (the content of the lie), and the second is motivation, the intent to deceive. Interestingly, the definition does not specify "words" but rather the intent to create a false impression. In popular usage, and even among psychologists working in this area of research, a "lie" usually refers to words alone.

The misrepresentations of a psychotic person are not considered to be lies because the person believes them. Nor do we consider honest mistakes or statements made on the basis of misinformation to be lies. Thus, we can have a situation in which deliberately false information (a lie) is passed from one person to a second who believes it. The same information is then passed from the second person to a third person. This secondary transmission of the original lie would not be considered a lie, even though the content of the misinformation is the same for both statements.

As simple as the above definition appears to be, it does lead to some fascinating paradoxes. For instance, it is possible to tell the truth and yet have the intent to deceive (half of the practical definition of lying). For example, a secretary explains to her superior that she is 30 minutes late to work because there had been a terrible accident on the interstate highway. She was technically correct, but she told only part of the truth. In fact, the accident was on the other side of the highway on which she was traveling, and it delayed her only a minute or two. By telling only half the truth, she had effectively deceived.

In yet another situation, one may tell "the truth" but may lie! If one incorrectly believes something to be true and deliberately states the opposite (which *is* true) in an effort to deceive, then the full definition of lying has been met because of the intent to deceive, even though the truth was spoken.

Language of Lying

The English language has many terms and euphemisms to describe lying (see Table 17.1). Karpman (1953) commented that the number of synonyms for "truth" is small, but those related to lying might fill several pages in a dictionary. Shibles (1985) noted that a rich vocabulary of deceit is not unique to English and provided a long list of German words descriptive of lying. "Lying" is a remarkably emotional word, and to accuse a person of being a "liar" is regarded as an attack. To call someone a liar might, in some cultures, be tantamount to a challenge for a duel. The use of euphemisms softens the aggressive nature of words referring to deceit and also provides gradations of culpability. I define and briefly discuss a few of these words.

Prevarication means deviation from the truth. It is derived from the Latin term meaning to walk crookedly. To *perjure* oneself is to voluntarily (knowingly) provide false statements while under oath. A *fib* is a lie, but it implies one that is trivial or childish. A *mendacious* person is characterized by deception or falsehood. Two words frequently used by historians are *dissemble* and *ingenuous.* The former means to put on a false appearance—to conceal facts, feelings, or intentions. The latter suggests showing a childlike simplicity or naivete, but with a hint of a self-deceptive quality.

New words periodically creep into usage, which are probably attempts to soften the emotional impact of words such as *lies* or *liar.* During the Rea-

Explaining Ideas

How would you explain on-line lying? What types of lies do you encounter the most in online communication? How are these similar or different from the lies you come into contact with in face-to-face situations?

TABLE 17.1 Examples of Words that Connote Deceit

Verbs	Nouns	Adjectives
Belie	Affectation	Clandestine
Bluff	Canard	Double-dealing
Cant	Casuistry	Sham
Cheat	Dishonesty	Surreptitious
Conceal	Disinformation	Untruthful
Connive	Dissimulation	
Contrive	Double-face	
Counterfeit	Duplicity	
Deceive	Fallacy	
Defraud	False-hearted	
Dissemble	Falsehood	
Exaggerate	Fraud	
Fabricate	Humbug	
Fake	Hypocrisy	
Feign	Perfidy	
Fib	Pretension	
Impersonate	Sophistry	
Lie	Stealth	
Malinger	Treachery	
Misrepresent	Trickery	
Perjure	Understatement	
Plagiarize		
Pretend		
Prevaricate		
Slander		

gan administration, the word "disinformation" emerged as a description of deliberate misinformation. During the Iran-Contra investigation, witnesses "groped for polite ways to say the L word. They have confessed to having told half-truths (as opposed to half-lies), or having told the literal truth instead of the real truth." (Baldwin 1989, p. 35). Euphemisms for lying are not limited to American politicians. Winston Churchill used "terminological inexactitude" to describe deceit, and a subsequent British government employed "an economy of the truth" to describe its deceptions (W. P. Robinson 1993).

Levels of Lying

Lies differ in their complexity and sophistication. Leekam (1992) proposed three levels of lying. She describes the first level as manipulating the behavior of another person without the intent (or even the idea) of influencing the other's beliefs. Leekam suggests that such lies are told by small children who may deny misbehaviors to avoid punishment or falsely claim to have done something good to get a reward. These are generally "learned" strategies, employed without understanding that saying something untrue can affect the listener's beliefs. Obviously, these simple lies often fail because small children tend to lie at the wrong time or neglect important issues such as covering their tracks (e.g., leaving cookie crumbs).

The second level of lying takes into account the liar's awareness of the listener's beliefs. The liar must now keep in mind that the false statement (lie) may manipulate the listener's beliefs, that the listener will evaluate the statement as being true or false, and that the listener will, on the basis of the new belief (if the lie has been accepted), evaluate future statements in the light of the new belief. Liars who have reached this level of developmental sophistication are much more effective at deception than are first-level liars. For example, a car salesperson may size up a customer and be deceitful as to certain attributes (e.g., fuel economy, safety, or reliability record) of the car that he or she is selling.

On reaching the third level of lying competence, the liar recognizes not only the effect of the words spoken on the listener's beliefs but also that the listener may be evaluating the liar's own beliefs about the words. In other words, how sincere is the liar? Thus, skilled lying involves convincing the listener that the speaker believes what he or she is saying and has a truthful intention. A skilled liar also continuously "reads" the listener's nonverbal behavior and, in response to "feedback" from the listener, adjusts both verbal and nonverbal communications to be more credible. This skill markedly enhances one's capacity to manipulate other peoples' beliefs and behaviors. Leekam suggests that this ability may be the hallmark of subtle acts of tact, persuasion, and diplomacy. An example of this skill is that the aforementioned car salesperson could "read" the effect of his or her sales pitch on the potential customer. If any disbelief were detected, the salesperson would immediately alter his or her behavior to appear more sincere and credible.

These levels of lying are developmental steps that are not mastered by all people, although most people can learn to lie at the second level.

There is yet another level of skill at other-deception that we can term *advanced lying*. Relatively few persons achieve this sophistication in deceit, but among those that do are certain charismatic politicians, evangelists, sales professionals, poker players, and con artists. These persons, especially the con artists, use psychological ploys to quickly convince their "marks" of their complete trustworthiness, even to the point that life's savings may be handed over to almost complete strangers. Persons with these skills have mastered techniques of monitoring their own nonverbal behavior and controlling it as a means of conscious communication that is simultaneous with their speech.

One politician was notably skillful at dissembling and controlling his nonverbal messages. He always made it a point to make only positive comments about anyone. If, however, he wanted the listener to think poorly of another person, he would provide subtle nonverbal hints of disgust while extolling the person's virtues. The message being broadcast was: "I am really

Communicating Skillfully

Your teenage son is going to his first dance and feels terribly inadequate. The truth of the matter is that he is inadequate in several important social skills—for example, he doesn't dance, is awkward communicating, rarely maintains eye contact, and has the annoying habit of telling long and boring stories. What do you say as he gets ready to go to the dance?

a nice person who likes everybody, but this guy is really a sleazeball." Predictably, some of the people discredited by this manipulative politician were actually fine, upright, and decent people who were slandered through deceptive nonverbal communication (see section, "Nonverbal Deceit," later in this chapter).

Classification of Lies

The existence of numerous terms for lying suggests the need in the English language to differentiate various, perhaps subtle, distinctions of the types of lies. Some authors have also classified lies into separate categories depending on the malignancy, personal psychopathology of the liar, and target of the lie (Bok 1978a; Davidoff 1942; Karpman 1953). Such classifications must be viewed with caution because they may have moral implications. Table 17.2 provides one such classification.

Different types of lies.

The terminology used to classify lies is often obvious. However, it may also be subject to individual or idiosyncratic interpretation. Some commonly used terms are described below.

White lies are basically social lies that serve to lubricate interpersonal relationships. They are frequently provided in such an automatic manner as not even to register in consciousness. For example,

- "I enjoyed your party. Thank you so much for inviting me." (The truth is that the invitation was accepted because of occupational necessity, and the party was deadly boring.)

- "I'm sorry that I can't go out with you Saturday night. I have a previous engagement." (The truth is that the girl wouldn't be "caught dead" in public with the nerd who is asking her for a date, and the previous engagement is washing her hair.)

- "I'm fine. How are you?" in response to "Hi. How are you today?" from a salesclerk. (The truth is that the person has a terrible headache and under the best of circumstances couldn't care less about the health of a stranger.)

> **Cultural Analysis**
>
> What kinds of lies does your culture consider "harmless"? What kinds of lies does it consider "harmful"? Is it more "wrong" to lie to a member of your own culture than it is to lie to someone from another culture?

In general, white lies are social conventions that convey little intention to deceive. They primarily serve to respect the sensitivity and dignity of others. Yet many persons regard any lie as morally reprehensible and will strive to make their statements as factually accurate as possible, sometimes by telling only a portion of the truth. For example, in the first situation, the individual might reword the thanks to: "I really appreciate it that you thought enough of us to invite us to your party."

Humorous lies are those aimed at amusing the listener, and any intent to deceive is transient and teasing. Characteristically, they involve some degree of preposterous exaggeration. For example,

- "Oh, darling! We are so happy to be at your party. When we received your invitation, we interrupted our vacation in Monte Carlo and immediately

TABLE 17.2 A CLASSIFICATION OF LYING	
Type of lie	**Motive**
Benign and salutary lies	To effect social conventions
Hysterical lies	To attract attention
Defensive lies	To extricate oneself from a difficult situation
Compensatory lies	To impress another person
Malicious lies	To deceive for personal gain
Gossip	To exaggerate rumors maliciously
Implied lies	To mislead by partial truths
"Love intoxication" lies	To exaggerate idealistically
Pathological lies	To lie self-destructively

Source. Adapted from Karpman B: "Lying," in *Encyclopedia of Aberrations: A Psychiatric Handbook.* Edited by Podolsky E. New York, Philosophical Library, 1953, pp. 288–300.

flew back." (This statement was made by a neighbor who was invited to a backyard barbecue.)

- "I sold so much dog food last week that no horse within 50 miles was safe." (This statement was made by a sales manager for a dog-food company.)

Altruistic lies are those lies that are told to benefit someone else, to reduce suffering, or to help increase self-esteem. The most commonly cited altruistic lies are those told by professionals to persons for whom they are caring. For example,

Ethical Judgments

Lots of people would say that lying to make a person feel better is not really lying and would not be considered unethical. Can you think of other types of lying that most people would *not* consider unethical? Do you consider it ethical or unethical to lie to make someone feel better? To advance a good cause, for example, to stop teenagers from smoking? To avoid an argument that could possibly damage an otherwise good relationship?

- "Mrs. Jones, you don't have anything to worry about. We will have this cancer licked with chemotherapy." (This was told to a woman with widespread metastatic ovarian cancer.)
- "I know that it's painful now, but you will be united with her in Heaven." (This statement was made by a hospital chaplain to a couple whose daughter had just died of a cocaine overdose.)
- "Of course you are attractive, and there is someone who will want to marry you." (This statement was made by the mother of an unattractive and borderline mentally retarded teenage daughter.)

Although the ostensible purpose of the altruistic lie is to serve the needs of the person to whom the lie is told, such lies may actually be motivated by the lying person's discomfort with the situation (Bok 1978b).

Defensive lies are those told to protect oneself and others. They may be told to avoid punishment or attack from others or to preserve self-esteem. For example,

- "No, I didn't get into the cookie jar." (This was said to a mother by her 4-year-old son who had chocolate smeared on his face.)

- "There is no one here except our family members." (This was told to German Gestapo agents by a Dutch family hiding Jews during World War II.)

- "I don't know what happened. All of a sudden the computer malfunctioned." (This was said by a secretary who accidentally deleted an entire file, an essential manuscript, from her computer's hard drive memory.)

Defensive lies are among those that are easiest to understand and perhaps justify. People who lie to protect themselves or others are acting in self-defense, a time-honored behavior. A lie told in defense of others may also be seen as altruistic.

Aggressive lies are told in an effort to hurt someone else or to gain an advantage for oneself. For example,

- " ... and he was so cheap, he wouldn't buy me dinner!" (This was told to friends by a young woman who was angry that a man had not asked her out for a second date.)

- "I type 60 words per minute." (This was told by an applicant for a receptionist job. Her actual typing rate was 40 words per minute with multiple errors.)

- "Our ships in the Tonkin Gulf were attacked last night by forces of the North Vietnamese Navy." (This was told by the president of the United States to obtain approval for bombing attacks on Hanoi. No evidence of such an attack was ever discovered.)

Aggressive lies are self-serving and may potentially damage others, and therefore, most people would see them as clearly immoral.

Pathological lies (compulsive lies) are of special interest to persons studying the psychology of lying. As used in this book, pathological lies are those that are told even when there is little or no apparent gain to the person who is lying. In fact, the lying often occurs even when the results would be better if the truth were told. Furthermore, the lie is not determined solely by situational factors and appears to be compulsive or fantastic (Selling 1942). In general, lies are termed pathological when they interfere with normal development or are destructive to the quality of the life of the person who tells the lie.

Pseudologia fantastica is a specific form of pathological lying in which the pseudologue (the liar) tells involved stories about life circumstances, both present and past (King and Ford 1988). At first, the stories may seem believable, but with time the inconsistencies often betray their fantastic qualities. Detecting the falsehood is often difficult because there may be a skillful blending of fact and fantasy. The stories are told as if they were real, and the person's emotional state may be consistent with the content provided, thereby supporting the story's apparent authenticity. For example, one pseudologue told the convincing story, while weeping genuine tears, of a car wreck that killed his fiancée and her two young children. The entire story was later proved to be a fabrication. A Munchausen patient who was simulating

Ethical Judgments

Would it be ethical to lie to a romantic partner of long-standing about your current romantic feelings? About your current romantic behavior? About your romantic past? About your romantic fantasies?

Evaluating Ideas

Can you classify the lies you hear in an average day into the categories identified by Ford: white lies, humorous lies, altruistic lies, defensive lies, aggressive lies, and pathological lies? Which seem to occur more often? Can you think of lies that would not fit into these categories? Can you think of lies that would fit two or three categories?

chest pain claimed to be a commercial airline pilot. He stated that because of pain, while landing at Detroit, he had to turn the controls over to his copilot. He further stated that as an Air Force pilot during World War II he had been forced to eject from his burning plane and received shrapnel injuries. In fact, this "patient" was not a pilot, but he did have a police record of 33 arrests and convictions for forgery, alcohol-related disturbances, and other misdemeanors (Heym 1973).

When vigorously confronted with their fabrications, pseudologues can acknowledge that they are not true, thereby demonstrating that the stories are not the delusional products of a psychotic person. However, in their explanations of the discrepancies, they may (convincingly) provide new fabrications. Attempting to determine the "truth" from these persons is like trying to catch a greased pig.

Nonverbal Deceit

Communication is not limited to the words we use. Humans also communicate by a variety of nonverbal means, including the emotions displayed (or concealed) and characteristic symbolic gestures (emblems) (H. G. Johnson et al. 1975). For example, every adult American knows what it means to "give someone the finger." These nonverbal communications may stand on their own as messages or serve as metacommunications to modify the verbal messages being delivered. Affect (emotional display) can be used to emphasize a verbal statement or to negate it (Ekman and Friesen 1969a). Furthermore, just as one can use words to deceive, one can also use nonverbal channels of communication to deceive. Skilled liars, as noted earlier in this chapter, have some measure of control over their nonverbal behavior and expression of emotions.

B. M. DePaulo (1988) suggests that nonverbal deceit is more common than many people realize. Such deceit may be difficult to articulate in words or store into memory simply because it is non-verbal. An example of nonverbal deceit was provided by C. R. Snyder and Higgins (1988). A baseball pitcher whose pitches were being hit by the other team was pulled from the game by his manager. As he left the mound, he began rubbing his pitching arm. The nonverbal message was: "I'm really not that bad of a pitcher. I have a sore arm today." Simulation of physical symptoms may be a common form of nonverbal deceit.

Four major strategies can be used to modify nonverbal behavior: minimization, exaggeration, neutralization, and substitution of emotions and behaviors (Ekman and Friesen 1969a; Saarni 1982).

MINIMIZATION. The result of an individual's attempt to dampen the external appearance of a more deeply experienced emotion is minimization of emotional expression. For example, a surgeon whose patient is failing rapidly after an operation may present himself to the family as "concerned"

Brain Talk

A useful critical tool in dealing with lying is to distinguish facts from inferences and to act on inferences as if they are guesses or hypotheses and not necessarily true. Liars frequently give off a variety of nonverbal cues that many take as signs of lying—shifting posture a lot, touching their face or hair, using many long pauses, avoiding direct eye contact, and making more speech errors. Regardless of how many of these cues are present, remember that you can only make inferences about someone's lying. Treat these inferences as guesses and seek additional confirmatory evidence before drawing any conclusions. Even after you've drawn conclusions, treat them, too, as tentative and be willing to change them when the evidence tells you to.

but outwardly calm, while inwardly he feels panicky as he perceives the looming disaster.

EXAGGERATION. Maximization of felt emotions reflects a dramatic attempt to influence another person. Saarni (1982) suggests that this non-verbal deceit may be the first type of deceit to emerge developmentally. Children are more likely to cry after experiencing a minor injury when they believe that they are being observed than when they believe that no one is attending to them. Persons with a histrionic personality style are more likely to exaggerate their emotions in an attention-seeking manner.

NEUTRALIZATION. An effort to mask emotional response by adapting a "poker face" is known as neutralization. Psychoanalysts and other professionals may display relatively little response in their efforts to appear non-judgmental of the patient's or client's statements. Ekman and Friesen (1974) contend, however, that it is difficult to maintain strict neutrality of emotion and that one's true emotions tend to leak out.

SUBSTITUTION. A common mechanism of hiding one's true feelings is substitution of emotions. One of the most common techniques employed for this purpose is to substitute "pleasure" for a negative emotion. Smiling is one of the easiest nonverbal communications to produce and may be used to mask feelings of arrogance, anxiety, or boredom (Ekman et al. 1988). A shopkeeper may keep smiling even when he or she wishes that a demanding customer, who is unlikely to make a purchase, would leave the store. An employee may smile and graciously accept constructive criticism from a supervisor, even when he or she feels it is unjust.

The importance of nonverbal behavior is so great that no study of deceit can be intelligently pursued without considering this channel of communication.

Ethical Judgments

When would you consider the use of any of the four major strategies to modify verbal behavior to be unethical? Can you identify an unethical example of each of the four strategies?

How to E-Mail Politely

E-mail is often, but not always, a type of interpersonal interaction. In this article, etiquette expert Letitia Baldrige discusses ways to make your e-mails more polite and hence more effective. She offers eight e-mail suggestions that should prove of value to anyone using e-mail. These suggestions, as you'll discover, are equally useful for all types of e-mail, personal as well as business.

Want to learn more? See the excellent article by Philip Vassallo, "U-Mail, I-Mail—More Effective Business E-Mail," *Et cetera: A Review of General Semantics* (Summer 1998): 195–203 or browse through the computer books at your bookstore for suggestions for making your e-mail more effective.

When it comes to communication, the difference between today and 10 years ago is like the difference between the first century and the 18th century. A laptop or a gadget that sits in the palm of the hand makes our investments, orders our groceries, pays our bills and hooks us up with a merchant in Hong Kong or an Alpine guide on Mont Blanc. Forget the gentle manners that were taught before the advent of the cyberage. Gone. Finito.

But even if the traditional forms of civility have evaporated, we still need to greet one another, comfort one another and entertain and learn from one another. In the next century, innovations could allow us to embrace via computer (I wonder what a computerized hug feels like? A robot's kiss?). But in the meantime, let's draw up a set of rules that make the electronic age function more efficiently, predictably, considerately and kindly.

1. Please don't send e-mails that make angry demands on me. How offputting when you scream: "I must have an answer by 2 p.m. tomorrow. Repeat, by 2 p.m. tomorrow." You don't know what's happening in my life, and if you did, you might just change your threatening language.

2. Please don't waste my time with the latest "jokes du jour," sent to hundreds of e-mail addresses, including mine. I don't have time for the jokes, and I am not going to be impressed that you know 200 people to send them to. I start to regard the other names with suspicion. Do they have so little work

---

Letitia Baldrige, "E-Etiquette," *The New York Times* (December 6, 1999), p. A31. Copyright © The New York Times Co. Reprinted by permission.

to do that they can read jokes all day, or am I the only one working under inhuman pressure?

3. Please don't order me to visit your Web page. Ask me nicely, and maybe I will. Most important, don't ask me what I think of your Web page. I don't have time to write a thoughtful response, and besides, you might not want to hear what I think.

4. When I e-mail you a thoughtful note, please don't treat it as if it never existed. At some point, you should send me a short acknowledgment: "Thanks for the important info about the oil company merger. Needed to know that. Best wishes, John." It's frustrating not to know whether or not you received my communication.

5. In my e-mails, I will be careful with my grammar, spelling, sentence structure and punctuation. I realize that if I send a carelessly written missive, I am only diminishing myself in the eyes of everyone who reads it.

6. I will keep my e-mails, those of my staff and those of my children free of foul language.

7. I will not send messages with insulting comments about others. Nor will I spread rumors on line. I realize that what I write in cyberspace, intended for only one other pair of eyes, can be spread to millions of pairs of eyes in a split second.

8. I will send messages of congratulation to those who achieve, messages of consolation to those who are having bad luck and messages of encouragement to those who need jump starts in their lives. In addition, I may write a long, beautiful letter on good stationery.

9. In my e-letters, I will use a salutation and a closing, and state the purpose of the communication up front. I will also add a personal touch: "It was great seeing you at the Convention Hall yesterday" or, "I hope your husband has recovered from his flu by now."

To me, the great promise of cyberspace is speed. Along with the grinding efficiency of it all, just a few thoughtful words can change the entire nature of the communication. Good manners mean a quiet touch of warmth in the cold, new, techno world.

Cultural Analysis

How does your organizational culture treat e-mail? For example, does it have rules regulating potentially offensive e-mail such as sexist jokes or sexual pictures and Web sites?

Communicating Skillfully

Let's say you're a manager of a division employing 12 people. Recently, one of your employees sent a racist e-mail to someone outside the company but, for some reason, it got sent to the entire division. What do you say to the e-mail sender? What do you say to the members of your division?

Evaluating Ideas

How useful are the eight e-mail tips? Would you take issue with any of these suggestions? Would you alter any? Add any?

Evaluating Ideas

How would you evaluate the readings in this volume? Have they been of value to you? Write an e-mail to your instructor in which you state the positive and the negative reactions you've had to the articles you've read so far.

part three

Interpersonal Relationships

Communication is to a relationship what breathing is to maintaining life.

—Virginia Satir

How to Get the Most Out of Relationships

In this article, the authors discuss the importance of interpersonal relationships in securing needed stimulation, in helping each other, and in maintaining physical and emotional health.

Want to learn more? The many and varied articles in Ann L. Weber and John H. Harvey's (eds.) *Perspectives on Close Relationships* (Boston: Allyn and Bacon, 1994) will give you added insights into the importance of interpersonal relationships as will the insights from Albert Ellis and Ted Crawford, *Making Intimate Connections: Seven Guides for Great Relationships and Better Communication* (Manassas Park, VA: Impact Publications, 2001). Research on the gender differences in close relationships is thoroughly covered in Barbara A. Winstead, Valerian J. Derlega, and Suzanna Rose's *Gender and Close Relationships* (Thousand Oaks, CA: Sage, 2000).

Explaining Ideas

Before reading this article, jot down three or four reasons why you feel relationships are important in your life or in the lives of most people you know. Can you explain with specific examples, how your relationships have fulfilled (or not fulfilled) these needs?

Are you happy or unhappy? It can depend greatly on other people—on the help and emotional support they give you and the stimulation they bring into your life. Benefits such as these can flow in some degree from the most casual encounters, but they come especially from established successful relationships. Even your physical health can be affected by the level of emotional support you receive from friends, family and your marriage partner in times of stress.

Stimulating Company and Support

Any company is enlivening to some degree. You can never be completely sure even of what your oldest acquaintances will say next, and this unpredictability contributes to their value, for we are creatures who need a particularly high level of stimulation.

Other creatures need stimulation too, and the penalties for having too little can sometimes be seen in zoo animals. Deprived of enough space to move about in and explore, or deprived of the social life that is natural to their species, animals suffering the stress of boredom pace mechanically back and forth in their cages, pull out their own feathers or fur or withdraw to sit in corners staring blankly. They can also receive too much stimula-

---

Barry McCarthy, Robin Gilmour, and Ian H. Gotlib, "Why Relationships Matter," in *Eye to Eye: How People Interact*, ed. Peter Marsh (Topsfield, MA: Salem House Publishers, 1988), pp. 130–137. Reprinted by permission of Ian H. Gotlib.

tion—for example, in crowded conditions—and the symptoms are similar, but between the extremes there is a happy medium that, given the opportunity, each will find.

For humans too, there is a happy medium of stimulation, but individual differences greatly affect it. Extroverts are thought to have central nervous systems that are less easily aroused than those of introverts. As a consequence, to achieve an optimum level of arousal, extroverts choose brighter colors, listen to louder, more exciting music and mix more with other people. Only the most extreme introverts, however, shy away from all forms of social contact. Age also makes a difference. An old person might find one or two friendly conversations in a day very refreshing while many an adolescent longs to be doing exciting things with friends in noisy surroundings.

Encounters with strangers, distant acquaintances, old friends and those nearest to us can all contribute to the stimulations we need. When we meet and interact with strangers, they are novel and, therefore, interesting in themselves. The people we work with give us challenges that we must rise to, and they share ideas and experiences. People we know also bring novelty into our lives by telling us jokes and bringing us news of themselves and of mutual acquaintances. The ones we know best know from experience what most amuses, entertains or excites us.

Stimulating activity can be solitary, and activity is a recommended therapy for loneliness. But generally people prefer to share it with others.

Perhaps the most pervasive and insistent of human social needs is for self-esteem. We all need our egos supported by receiving some combination of assurances that we are noticed, valued, liked or loved, recognized for what we have achieved and considered right or at least acceptable in what we think or have done. We also need to feel secure, to be reassured that the benefits we enjoy in life will probably continue at an acceptable level. Both security and support for our self-esteem contribute to the *emotional support* that we receive from others.

Very casual—even barely noticeable—relationships give some emotional support. These are "familiar strangers" who affect us simply by always being there. The same waiter standing by the door of the same restaurant that you never go into lends a comforting stability to daily life. This is a stability you may not even notice until one day he is no longer there.

People often make a social display to familiar strangers, a nod and a smile, and perhaps a "Good morning" between distant neighbors who do not know each other's names. If matters are to go no further, why do they bother? The point is that greetings are almost impossible to ignore. You are bound to get a response, and usually it will be a pleasant one. People like to be recognized and acknowledged by familiar figures—the mailman, newspaper sellers, neighbors. It gives a small but important fillip to their day, which they return in kind. In the simple act of exchanging greetings we reinforce each other's self-esteem. So it is when people respond in a positive way to one another in everyday encounters of any sort.

Mostly, however, we turn to people we know well for emotional support. The potential of a person—through similarity of attitude, background and opinion—to make us feel right about ourselves is a main element in making them attractive as a friend. For just the same reason, couples are drawn together by similarity. For friends, husbands, wives and lovers, we tend to choose people who will reinforce our way of looking at ourselves and the world. Close friends and intimates also support us by giving sympathy when we are unhappy, by listening to troubles that we would not reveal to others and by making us feel liked and loved.

We are also dependent for emotional support on relationships that we do no choose. When you must work with someone, the work will be less stressful and more rewarding if you feel recognized for your contribution and liked, and if you receive reassurances when the job seems to be getting on top of you.

Family life is happier and children develop more confidence and more skills when they feel loved and secure and their self-esteem is strongly supported by parents who avoid excessive criticism and give them ample recognition for their achievements. Parents list the love and affection that they receive from their children as the chief value of having them.

Relationships also give emotional support by helping people to fulfill their role expectations and to have a sense of identity. We grow up expecting to be parents, for example—expecting not simply to have a biological relation to children but to be *like* a mother or father to them. Fulfilling this role makes people feel valuable, and it helps them to feel that they are an important part of the wider family and community to whose biological and cultural continuity they are contributing. Similarly, we maintain contact with kin and cultivate good relations with them, and we want to be friends with people at work, partly because this is what "belonging" to the family or the workplace means.

A Helping Hand

Almost always, having a relationship with someone involves mutual help. Some of the help we exchange is tangible. Children help their parents by doing chores around the house, workmates give each other lifts to the office, one sister looks after the children of another. Sometimes we help with information—a friend gives you a useful tip or a parent shows a child how to do a piece of homework. Others also help us by appraising us—they help us to understand, clarify and evaluate our problems so that they are easier to deal with. Out of concern, they may also help to motivate us to overcome problems such as smoking or excess weight. Utter strangers help each other, but usually when someone is in trouble and no one else is available. Neighbors do more, even when they are not friends. They watch out for the repairman, lend tools and cups of sugar and exchange gardening tips, but normally they do not feel close enough to ask for much more than this. Nor do circumstances usually justify it. Formerly, neighbors were more dependent on each other. In a rural community, there may have been no other way

---

Communicating Skillfully

Steve wants to become closer friends with John and wants to show John that he's an appropriate confidant and that John can discuss just about anything with him. What might Steve do or say to demonstrate that he is an appropriate confidant?

of getting a barn built than to ask for help from people who happened to live nearby. Before they had cars, people made more friends in their own street, and relied on them.

Work relationships also produce mutual help—more than neighborhood relationships do, because workmates spend more time together and the time is mainly devoted to getting something done. (Neighbors mainly talk when they are together, at the garden fence or in the street.)

Voluntary relationships can involve higher expectations of help, but these expectations are not uniform. Many friendships mainly involve socializing—the friends see each other for entertainment and seldom ask favors. Other friendships are centered on a shared activity, such as a team sport, and although there may be a high level of loyalty and reliance on one another during practice and play, the friends do not help each other, or meet each other very much, in other areas of life. Close friends, however, sometimes help each other significantly—lending money, providing useful introductions and helping each other and each other's offspring to get jobs.

When we need a lot of help, especially if we have no clear opportunity to pay the favor back—money to meet an emergency, or someone to look after the children while we go out to work—we tend to turn to our families, parents especially but also adult brothers and sisters. Mutual help is most intense in families living under the same roof, usually with some members contributing earnings and all sharing in different degrees the work of looking after the home and each other's daily needs.

The Effect of Close Relationships

A consistent correlation has been found between marital status and reported well-being, and between marital status and mortality rates. Married people are healthier and live longer than people who are single, widowed or divorced, and this applies equally to every age group and to both men and women. And you do not need a marriage certificate to gain these benefits: those cohabitating or in similar long-term intimate relationships do nearly as well as married couples.

There are some simple explanations for this. Intimate partners tend to look after each other, make sure that they are properly nourished and care for each other when ill. Those living alone often develop bad health habits such as an inadequate diet, smoking and/or drinking too much.

However, researchers who have examined more closely the connection between marriage and health have found that not only is *being* married healthier than remaining single, but the *quality* of the relationship may further enhance its protective effects. In England, sociologists found working-class women whose husbands act as intimate confidants to be less susceptible to depression during stressful episodes in their lives. Of those who did not have a husband-confidant and were under stress, more than 40 percent developed clinically significant depression, while only 10 percent of those with a husband-confidant became so depressed.

Cultural Analysis

How would you explain the differences between men and women in the way they approach and deal with interpersonal relationships? For example, do men and women enter relationships to satisfy the same needs? Do they place the same degree of importance on interpersonal relationships? Do they break up relationships for the same reasons or in the same ways?

Explaining Ideas

How would you explain the similarities and differences in the advantages and disadvantages of face-to-face and online relationships?

Another study suggests that people who express their feelings are less prone to develop cancer. Women with breast tumors were interviewed before exploratory surgery. Women who spoke easily about their grievances and disappointments tended to be among those whose tumors were later found to be benign. Those who had more difficulty about communicating grievances were more likely to have cancerous tumors.

Couples with a good supportive relationship are less likely to suffer ill health if either partner becomes unemployed. Among men who lost their jobs as a result of a factory shutdown, those with wives who gave them emotional support had fewer symptoms of illness and lower cholesterol levels, and did not blame themselves for their unemployment. Although they did not find jobs any sooner, they did make a better adjustment.

The likelihood of a schizophrenic suffering a relapse and returning to hospital has been found to reflect the amount of sensitive support given by family members. Hostility and intrusiveness on the part of the sufferer's family results in a poor prospect of recovery.

It also seems that those with children tend to live longer than those with none. This is true despite the dangers to women of pregnancy and childbirth, and the fact that both young babies and adolescents produce a great deal of stress in their parents.

Life Crises and Support

A life-event or life-crisis—such as bereavement, divorce, job loss, or even the excitement of winning a lottery—can upset the balance of a person's life. This means a period of readjustment, a particularly stressful time in which the risk of illness rises.

The amount and type of support needed differs from one recipient to another, depending on their ability to cope. However, support may not be forthcoming, even from those closest to the victim. People in distress are often seen as threatening by others—perhaps because they feel that they, too, could share a similar fate. And the more severe a person's problems, the less likely they are to receive support. For example, studies show that it is more unlikely for those with the worst cases of cancer to receive support than those less seriously afflicted. People who show that they are coping well with a crisis attract social support. However, those in greatest need may be the least likely to get it.

Those who experience crises turn only seldomly to the professionals for help. They are much more apt to turn to informal support systems—family, friends and neighbors and people who have undergone similar experiences. As our need for social support has been increasingly understood, however, hundreds of support groups have come into being. Alongside the well-established ones such as Alcoholics Anonymous and suicide hotlines, there are those for migraine sufferers, battered wives, widows and widowers, parents of hyperactive children—in fact, there are support groups for those affected by almost every misfortune.

The effectiveness of social support is greatly enhanced when the victim can identify with the helper. For example, a woman with breast cancer may be more likely to accept emotional support and practical advice from someone who previously went through the same experience than from a well-meaning but uninformed friend.

Tending Your Social Network

Generally speaking, women make the most of the support offered by family, friends and neighbors, whereas men depend almost exclusively on their relationships with their wives and with workmates. In fact, marriage and other long-term intimate relationships benefit men far more than women, and this may be because women tend to be the supportive partners within them. When men become widowers, they suffer far more illness and depression than widows—perhaps because they have lost more support.

While women have the social skills for generating and maintaining one-to-one relationships with a variety of different people, men tend to derive the rest of their social support from their colleagues at work, and identify more with groups than with individuals. This concentration of all social effort into a very small number of relationships can be dangerous—if, for example, a man loses his job or gets divorced, there may be no friends to rally round and fill the emotional gap.

Your social class will also affect your relationships. On the whole, the marriages of working-class people tend to be less resilient than those of higher classes and more often end in divorce. However, ties between family members are usually far stronger. Relationships among working-class workmates can also be more supportive than those between middle-class colleagues, who are more likely to feel a sense of competition with each other.

Given the association between happiness, health and relationships, it may be possible to have a happier life and reduce the incidence of illness by improving your own and others' levels of social support.

There are a number of ways that this could be done. An awareness of the importance of relationships and social support can make you more determined to create new support systems. This does not mean that you should go out with the express purpose of meeting dozens of new people. The average network of friends and relatives seen frequently is not particularly large—it generally includes some nine or ten people. Moreover, the effects of social support are not necessarily cumulative—having dozens of acquaintances may be far less beneficial than having two or three close friends or one intimate relationship. The best preventive medicine may be simply to strengthen your existing sources of support by enhancing the relationships that you have already.

Brain Talk

Much as anecdotal evidence should not be substituted for research-discovered generalizations, neither should generalizations substitute for universal truths—which we really don't have in the field of interpersonal communication. Results from experimental studies, for example, are generally applicable to a broad range of the population but not to everyone. Therefore, when you read that people do this or that, remember that these are generalizations and do not describe all people. Remember, too, that results from academic research reports are often obtained from college students in the United States. Be careful in applying these results to people who are unlike United States college students, such as people who are significantly older or from difficult cultures.

20

How to Think Clearly about Relationships

In this article, critical thinking and relationship expert, Robert Sternberg discusses six myths about relationships that cause difficulties because people believe them to be true when they aren't. As you read these myths think about your own beliefs. Do (did) you believe these myths?

Want to learn more? If you'd like to explore further the research and theory basis of Sternberg's observations see the book from which this article is taken; it covers four additional myths. Also see Robert J. Sternberg and M. L. Barnes, eds., *The Psychology of Love* (New Haven, CT: Yale University Press, 1988) and Robert J. Sternberg, *The Triangle of Love* (New York: Basic Books, 1988). Also, search the *Psychlit* database for Sternberg's more research-oriented writings.

Do you look at your love life and find yourself asking:

- How did I ever get into this relationship?
- Why am I still in this relationship?
- How could I have lost him/her?
- Why do I keep making the same mistakes over and over again with him/her?
- Why do we keep talking past each other instead of talking to each other?
- Why can't I figure out what is wrong with this relationship?
- Why can't I get him/her to change?

If you are like most people, you're no stranger to some or all of these questions. No matter how intelligent, competent, or skillful you are in other domains, you may find yourself repeatedly frustrated when you try to transfer these abilities to the art of loving.

This dilemma causes great pain for many people. Every year, millions of men and women flock to the bookstores or tune into popular television talk shows looking for some insight into why they can't make their relationships

---

work. They're seeking a new key to unlock the mystery, but they often walk away feeling dissatisfied. In fact, the popular wisdom about achieving success in love hasn't changed much over the years, in spite of the careful examination it has received in the media. We may be more aggressive about looking for solutions than were previous generations, but most of us basically trust the old wisdom without really questioning its validity. When our relationships fail, we blame ourselves. It rarely occurs to us that we should question our fundamental assumptions.

Although certain ideas about love are commonly accepted as fact, scientific research on relationships has shown each of them to be flawed. We get into trouble in our relationships when we measure our reality against these myths—saying, for example, "If he loved me, he wouldn't . . ." or "I thought people who loved each other were supposed to . . ." As the gap between our culturally inspired expectations and our actual circumstances widens, we assume that something is wrong with us.

We readily accept these myths about relationships because they seem to supply the "markers" we need as we travel the uncertain paths of love. No other arena of our lives seems filled with the same degree of confusion and ambiguity; in no other arena are we so consistently at a loss for solutions. In the absence of guidelines, we place our trust in popular assumptions, even when they do not seem consistent with our experiences. Our literature is filled with "answers" that let us off the hook or, conversely, fill us with guilt.

The first step in developing Relationship Intelligence is to see why the common myths of love are not true. There are many such myths; people live them out every day. I have chosen six very common myths to illustrate the chasm that often exists between our love ideology and our real lives.

Myth #1

The best predictor of happiness in a relationship is how deeply you feel about each other.

Explaining Ideas

How would you explain your own beliefs about relationships? Can you list five or six beliefs you have about what constitutes a good relationship? Might some of these beliefs be myths? What evidence do you have for these beliefs?

When Michael Barnes, a graduate student at Yale, and I studied what predicts success in relationships, we found that, contrary to popular belief, the best predictor is not how deeply you feel about one another. Rather, success in relationships is measured by the difference between the way you would ideally like your partner to feel about you and the way you actually perceive your partner to feel. Simply put, it is the difference between what you think you want and what you think you are getting.

Jason and Cynthia have been dating for three months, but Jason feels constantly on guard because he's afraid that Cynthia is pushing for an early commitment. That's the last thing he wants right now, having ended a seven-year marriage just two years ago. His feelings for Cynthia are strong, but he thinks he needs more time before he settles down again.

Why does Jason think Cynthia wants to force a commitment he's not ready for? He has trouble putting his finger on it, but there are a number of signs: The way she asks so many questions and seems overly interested in the answers; the concern he glimpses when he mentions going out with other women; the way she's so solicitous of him; the way she gets so emotional about things he says and does.

If you were to ask Cynthia for her perspective on the relationship, she would say, "There's such a bond between us. I feel as though we were meant to be together." It bothers Cynthia that Jason sometimes seems withdrawn, but she is counting on that to change with time. And there will be time; Cynthia expects them to be together forever.

Clearly, there is a tremendous gap between the way Jason and Cynthia perceive the future of their relationship. But consider a different scenario. What if Cynthia and Jason both felt deeply in love, and could hardly wait for every moment they would be together? What if Jason were as passionately involved in the relationship as Cynthia? Even if they shared this depth of feeling, it would not necessarily tell them very much about their overall prospects as a couple. Jason might *feel* filled with love for Cynthia, but still be unwilling to make a commitment. His perception of what his feelings mean might be quite different from Cynthia's.*

Perhaps the greatest myth of love is that the more deeply it is felt, the more "true" it is—and therefore, the more likely there is to be a successful love match. But when you fail to make the connection between your feelings and your perceptions, you are often left wondering why the most promising relationships don't work out.

In matters of love, we tend to place an overwhelming trust in feelings: a quickening heartbeat, sweaty palms, the dizzying sensations of desire and passion. When these feelings are present, they stand as proof that we are legitimately "in love." But feelings provide a shaky basis for drawing conclusions about the potential of relationships. If our perceptions and expectations are mismatched, all the feelings in the world won't change that fact.

Cultural Analysis	**Myth #2**
As you read these myths, think about whether you were taught any of them. For example, did your parents, teachers, the media, or religious leaders teach you any of these six myths? How? Have you assisted in teaching any of these myths to others?	Living together before marriage will demonstrate whether you will succeed together once you are married.

Nick and Charlene lived together for almost three years before they got married. Both had successful careers—Nick as a lawyer and Charlene as the buyer for a major department store chain. During the time they lived together, they were both satisfied with the arrangement. Each felt available for

---

*The examples in this book are drawn from actual experiences. To protect the privacy of the individuals who told me about their relationships, however, names and other identifying details have been changed.

the other, but they avoided stepping on each other's toes. They were convinced they were right for each other and they got married.

Charlene's disappointment began only a few months after the wedding. Nick seemed to have changed. At first, the changes were slight but, as time went on, he seemed to grow more and more restless. When they argued, Nick often accused Charlene of trying to hold him back, and this attitude confused her because their relationship had always been one of equal sharing—interdependent, rather than dependent.

Charlene also felt Nick was backing down on some of the important agreements they had made before they were married, such as having children and buying a house. He said they weren't ready to make such big commitments, but Charlene wondered how they could not be ready. They had lived together for three years before marriage. She thought getting married was a sign that they *were* ready for the big commitments.

How could Nick and Charlene have such separate views of their relationship after they had lived together for three years?

Actually, people who live together before marriage are statistically more likely to get divorced than people who do not live together before marriage. Yet, the living together was supposed to be a test of how the couple would function together. Why doesn't it necessarily work? It's probably a combination of several factors.

First, people who live together before marriage are likely to be more shy of commitment than those who do not. By living together first, they hope to convince themselves beyond any reasonable doubt that things will work out in the long run. But once they are married, they often continue to be shy of commitment. They still test their partners as they did before the marriage. As they discover the seriousness of the commitment they have made, they may find it hard to accept what they have done, especially when things get difficult. And at some point, things do get difficult in *any* marriage.

A second explanation of why people who live together first are more likely to have trouble after marriage has to do with a psychological condition called "reactance." Reactance is rebellion against a perceived threat to freedom. We sometimes call it the "trapped wolf" syndrome. People differ in how prone they are to reactance, just as their reactions would differ if they were actually caged in a prison or under house arrest. People who live together before marriage may be more susceptible to reactance. In fact, this disposition might be part of what led them to live together in the first place, since living together left them the option of walking away if they started to feel trapped. But after marriage, it is much harder to walk away. They may feel that their freedom is restricted.

Today, many couples accept the idea that living together before marriage is the best way to test the endurance of their commitment. They want a guarantee that everything will work out. But there are no guarantees in life or love, and often living together achieves the opposite of what is intended.

Communicating
Skillfully

Pat and Chris have been romantic partners for three years and recently Pat suggested that they move in together; Pat's argument, basically, is that by living together they'll see if they're compatible enough for a more permanent arrangement. But, Chris has read this article and realizes that living together is not a good predictor of relationship success. What additional arguments might Pat advance for living together? What arguments can you advance against it?

Myth #3

Love conquers all—even a partner's greatest barriers to self-esteem.

Tina was a woman with low self-esteem. She had a history of failed relationships and she finally sought counseling to find out why she always seemed to choose men who belittled her. Her relationships normally followed a set pattern. The men treated her well in the beginning of the relationship, but as they got to know her, they treated her worse and worse. This only reinforced her deep-seated view that she was essentially worthless. It was a message that had been hammered home all her life—first by her parents, then by the teachers at school, and now by the men she met. She wanted the counselor to help her find a way she could present herself to men that would mask her many inadequacies.

The counselor recognized the pattern in the way men's attitudes toward Tina changed over time. And after several months of therapy, Tina began to see for herself that she was seriously misreading the course of her relationships. Because of her poor self-image, she was baiting men to treat her poorly. When men treated her well, she responded in a way that suggested she didn't think much of their judgment, either of herself or of people in general. When, in turn, they demeaned her, she reinforced their behavior, subconsciously indicating that their appraisal was on target. Because the men were rewarded for treating her poorly, their behavior became shaped by the reward system Tina set up. They treated her in the way she thought she deserved. But ironically, when they won her, they lost her. Once they treated her badly enough, she either left them, claiming she was being demeaned, or they left her, having bought the message that she wasn't good enough for them.

This self-destructive dance is not uncommon in relationships where one person has a problem with self-esteem. But it is contrary to the popular wisdom, which suggests that a person with a low opinion of himself or herself need only receive positive reinforcement to bolster his or her self-esteem. Why did Tina not respond to the positive feedback she received from men early in her relationships?

A person with low self-esteem is more likely to feel comfortable with a partner who reinforces his or her self-story than with someone who presents a challenge to that self-image. It is too threatening to be bombarded with new data that are affirming. Without being aware of it, persons with low self-esteem tend to choose partners who feel as they do. When they are paired with a person who thinks too highly of them, they find it impossible to cope with the clash in views. They cannot bring themselves to trust someone whose view of them is in such contrast to their own.

Tina automatically mistrusted men who built her up. She assumed they were only nice to her because they didn't know her well enough to see her many failings. Or, even worse, she suspected they might be deliberately deceiving her, leading her on in order to get something from her. Changing

Tina's view of herself was a task that required several years of therapy. Her self-story was too deeply rooted. It was not enough, as our romantic mythology would have it, for a loving man to come along, sweep her off her feet, and shower her with affirmation.

It is a common relationship myth that one person can change the other by the sheer force of his or her love. But when one person is suffering from low self-esteem or other blocks to intimacy, a solution cannot be forced from the outside. We like to believe that we can rescue our loved ones and eliminate these barriers. We like to believe that love—specifically, *our* love—can conquer all. But true change and growth must come from within. It cannot be controlled from the outside, no matter how hard we try.

This myth is often acted out with couples when one person is addicted to alcohol or drugs. A woman whose husband was an alcoholic once told me, "I know he drinks because he doesn't have enough confidence in himself. If I can show him that I really love and respect him for who he is, he might not need to drink so much." This woman had been trying to do just that for five years, to no avail. Her words of support sounded hollow to her husband, and often he resented her for her attempts to control him. She, in turn, resented him for not getting better. Until she acknowledged that her husband's addiction was beyond her power to change, she would continue to be trapped in this destructive relationship.

Myth #4

"Chemistry" is the unpredictable wild card in a relationship.

We usually think of chemistry as a mysterious "wild card"—totally unpredictable. But scientific research indicates that we tend to repeat the attachment styles we developed in infancy in our adult relationships. When we believe the myth that love "happens" to us, we fail to recognize—and avoid—destructive patterns.

Jeffrey Young, a brilliant psychotherapist in New York City, has devised a form of therapy called "schema therapy." According to Young, all of us grow up with "early maladaptive schemas," resulting from early experiences coping with life. One such schema, called vulnerability, leads a person to perceive constant threats to his or her personal integrity, whether they be financial, emotional, intellectual, occupational, or some other. Such a person may have grown up feeling insecure or seeing weaknesses or helplessness in those around him or her. Another schema, abandonment, is likely to result from feelings of being left alone and helpless in childhood. It is the fear that those who are most loved will leave and it leads to a reluctance to commit totally to love. Other schemas include dependence, fear of losing emotional control, unlovability, emotional deprivation, social exclusion, sexual undesirability, mistrust, poor judgment, incompetence, shame/inferiority, unrealistic standards, excessive self-control, guilt, inadequate self-discipline, and unrealistic freedom.

When people talk about "chemistry" in a relationship, they are often not aware that one predictable aspect of chemistry is the tendency to seek out and feel attraction for people who reinforce our early maladaptive schemas. These schemas, typically primitive and subconscious, cling to us like electrostatically charged underwear. They are so much a part of our identity that, even if we are aware of them, we are often reluctant to give them up—which, according to Young, is one of the reasons we are attracted to those people who reinforce them.

Not all early schemas are maladaptive. But chemistry has a way of generating explosive reactions—and those reactions often play upon early maladaptive schemas.

Lucy learned from the time she was very young that the best way to survive in her family was to avoid getting too close to anyone. The relationships in her family were cool—whenever a family member would start to get too close, other members would back off. It was believed that family members should treat one another with respect, which meant no meddling in personal matters. Lucy's parents were distant and discouraged open displays of affection; as Lucy grew up, she preferred to maintain some distance from other people. When she entered into romantic relationships, she found herself attracted to men who could not deal with being close. Although she admired men who could relate to her intimately, she found that they didn't turn her on. Thus, chemical reactions were following Lucy's early maladaptive schema of seeking distance, even when she consciously desired intimacy.

According to Mary Ainsworth, a professor at the University of Virginia who has studied infant-attachment patterns, an infant who is separated from his or her mother for relatively brief periods of time tends to react in one of three ways when the mother reenters the room. One type, the secure infant, seeks out the mother gladly, showing only minor distress at having been separated. The secure infant contrasts with the avoidant infant, who, upon the mother's return, actively avoids her. Both of these infants are in contrast to the anxious/ambivalent infant, who desperately seeks out the mother upon her return, and has tremendous difficulty in dealing with the separation.

What does this have to do with adult relationships? Phillip Shaver, Ph.D., of the State University of New York at Buffalo and his colleagues have found that we tend to repeat in our adulthood the attachment style we developed in infancy. The adult who was secure as an infant will tend to be secure as an adult. But the adult who was either avoidant or anxious/ambivalent in infancy will tend to recapitulate these schemas in adulthood. The chemistry of a relationship, therefore, is at least somewhat predictable.

Research by Elliot Blass and his colleagues at Johns Hopkins University takes the question of chemistry one step further. Although his research was done with rats, it is conceivable that the results of the research may extend to humans. Blass studied baby rats born to mothers who had been immersed in a certain odorant. When the baby rats grew up and sought mates, they preferred rats that had been immersed in the same odorant as their mothers. In other words, the smell associated with the mother seemed to influence the chemical bonding of a rat with a mate.

Although we have a long way to go in understanding the phenomenon of chemistry—what attracts one person to another—we are beginning to understand that many predictable elements are involved. Chemistry does not appear to be the "wild card" in relationships that we once believed it to be.

Myth #5

The ability to communicate will improve as you get to know one another better.

As Harry and Ellen grew closer, Harry found himself opening up to Ellen about his past, including telling her about some of his bizarre sexual exploits. Harry had a voracious appetite for sex and had gotten himself into situations that made for interesting telling, especially when he found that Ellen was willing to accept him and his background.

Over time, Harry found himself less and less able to stay faithful to Ellen and he started regularly seeing other women on the side. Ellen wanted an exclusive relationship, but Harry, although he didn't want to lose Ellen, still longed for the adventures of the past.

Harry was able to be completely frank with Ellen about his past relationships, but he was like a clam when it came to leveling with her about his current activities. He was afraid of losing her and it was too big a risk to tell her what was happening. He became more and more secretive about his feelings and his activities. When Ellen eventually found out he was seeing other women, she left him, not so much because of what he was doing, but because he had broken faith with her by not telling the truth.

It often happens in relationships that the closer we become, the more we feel we have to lose by communicating honestly with one another. At the start of the relationship, we may hold back from disclosing our deepest, darkest secrets. As we get to know a person more intimately, we are more willing to tell him or her things about ourselves that perhaps we thought we would never reveal. But then, as time goes on, there is a tendency to close up again because we feel vulnerable to our loved one's opinion of us. If communication and trust are not established early in the relationship, we cannot hope that they will develop later when the stakes are much higher.

Many people harbor a secret view that, if people knew their "true self," they would not find it attractive. To a certain extent, we all wear public masks that allow us to present our most acceptable selves to the world. Choosing to trust another person enough to drop the masks is not easy, for we risk the possibility that our "true selves" will be rejected. But unless we are willing to drop our masks from the start, we can easily become mired in a web of deception. And even small deceptions become meaningful when they close doors on our ability to communicate.

Ethical Judgments

Was this man unethical in being unwilling to disclose his military experience to his wife? Was it unethical for the wife to be unwilling to accept his decision to not reveal these experiences? If you were asked to mediate this disagreement, what would you say to each of these people?

I know a man who told his wife, "I will share everything about myself with you except my experiences during the war. They're too hard to talk about." He could not see that by closing that door, he was making true communication impossible. His wife never felt as though she really knew him.

I know another man who committed a relatively small deception, but one that had great impact on his life. When he first met the woman he eventually married, he lied about his age, subtracting eight years. During the thirty years they were married, he never admitted the truth and went to great pains to make sure his wife never found out his real age. He took his secret with him to the grave, and it was only when his wife saw the death certificate that she learned the truth. She told me, sadly, "I can understand why he didn't tell me in the beginning. I might have thought he was too old for me. But later, when we were happily married and very close, he should have been able to trust me with the truth. Could he have really thought it would have mattered to me then?"

Explaining Ideas

What types of myths do you see perpetuated on television sitcoms and dramas? On television talk shows? On news and magazine shows? What are some of the popular myths about online relationships? Why do you think these beliefs are myths?

Myth #6

The best way to judge how your partner feels about you is to observe his or her actions.

Larry shopped for an engagement ring for Julia. He looked at a variety of diamond rings, but found them uninteresting. He couldn't understand how a stone that just looked like a fancy piece of glass could sell for so much money. He wanted a stone that showed how he really felt, that was unique and special. One day he came upon an antique turquoise ring that was an estate piece dating back about 200 years. It was marvelously hand-crafted, and its intricate design showed a degree of care he felt could not be found in any of the contemporary rings he had looked at. He happily bought the ring, planning to surprise Julia with his originality.

He succeeded on the first score. Julia was certainly surprised. But her reaction was nothing like what he had anticipated. She appreciated Larry's good intentions, but she could not hide her deep disappointment. She didn't see the symbolism in Larry's gesture. For her engagement, she wanted a diamond—that was an important symbol to her. In spite of her disappointment, Julia accepted the ring and they were married.

Three years later, Larry gave Julia a diamond eternity ring, which she started wearing as a wedding band. Larry and Julia are still happily married. They find they share many things in common, although taste in jewelry isn't one of them.

The point of this story is to illustrate that the very same action can symbolize different things to different people. For example, holding hands in public may be interpreted as a sign of affection on the part of one partner, but as a showy and inappropriate display by the other. Or one partner might view daily lovemaking as a sign of deeper love, while the other sees it as a dull routine. Often in relationships, an action means completely different things to the two partners. As such, the saying that "actions speak louder than words" is not necessarily accurate. It is not always possible to interpret a person's feelings by the way he or she acts.

Our acceptance of the false myths about love often gets in the way of our having effective relationships.

- When we believe our feelings are enough, we miss the vital signals that tell us what we really expect and need in a relationship.

- When we decide that living together before marriage will guarantee a smooth relationship, we sometimes fail to internalize our commitment to one another.

- When we think we can force our partner to change, we do not see that change must come from within. . . .

- When we allow ourselves to feel helpless against the flow of chemistry, we fail to acknowledge the negative triggers over which we have control.

- When we assume that good communication and trust will develop over time, we ignore the danger signals that might be present early in the relationship. . . .

- When we assume that actions are the sole indicator of feelings, we easily draw false conclusions from the way people behave.

Evaluating Ideas

How effectively did the author argue that these beliefs are in fact myths? Are you convinced? If not, what additional evidence would you want?

21

How to Fight Effectively

In this brief article, James L. Creighton identifies twelve principles for effective conflict resolution. These principles will help you avoid ways of communicating that may aggravate the conflict and seriously damage the interpersonal relationship. As you read this article, try to identify instances in which you did or did not use the various principles and especially what effect this use or nonuse had on the conflict and on your relationship.

Want to learn more? There are numerous popular and scholarly works on conflict that will give you greater insights and skills for dealing with the inevitable interpersonal conflicts you'll experience throughout life. For an academic perspective see, Daniel J. Canary, William R. Cupach, and Susan J. Messman, *Relationship Conflict: Conflict in Parent-Child, Friendship, and Romantic Relationships* (Thousand Oaks, CA: Sage, 1995) and Joseph P. Folger, Marshall Scott Poole, and Randall K. Stutman, *Working Through Conflict: A Communication Perspective,* 3rd ed. (New York: Allyn & Bacon, 1997). For more applied presentations see, Roger Fisher and William Ury with Bruce Patton, editor, *Getting to Yes: Negotiating Agreement Without Giving In,* 2nd ed. (New York: Penguin Books, 1991), the popular classic George R. Bach and Peter Wyden, *The Intimate Enemy: How to Fight Fair in Love and Marriage* (New York: Avon Books, 1968), or the more recent Kathy Dawson, *Diagnosis: Married: How to Deal with Marital Conflict, Heal Your Relationship, and Create a Rewarding and Fulfilling Marriage* (New York: Perigee, 2001) and Philip C. McGraw, *The Relationship Rescue Workbook* (New York: Hyperion, 2001). For conflict in the workplace, take a look at Richard Carlson, *Don't Sweat the Small Stuff at Work: Simple Ways to Minimize Stress and Conflict while Bringing Out the Best in Yourself and Others* (New York: Hyperion, 1999) and Lynne McClure, *Anger & Conflict in the Workplace: Nine Management Skills Everyone Needs* (Manassas Park, VA: Impact Publications, 2000).

Over the past twenty-five years, I have identified key characteristics of people who resolve conflicts successfully and perceive them as opportunities for

James L. Creighton, "Twelve Characteristics of People Who Resolve Conflicts Effectively," *Don't Go Away Mad: How to Make Peace with Your Partner.* Copyright © 1990 by James L. Creighton, Ph.D. Reprinted by permission of the author and the Sandra Dijkstra Agency.

building greater understanding and mutual support. I present these characteristics in the following twelve-point program. This same program is as effective for achieving greater intimacy and expression in your relationships with your spouse, lover, family members, or friends as it is for improving relations in your job or profession.

The following twelve points outline the skills and attitudes that characterize people who are consistently effective in resolving conflicts. Like them, you can develop the ability to:

1. Protect Your Relationship Even While In Conflict

At the top of our list is the "Golden Rule" which weaves through all the other eleven points in this program. It is this: Even as a conflict turns into a fight, the person continues to have a deep sense of responsibility for the relationship. There is a commitment to honor that relationship and keep it intact, ensuring that the "home base" it represents is still there when the fight is done.

People who are good at conflict resolution stay as aware of *what they are communicating about the relationship* as they are about the more obvious issues of the fight. They never lose sight of the fact that what they say or do will have either a positive or a negative impact on that relationship.

2. Accept Conflict as a Normal Part of Human Relationships

Conflict is an important part of every healthy relationship. When addressed, conflict can help relationships evolve slowly and peacefully, eliminating the need for violent upheavals. Through conflict, we confront our personal beliefs and differences, getting to know ourselves better and clarifying how our feelings and perceptions serve us or hinder us in our daily lives.

Conflict provides a safety valve for discharging some of the inner tensions naturally generated by the "limiting" aspects of a relationship.

When conflict is accepted as normal, we give ourselves permission to turn to it in constructive and positive ways. We focus on discovering how we can reap the greatest benefits from our conflicts while minimizing the discomfort and pain. Our attention shifts from being concerned about the number of fights we have to the positive results they produce.

3. Take Responsibility for the Outcome of Conflicts by Seeking New Skills to Ensure Resolution

Accept that *how you act*—your own skills and behavior, not fate, the gods, or "lucky" combinations of personalities—will shape the outcome of your efforts. Know that not all conflicts can be readily resolved, but you can make a significant contribution toward a positive outcome for everyone concerned.

When you develop this attitude, strengthening your relationships becomes your goal, replacing other objectives such as winning fights, proving a point, or asserting your power over others. This is not to suggest that there

Ethical Judgments

What ethical obligations do you have when you argue with your relationship partner? What ethical rules do you expect your partner to follow?

won't be times when you'll be so upset that you'll revert to defensive, adversarial, or hurtful behavior. To do so is only human. But as you become increasingly aware of the impact of what you say and do, you'll also become better and better at setting limits on your own behavior, even when you are most upset.

4. Make Room for Different Emotional Realities

Take responsibility for your own perceptions. Understand that the way the external world appears is actually a reflection of your own inner realities and no one else's. Accept that we all have the right to our own separate and unique ways of experiencing the same event. Each of us creates our own emotional experiences by deciding, consciously or unconsciously, what events mean. When we're in conflict, we may feel hurt, threatened, or angered by something that a person has said. When we're in this state, the other person really does seem to have "caused" our upset. We feel that we're the victims of their actions.

Explaining Ideas

Do you generally make room for different emotional realities? Can you recall a specific instance where you did or did not make room for such differences? What happened?

It's important to remind ourselves to make room for different emotional realities when disagreements heat up. When we can acknowledge that we can have entirely different emotional reactions to the same event, with both of us experiencing our reactions as "true and real," we are more likely to prevent the conflict from escalating.

5. Communicate Emotions, Not Judgments

Make room for different emotional realities by knowing how to communicate emotions rather than judgments. Here are two quick examples:

COMMUNICATION OF JUDGMENT:

"Only a callous and unfeeling SOB would forget to call me back after I specifically said how urgent it was!"

COMMUNICATION OF EMOTIONS:

"I was really hurt and angry when you didn't call me back. I really wanted to talk with you right away."

Making judgments not only increases defensiveness, but also discounts the other person's reality. Let's imagine that my wife and I go to a party. About two hours into it, I start getting bored. I get my wife off in the corner and tell her, "This is one of the dumbest parties I've ever attended. These people are boring and shallow. I don't see how anyone but a fool could enjoy this crowd!"

I have been so wrapped up in my own thoughts that I failed to recognize that my wife was having a grand time. As a result, everything I've said is not just a statement of my inner truth, but also an attack on my wife. After all, I've said these people are boring and shallow and that anyone who enjoyed them had to be a fool. Although I had just wanted to blow off some steam, I suddenly discover that I've dropped a bomb.

Yes, it is true that I'm bored. But it is equally true that my wife is having fun. I may find that difficult to accept but neither my acceptance nor rejection of it will change it.

Two different emotional truths can coexist. But two contradictory judgments can't. If, instead of communicating my judgments to my wife ("This is a really dumb party!"), I communicate my emotions ("I am really bored"), then the potential for a fight is reduced. Moreover, by communicating our feelings instead of our judgments, and recognizing them as such, we learn to value and respect both our own feelings and those of the people we love.

6. Listen to Understand the Other Person's Point of View, Not to "Build Your Case"

Effective listening is a key skill for preventing disagreements from turning into fights. People who do it well know how to stop focusing on the chatter in their own minds. This chatter usually consists of arguments and defenses against what the other person is saying. When we begin concentrating on the emotions being expressed, some very interesting changes take place. We begin to hear what the other person is saying not as a challenge to our own beliefs but as an expression of the other person's needs, perceptions, and sensitivities. Our reflex for argument and defense is often significantly reduced, and suddenly we may have the feeling that we are truly understanding the other person for the first time. There are times when everyone gets defensive no matter how skilled they may be as a listener. There will be times when one or both people involved will be so emotionally tied up by the issues that they will not be able to do a good job of listening. With this in mind, set up ground rules and procedures to ensure that both people feel that they will eventually be heard even when communications have momentarily broken down. These alternatives are an important part of learning to listen.

7. Recognize That Conflicts Can Occur at Many Different Levels Simultaneously

There's not just one kind of conflict. Some are over facts. Others are over issues such as feeling unloved or unneeded or having one's feelings suppressed or discounted. Others involve beliefs about responsibility, fairness, justice, morality, or ethics. Still others are over resources such as money, time, personal space, land, or valuable objects.

Although a dispute may seem to focus on just one of these areas, it is rare that only a single issue is involved. An argument over the household budget, for example, may appear to be only over money. But as the argument progresses, we often discover that behind the money issue are strong feelings involving who has the right to control the family resources and whose needs come first. Beyond this, the same conflict may involve beliefs about what's important in life: security, pleasure, getting ahead, etc.

Disputes can also revolve around two people being in possession of very different facts. They might have conflicting information about how

Communicating Skillfully

How would you describe the conflicts in your own life? As you look back on them would you describe them as mostly positive? Mostly negative? What might you have done to make them more positive?

much something will cost, which can get resolved the moment they both have the same facts in front of them. But until both people can agree on how to get credible information, their conflict may spill over into areas such as who has control of the family budget.

Since most disputes involve two or more levels—a couple may be arguing simultaneously about money issues as well as whose needs should come first—we must learn to be sensitive to these different levels and take the time to identify them.

8. Put Limits on Fights

Seemingly trivial disagreements can escalate into arguments, then into "wars" where hurting each other becomes more important than solving problems.

Take the time to actually set limits on fights. The object is to protect yourself and your loved one from behavior that could threaten the foundation of your relationship. These rules should be set at a time when both people feel good about each other, rather than in the midst of a battle. Once we're in a fight, we're in no position to discuss something as sensitive as setting limits on our behavior. To even attempt to do so could escalate a fight.

Setting limits on our behavior is an important statement about our relationship. It says that we really do look upon conflicts as normal and we are willing to develop effective skills for dealing with them. Setting limits also provides some assurance that fight tactics which proved to be particularly painful in the past will not be repeated.

9. Use the Recovery Period After a Fight for Self-Knowledge and Self-Growth as a Couple

What does a fight mean to your relationship? Does it mean the beginning of the end? Or does it mean you're getting better at resolving major issues, that you're able to talk about feelings which you once held on to or hid from the other person? What a fight means depends a great deal on what you do after the screaming has stopped. We derive our greatest benefits from conflict when we take time afterward to reflect on what happened. Ideally, this is a time to accept responsibility for the emotions we brought into the conflict. But this is a delicate process. What makes self-knowledge possible is the ability to focus solely on our own contributions to the fight—both the positive and the negative. A period of reflection can bring much emotional healing. The results can turn even the worst fight into a moment which spurs the growth of your relationship and your own growth as an individual.

10. Concentrate on Meeting Needs Rather Than Cutting Deals

Most of us have been taught that the way to resolve conflicts is to "cut deals," or make compromises. To be sure, compromise is sometimes the only alternative we can manage. But continued compromise can threaten the health of any relationship. As someone once said, "Compromise is the art of negotiating a settlement in which everyone is equally dissatisfied."

There's no law that says I must give up my needs so that yours can be met. But neither is there one that says you must give up your needs to meet mine. In ongoing relationships, one-sided settlements are never stable. For this reason, we must learn to seek solutions that truly meet the needs of everyone involved. Here, the emphasis is always on both people getting what they need, rather than on one person winning, compromising, "giving in," or withdrawing so that the other person can have his or her way.

11. Agree on a Process of Collaborative Problem Solving

In recent years there has been extensive research on collaborative problem solving. As a result, we now have definite guidelines for creating solutions everyone can be happy with. People who know these skills take the time to sit down together when there is no conflict and agree upon a process for resolving any conflicts that might arise between them.

This process serves as a "road map" to guide everything from the first step of defining problems, through brainstorming for alternatives, to the final stages of carrying out agreed-upon solutions. This way we reduce the chances of falling back into old, often destructive patterns of fighting. Collaborative problem solving is an alternative to the destructive behavior which occurs when we feel so threatened, frightened, or outraged that we abandon all rules and go for blood, engaging in actions that seriously wound those we love.

Cultural Analysis

In some Middle Eastern cultures, for example, when there is a relationship conflict the man gets his way, and the woman is expected to abide by the man's decision. Are there gender rules in male-female conflict in your own culture? What are they?

12. Recognize When a "Referee" Can Be Helpful

Couples and long-term coworkers can become so familiar with each other's responses that soon they are a part of a "system" of expectations, roles, and predictable behavior which feels natural and normal. Even if the interaction is painful for one or more people, it is often perceived as "just the way we are." When, as sometimes happens, the relationship becomes destructive, unfulfilling, or frustrating, it may require someone from the outside to identify what isn't working so that both parties can seek alternative ways of acting.

In most cases, we turn to close friends when our relationship systems break down. Close friends can certainly be comforting, but more often than not they are, without knowing it, part of that system. They become participants, for example, by consciously or unconsciously taking sides, which only deepens whatever wounds have already been inflicted.

Evaluating Ideas

How effective do you think these twelve principles will be in your own interpersonal conflicts?

How to Communicate to Help

Talking with people who are grieving is an especially difficult task. But, it is also an extremely important one. Knowing what to say and what not to say will prove helpful in a wide variety of situations. In this brief, but especially helpful article, the Zunins offer ten suggestions for communicating with someone experiencing grief.

Want to learn more? There are a variety of Web sites, chat groups, and newsgroups devoted to giving support for people experiencing grief. Visit some of these sites and become familiar with the services available. For a discussion of the differences between men and women in expressing grief see Terry L. Martin and Kenneth J. Doka, *Men Don't Cry . . . Women Do: Transcending Gender Stereotypes of Grief* (Levittown, PA: Brunner-Routledge [Taylor and Francis], 2000). Carol Staudacher in her *Men and grief: A guide for men surviving the death of a loved one* (New Harbinger, 1991) offers an interesting perspective on the problems that men experience, but have difficulty talking about.

It's not uncommon to be fearful of saying the wrong thing to a friend in grief. As a result, many would-be condolers withdraw or hold back rather than reach out. They tell themselves they're doing this to respect the bereaved's privacy, but it is rarely the truth. Usually, they are just taking the easy way out.

As you approach and begin to converse with the bereaved, certainly there is a risk, but as Dr. Zunin points out in his book *Contact: The First Four Minutes,* "Human contact is always a challenge . . . which means a certain amount of risk-taking . . . an investment that earns interest in love, friendship, growth and a more positive self-image," both for the condoler and the bereaved. People in crisis often need others around them, but it may not always be evident to them or to those who care for them. With care and sensitivity your presence can be a gift, not a burden.

Once you have taken the time to listen, healing conversation can begin. Here are a few remarks you may find helpful in getting started:

I'm so sorry. Was your father ill for a long time?

Leonard M. Zunin and Hilary Stanton Zunin, "Suggestions for Positive and Healing Communication," in *The Art of Condolence* (New York: HarperCollins, 1991), pp. 149–153. Copyright © 1991 by Leonard M. Zunin, M.D. and Hilary Stanton Zunin. Reprinted by permission of HarperCollins Publishers, Inc.

I am at a loss to know what to say, but I sense how very difficult this must be for you.

I've been thinking about you and wanted to know how (what) you've been doing.

This must be a bewildering and incredibly complicated time. It must be very hard for you (and your family).

What's it like for you these days? How are you coping?

Do you feel like talking for a while?

The following are suggestions for continued positive communication with those in grief. They may not only help you to avoid pitfalls, but they may help you to overcome some realistic concerns.

1. *Perhaps another time.* Even though you may be totally prepared to listen, the time may not be right. Don't burden the bereaved because you have decided you are ready and willing to listen. If you are caring, receptive, and patient, the time will eventually present itself.

2. *Listen without judgment.* Don't prejudge; don't moralize; don't condemn. Though there will be times when what the person is feeling seems to you to be inaccurate or inappropriate, don't tell the bereaved how or what they should be feeling. The really attentive listener remains alert, present, and receptive, and avoids drawing conclusions.

3. *Focus your attention.* Concentrate on the person and what is being said by giving your undivided attention. This does not mean being silently impatient or apathetically quiet. And try not to think about what you're going to say as soon as the other person stops talking. Such nonverbal cues as maintaining good eye contact, leaning forward, nodding your head affirmatively, and using facial expressions indicate encouragement and confirm your attentiveness.

4. *Avoid interrupting.* Allow the bereaved to complete their sentences and their thoughts even though the words may seem confused or fragmented. Try not to jump in at any opening, finish a statement, or hurry the bereaved along. In addition, when we suggest that you avoid interrupting, we mean not only the bereaved's words but their silences as well. The silence of grief can be remarkably eloquent.

5. *Maintain a positive outlook on life.* Conversing with the bereaved doesn't always mean discussing pain and sorrow. Be attuned to what they want to talk about. There will be times when the bereaved want to discuss ordinary things and other times when they wish to share some of their anguish. It is immensely helpful if you can maintain a positive outlook on life and a quality of affirmation. Your attitude will be conveyed in many subtle ways, especially by supporting the bereaved in whatever they are feeling. You might also talk about how either the bereaved or the deceased has touched,

Explaining Ideas

How would you explain the difference between talking with someone who is grief stricken because of the loss of a friend, family member, or pet, and talking with someone who just received fantastically good news, say a scholarship to graduate school, a lottery winning, or a gift of a brand new Jaguar?

enriched, or even inspired your life. Mention the positive qualities and strengths you and others have noticed about them or relate memories that you cherish.

6. *Rational answers are irrational.* The death of a loved one can never be explained away with logic. Don't try. It rarely helps to offer "rational" explanations about death to someone in grief.

7. *Suggestions are better than advice.* Grief is an intensely personal experience. The true friend is one who does not advise but helps the other to become more alert, more aware, and more conscious of life's choices. You may offer some gentle suggestions, but do so without the mantle of authority or demand. Instead, help the bereaved to find their own way with courage and authenticity.

8. *Share, don't compare, experiences.* Those in the early stages of grief often feel their situation is so unique that no one can understand. They will be put off and shut off by any suggestion that your experience—or the experience of others you know—has been more intense or more profound. If you choose to discuss your own experiences with grief, share without comparing or professing complete understanding. The bereaved may find comfort, understanding, or ways of coping when you share your own experiences in this manner.

Another area in which one-upmanship may cause problems occurs when the condoler suggests that his or her love for the deceased was as great, if not greater, than that of the bereaved. Use judgment in sharing such feelings; the newly bereaved are highly vulnerable.

9. *Give occasional responses while listening.* There are many ways of conveying that you are engaged, that you understand, or that you want to know more:

- Soft, affirming conversational sounds that we all use without thinking (hmmm, uh huh) denote interest, agreement, and concern.
- Asking for clarification, whether in the form of questioning, repeating, or paraphrasing, checks to see that you've understood what the bereaved has said (e.g., if the bereaved mentions that she doesn't know how she's going to get to her doctor's appointment, the condoler might respond by asking, "Would you like me to give you a lift?").
- Simple requests for more information are helpful. While it's possible to ask for too much disclosure, most condolers err on the side of asking too little. Typically, the bereaved have a compelling need to talk about the who, what, when, and why of their loss. Inquiries may be general ("Tell me more about it") or specific ("How did you find out?").
- Reflective questioning is another way of encouraging the bereaved to talk. By occasionally repeating key words or phrases just spoken by the bereaved, you validate their remarks, demonstrate your attentiveness,

Ethical Judgments

What ethical obligations do you have when a close friend or partner experiences grief? Are these obligations different from what you might experience if you're at the scene of an accident and find yourself next to the mother of a child who was just killed in a drive-by shooting?

Communicating Skillfully

Assume you've been communicating with someone online almost daily for the last four months. You've developed a close friendship and have disclosed a great deal of personal information over this time. During one chat, your online partner says, without any warning and without any preliminary remarks, "I went to the doctor's yesterday; I'm HIV+." What do you say? What are some things you'd want to make sure you don't say?

and confirm your interest. (Bereaved: "I feel that I'm behaving like an angry ten-year-old kid." Condoler: "An angry ten-year-old?")

10. *Consider before using these remarks.* Many of the following reflect more about the condoler's own difficulty in coping with loss than about their sympathy for the bereaved:

Be thankful you have another child.

You must get on with your life.

You're not the first person this has happened to.

Don't cry; try to keep control of yourself.

You're young; there's plenty of time to have children.

I know exactly what you are going through.

It was really a blessing; you must be relieved.

You are lucky to have had him for so long.

Don't worry. It's probably for the best.

It's better this way.

It's a blessing in disguise.

He's better off this way; if he'd lived it would have been more painful for him.

Don't take it so hard.

Try to keep yourself together.

We have no right to question God's will.

Why didn't you call me?

I heard you're not taking it well.

It's just as well that you never got to know the baby.

Sensitivity is so important. When people share their suffering, they often feel vulnerable, foolish, and fearful that their self-disclosure will negatively impact your relationship with them. Often in grief there is a temporary impairment of self-esteem along with feelings of insecurity. The bereaved needs to know that no matter what is said, your friendship will remain intact. You will communicate simple acceptance and genuine caring with statements such as "I now more fully understand much of what you've been experiencing and I admire your courage and the difficult decisions you've made." Let the bereaved know you're really trying to understand what they are going through and that you respect how they are coping.

Evaluating Ideas

Recall a recent situation in which you talked with someone who was experiencing grief. Try to recall as closely as you can, what you said and what you felt. Would these ten suggestions have helped you? If so, what would you have said differently?

How to Communicate in Close Relationships

In this article, Mary Anne Fitzpatrick discusses her research program on relationship communication. From this research three major types of couples have emerged: traditionals, independents, and separates. As you read this article try to identify your own relationship style.

Want to learn more? If you wish to read more of Fitzpatrick's work see her *Between Husbands and Wives: Communication in Marriage* (Thousand Oaks, CA: Sage, 1988) and Patricia Noller and Mary Anne Fitzpatrick, *Communication in Family Relationships* (Boston: Allyn & Bacon, 1993). An excellent work on family communication, offering both reviews of the research and theory and useful insights into how to improve your own family communication is Kathleen Galvin and Bernard Brommel's, *Family Communication: Cohesion and Change,* 6th ed. (Boston: Allyn & Bacon, 2000). Another useful work is John Mordechai Gottman's *The Seven Principles for Making Marriage Work* (New York: Three Rivers Press [Random House, Crown Publishers], 2000).

Nearly all Americans get married at least once. Even people who divorce usually remarry within five years, although few people marry more than twice. Marriage may be common, but it is not easily understood. Personal experiences, fiction, and folklore can provide colorful examples and anecdotes, but they often contradict each other. Systematic, scientific observations can provide more reliable generalizations and improve our understanding of marriage.

Throughout this century, scholars have been searching for social or demographic factors—such as income, education, age at marriage, and age differences between spouses—that can predict whether marriages will succeed or fail. Many social scientists now believe, however, that such factors are far less important than the communication that occurs between partners. For example, a lack of money in itself doesn't cause marital problems. What is important is how a couple discusses and makes decisions about its economic difficulties.

For the past decade, my students and I have been conducting research aimed at illuminating marital communication. As the foundation of this re-

---

Mary Anne Fitzpatrick, "Studying Communication in Marriage." Reprinted by permission of the author.

search, we have delineated a descriptive classification system for marriage—what we call the "marital typology." Numerous studies conducted here and abroad have validated this typology, which is described below. In our studies alone, over twenty-five hundred married couples from all social classes have participated. Within any sample of these married couples, a few recognizable, recurring patterns of relationships have emerged. The basic premise of our program of research is that different types of couples, communicate in significantly different ways, and understanding such patterns can help us to understand why marriages succeed or fail.

Three concepts underlie our scheme for categorizing couples: interdependence, ideology, and conflict. We measure interdependence by assessing the amount of sharing and companionship in the marriage was well as by the couple's organization of time and household space. The more interdependent the couple, the higher the level of companionship, the more time they spend together on a regular basis, and the more they organize their time and space to promote togetherness.

The beliefs, standards, and values that individuals hold concerning relationships form the ideology that interests us. People generally see love and marriage in one of two contrasting ways. The "therapeutic" orientation views love and marriage primarily in terms of the psychological gratifications these give to individuals. The "traditional" orientation views love and marriage primarily as providing people with stable, committed relationships that tie them to the larger society.

Individuals in ongoing relationships inevitably come into conflict with one another, but how people try to resolve their differences varies. Some go to extreme lengths to avoid discussing any serious issue of disagreement with their spouses. Others plunge into disagreements with their spouses without hesitation.

To give us the basic data on couples in our marital communication studies, we employ a questionnaire I developed that measures interdependence, ideology, and conflict in marriage. The responses of large numbers of married couples to this questionnaire suggest three fundamental definitions of marriage: Traditional, Independent, and Separate.

To understand a marriage, both the husband's and the wife's perspective must be considered. Until the mid-seventies, though, marital researchers commonly interviewed only one member of a couple. (For example, a rather famous book, called *Husbands and Wives,* was based on interviews with wives alone, because the authors assumed wives could answer for their husbands.) My research group defines a marital type by comparing how a husband's definition of the relationship differs or agrees with his wife's. Therefore, in our scheme we first assess the marital type of each individual. If both a husband and a wife are Independents, for example, their communication pattern will be different than if he is a Traditional and she is an Independent.

Individuals categorized as Traditionals are very interdependent. Their use of time and space reinforces the companionship in the marriage. They

Explaining Ideas

How would you explain the types of relationships portrayed in television sitcoms in terms of Fitzpatrick's typology of traditionals, independents, and separates? For example, what kind of relationship exists between Will and Grace from *Will and Grace*? Between Niles and Maris Crane from *Frasier*? Between the Hughleys from *The Hughleys*?

keep regular daily time schedules to ensure interaction with their spouses, and they do not particularly like having autonomous physical spaces in their own homes. Traditionals emphasize stability more than satisfaction in marriage, and they hold conventional values about relationships. They describe their communication style as non-assertive, although they are willing to engage in conflict when the issues are serious ones.

Independents see marriage in a qualitatively different light than do Traditionals, although they are also very interdependent. While trying to stay psychologically close to their spouses, Independents keep unpredictable schedules and maintain separate physical spaces in the home to achieve some control over the accessibility their spouses have to them. Ideologically, they are at the opposite end of the scale from Traditionals. For example, Independents believe marriage should not constrain individual freedom. In their interactions with their spouses, they describe themselves as assertive and willing to fight over issues both large and small.

Separates are much less interdependent than others and carefully control the access their spouses have to them. The major way that Separates show any interdependence at all is by keeping regular daily time schedules. Separates may espouse traditional values but admit that sometimes they are unsure of those values. Emotionally divorced from their spouses, Separates report going to extraordinary lengths to avoid open conflict with them.

The pure couple types (Traditional, Independent, Separate) are those in which a husband and a wife share the same definition of the marriage. Approximately 60 percent of the couples who have completed the questionnaire agree on a definition of their marriage. The mixed types are those in which the husband holds one definition and the wife another (for example, Separate/Traditional, in which the husband is a Separate and the wife is a Traditional). The 40 percent disagreement coincides with most other programs of research on marriage. Such discrepancies in the reports of husbands and wives are relatively commonplace, leading one social scientist to remark that "his marriage" is not the same as "her marriage."

Building a typology of marriage would be a useless exercise if the types of marriage did not relate to other areas of interest. Throughout our program of research we have repeatedly tested what individuals say about themselves, their marriages, and their spouses against their behavior in actual and simulated situations. In essence, a couple's level of interdependence, its ideological orientation toward marital and family values, and the approach each individual takes to conflict predict a broad range of communication behaviors between spouses.

For instance, in one of the many studies conducted here at the Center for Communication Research, fifty-one couples engaged in role plays in which spouses attempted to get each other to comply with competing courses of action. The strategies for gaining compliance used by these couples differed markedly between the types. The bases of power that the couple types referred to in attempting to win their spouses over differed as did the intensity with which individuals pursued their own aims in these interactions.

Communicating Skillfully

Pat and Chris have been together for ten years and are having a big argument over where to spend their vacation. Pat wants to go to Las Vegas to gamble and see the shows. Chris wants a quieter vacation, something like taking a cruise to the Bahamas. How would Pat and Chris resolve this dispute if they were traditionals? If they were independents? If they were separates? Which resolution do you find most reasonable and satisfying?

Evaluating Ideas

How helpful do you find this typology and this discussion in understanding your own relationship interactions and also the relationships of people you know? How effective is this typology in describing the online relationships with which you're familiar?

Traditionals tended to discuss the advantages or disadvantages of the particular activity, to ask directly for their spouses to comply, to search for information in the conversation about their spouse's wants or needs, and to offer to compromise.

Independents seemed to demand that their spouses comply. They relied on power plays and pointed out their spouses' negative attributes in order to get them to agree to what they wanted.

Separates attempted to persuade their spouses to follow a given course of action by citing external reasons for it. Separate/Traditionals stressed their own positive attributes, the attributes of their spouses, or the relationship *per se* as reasons for their spouses to go along with them. Finally, other mixed couple types tended to focus on the attributes of the activity they wished to pursue, used power plays, and offered compromises when they tried to persuade their spouses of a given course of action.

Ethical Judgments

Are all three relationship styles ethically neutral? Or, do you find one type of relationship style to be more (or less) ethical than another?

In another study, couples of different types displayed different patterns in their verbal interactions. These patterns related to who controls the relationship. The forty couples who participated in this study were audiotaped in their own homes as they engaged in two ten-minute discussions. In one, they discussed their most recent serious conflict; in the other, they discussed a neutral issue (What item would you take along if you had to start civilization over again?). We transcribed the eighty conversations and analyzed them with a series of complex statistical models.

The results showed that the Traditionals did not struggle for control when discussing casual issues, but they did when an issue was important to them. When discussing a casual issue, the husbands and wives engaged in a give and take style of communication. Sometimes the wife gave in to the husband, and at other times the husbands gave in to the wives. During conflict, however, these couples argued openly, and neither gave in to the other's attempt to control the situation. Usually this took the form of exchanging orders.

Husband: "You have got to let me have an encyclopedia."

Wife: "You have to get rid of that defensive tone."

Whether the discussion was casual or not, the Independents tended to match the control moves of their spouses. In the Independent couple, each spouse is concerned with maintaining equality in the relationship. At times in the conversations, each person was equally willing to relinquish control.

Husband: "What do you want to bring?"

Wife: "Oh, I don't know. What do you want?"

At other times, the Independents were very competitive.

Husband: "The dictionary is a useless book. Why would you put down such a ridiculous choice?"

Wife: "That's not ridiculous. Without a dictionary, you can't expand your vocabulary and knowledge."

Husband: "You think it is more important to speak properly than to survive?"

Wife: "Survival is only one choice. The other is obviously literacy."

During casual discussion, Separates avoided intense exchanges of any kind. Whether or not the interchange was casual or potentially explosive, Separates tended to agree with their spouses, although the agreement was usually not very strong. Their struggle was not so much with their spouses as it was to maintain surface harmony in the relationship.

The mixed types talked more during conflict than during the neutral discussion, although strong competition characterized both conditions. Their disagreement over the nature of the relationship showed up in the dialogues of these couples with even more struggle over the control of the relationship than seen with the Independents. The mixed types also favored the use of challenges and justifications.

Husband: "You put in a novel. While we're starving, you'd read?"

Wife: "I put it in so I wouldn't get bored."

In conflict, only the couples in which one spouse was a Traditional and the other a Separate refrained from personal attacks. Instead, these couples stayed with the issue at hand.

Husband: "Why do you say your job is more demanding than mine?"

Wife: "I not only teach five classes, but I have drill team practice every night."

Husband: "So what. Why don't you quit your job?"

Wife: "I've worked hard to get where I am."

In another study, we found that the number of times couples related to each other in certain ways varied according to type. We audiotaped fifty-one couples as they were waiting for an experiment to begin. The middle four minutes of the interaction were later coded and analyzed statistically. During the four minute segment, Independents accounted for most of the statements that revealed a personal feeling, while couples in which the husband was a Separate and the wife a Traditional accounted for the fewest.

The Separates were significantly less likely, and the Separate/Traditionals significantly more likely, than the other couple types to express their attitudes or opinions to their spouses. Finally, despite the fact that all the couples reported enjoying this conversation, the Separates spoke less frequently to their spouses than did the other couples. This study validated what these couples reported about themselves concerning how expressive they are to their spouses.

The three examples briefly described above should give you a general idea of the research we have been conducting in the interests of illuminating how marital communication works within different types of couples. Research continues on the typology. Recently my students and I have conducted a series of studies testing whether couples have theories about their

Brain Talk

When thinking about relationships, try to identify your underlying assumptions and how they influence the way you view a topic. For example, think of how your attitudes, beliefs, and values influence your responses to questions such as: Should same sex marriages be legalized? Should safe-sex practices be taught in the schools? Should divorce be made easier to obtain?

Representative Statements from the Questionnaire

Ideology

Statements indicating traditional ideology:
- A woman should take her husband's last name when she marries.
- Our wedding ceremony was (will be) very important to us.
- Our society as we see it needs to regain faith in the law and in our institutions.

Statements indicating an ideology of uncertainty and change ("therapeutic" orientation)
- In marriage/close relationships there should be no constraints or restrictions on individual freedom.
- The ideal relationship is one marked by novelty, humor, and spontaneity.
- In a relationship, each individual should be permitted to establish the daily rhythm and time schedule that suits him/her best.

Conflict

Conflict Avoidance
- If I can avoid arguing about some problems, they will disappear.
- It is better to hide one's true feelings in order to avoid hurting your spouse/mate.
- In our relationship, we feel that it is better to engage in conflicts than to avoid them.

Assertiveness
- My spouse/mate forces me to do things that I do no want to do.
- My spouse/mate tries to persuade me to do something that I do not want to do.
- We are likely to argue in front of friends or in public places.

Interdependence

Sharing
- I think that we joke around and have more fun than most couples.
- We tell each other how much we love or care about each other.
- My spouse/mate reassures and comforts me when I am feeling low.

Autonomy
- I have my own private workspace (study, workshop, utility room, etc.).
- My spouse has his/her own private workspace.
- I think it is important for one to have some private space which is all his/her own and separate from one's mate.

Undifferentiated Space
- I feel free to interrupt my spouse/mate when he/she is concentrating on something if he/she is in my presence.
- I open my spouse/mate's personal mail without asking permission.
- I feel free to invite guests home without informing my spouse/mate.

Temporal Regularity
- We eat our meals (the ones at home) at the same time every day.
- We serve the main meal at the same time everyday.
- In our house, we keep a fairly regular daily time schedule.

communication that match the various types of marriages. Eventually, the systematic study of marriage and other personal relationships will help us to design practical programs and interventions to improve family life.

24

How to Deal with Verbal Abuse

This article reviews one of the most important issues in interpersonal communication but one that is often neglected in textbooks, namely verbal abuse. In this brief overview, you're asked to take a self-test to encourage you to think about the nature of verbal abuse and to examine your own tendencies toward verbal abuse. With this test as a foundation, the characteristics and effects of verbal abuse, the problems in recognizing and combating verbal abuse, and suggestions for dealing with verbal abuse.

Want to learn more? Here are four works you're sure to find useful: Patricia Evans, *The verbally abusive relationship: How to recognize it and how to respond* (Adams Media Corp., 1996), Suzette Haden Elgin, *You Can't Say That to Me!: Stopping the Pain of Verbal Abuse* (New York: Wiley, 1995). Albert Ellis and Marcia Grad Powers, *The Secret of Overcoming Verbal Abuse: Getting Off the Emotional Roller Coaster and Regaining Control of Your Life* (No. Hollywood, CA: Wilshire Book Co., 2001), and Barrie Levy, *In Love and in Danger: A Teen's Guide to Breaking Free of Abusive Relationships* (Seattle, WA: Seal Press, 1998). Also, try searching the Web for relationship abuse, verbal abuse, or abusive relationships. Newsgroups and chat groups are also available for victims of abusive relationships.

Before reading about verbal abuse, take the accompanying self-test; it will help you examine your own behavior and that of a partner on whom you might wish to focus.

Are You Verbally Abusive?

Indicate whether your relationship behavior is more likely to resemble the "A" or "B" responses. In reading these questions, visualize a specific relationship partner, for example, a friend, romantic partner, or family member, and respond to each question in terms of your relationship with this one person. The general term "partner" is used as a shorthand for any such relationship.

In interacting with my partner, I am generally likely to:

1. A reveal my feelings

1. B conceal my feelings

2. A listen to and encourage my partner to express his or her feelings

2. B discourage the expression of feelings

Joseph A. DeVito, *Verbally Abusive Relationships*. Revision of a unit from *The Interpersonal Communication Book*, 8th edition (New York: Longman, 1998), pp. 386–389. Copyright © 1998. Reprinted by permission of Addison Wesley Educational Publishers.

3. A become disturbed when my partner's feelings, attitudes, or beliefs about important issues differ from mine

3. B try to understand my partner's feelings, attitudes, or beliefs about important issues when they differ from mine

4. A assume that my partner knows that I understand what he or she is saying

4. B tell my partner that I understand what he or she is saying from his or her point of view

5. A evaluate and possibly criticize my partner's failures or unsatisfactory performance

5. B express support for my partner when he or she fails or does something poorly

6. A state my position or my interpretation of some issue with certainty

6. B state my position or my interpretation of some issue tentatively

7. A emphasize the positives of our relationship or of our interactions

7. B emphasize the negatives of our relationship or of our interactions

8. A compliment my partner rarely (once a day would be the most)

8. B compliment my partner frequently (at least three or four times a day)

9. A stress my own superior knowledge or abilities

9. B stress my partner's and my equality

10. A talk a great deal more than I listen

10. B talk and listen about equally

Scoring: These qualities of verbal abuse are derived from five qualities often identified as constituting interpersonal effectiveness (openness, empathy, supportiveness, positiveness, and equality). Responses considered verbally abusive are "A" responses for items 3, 4, 5, 6, 9, and 10 and "B" responses for items 1, 2, 7, and 8. Give yourself 1 point for each verbally abusive response. A score of 5 or higher probably indicates that your communications have the potential to prove verbally abusive to at least some reasonable people.

Let's spell out more clearly the interpersonal patterns in verbal abuse. The first two items under each of the five qualities are those included in the self-test.

Verbal Abusers:

lack *openness;* they:

1. refuse to reveal their feelings

2. refuse to admit there is a problem when their silence is questioned ("*Nothing's wrong; I'm just quiet.*")

3. discourage their partners' revealing feelings ("*Let's not get morbid; Why must you always talk about feelings; can't you just keep them to yourself?*") and the mutual sharing of thoughts and feelings ("*I'm really not in the mood to talk; watch the game.*")

4. avoid reacting openly and honestly to the feelings expressed by their partner

5. avoid taking responsibility for their own thoughts and feelings and instead attribute these to others; nothing seems to be their fault (*"Everyone thinks you should ask for a raise; No one likes the way you dress; Well, it was your decision that got us into this mess"*)

lack *empathy;* they:

6. become disturbed by their partners' disagreements or holding attitudes and beliefs different from their own (*"How can you possibly say that? You've got to be kidding!"*)

7. refuse to acknowledge any understanding of their partners' communications

8. refuse to grant their partners' feelings any validity (*"You're being silly; You're always complaining"*)

9. focus solely on what is said and ignore mixed messages

10. avoid checking or verifying their perceptions of their partner's feelings

lack *supportiveness;* they:

11. evaluate and judge their partners' accomplishments (*"Now that was fine; much better than last time"*)

12. criticize their partners' shortcomings (*"You never could fix the plumbing; You're afraid to try anything new, aren't you?"*)

13. state their own position as final and definitive, not allowing for any chance of change or alteration (*"Harrington is the best man for the job and that's it; there's no question about it"*)

14. assume that their partners are at fault when something goes wrong (*"What did you do wrong now?"*)

15. assume their partners will fail even before they try (*"Why bother; you know you'll never finish"*)

lack *positiveness;* they:

16. emphasize the negatives in their relationship, in their partners' behaviors

17. refuse to compliment their partners regardless of their accomplishments

18. blame their partner for difficulties (*"How can I accomplish anything with you always nagging me?"*)

19. use derogatory names to describe their partners or their partners' ways of behaving (often to their children) (*"Hey, big ears, come here a minute; Clumsy must be your middle name"*)

20. act indifferently to their partner and their partner's thoughts and feelings

lack a sense of *equality;* they:

21. emphasize their own superiority over their partners (*"Look, I studied accounting; you can't even balance a checkbook"*)

Communicating Skillfully

Your mother repeatedly criticizes the way you dress: "You always dress like a slob, like you just got out of bed. Why don't you dress like a responsible person?" You know that your mother loves you and cares for you but this kind of constant criticism makes you feel inadequate and makes having a positive self-image extremely difficult. You don't want to hurt your mother, but you really want her to stop this barrage of criticism. What do you say?

22. talk a great deal more than they listen and interrupt their partners to interject their own comments

23. refuse to grant their partners' thoughts any credibility or value (*"That's ridiculous; You're talking about economics?"*)

24. give ultimatums to get their way (*"If you don't want to go to London, then let's forget about a vacation all together."*)

25. give orders rather than ask or request compliance (*"Get me coffee before you go out; Buy butter pecan; I hate that vanilla you always buy"*)

The Characteristics and Effects of Verbal Abuse

Verbal abuse may be defined as a consistent pattern of attacking another person's self-concept and self-esteem through communication that is closed, non-empathic, unsupportive, negative, and unequal. Three essential characteristics are identified in this definition. First, to constitute verbal abuse, the behavior must be relatively *consistent*. Although isolated statements may prove abusive (e.g., cursing at someone), verbal abuse as an interpersonal relationship problem is a repeated pattern. It is, in fact, the consistency of such behavior that makes it so debilitating.

Second, verbal abuse *attacks the person's concept of self*. It is not, for example, merely negative behaviors, but negative behaviors that are directed at the self-image of the other person. It is not simply critical and evaluative behaviors, but it is those behaviors directed at another's self-concept. It is relatively unimportant what issue or content they address, and, in fact, may frequently address quite trivial issues. Their defining characteristic is that they comment in some way on the person's self-image (attacking and lowering it) and on the way in which the person is defined in this specific relationship (of little competence, importance, or consequence).

Third, verbal abuse consists of a *variety of communication patterns* that can be grouped conveniently as violations of the five qualities of interpersonal effectiveness. This is not to imply that other patterns could not be identified. The five qualities focused on here are offered as an introductory description of this type of interpersonal behavior.

Just as physical abuse attacks and weakens the body, verbal abuse attacks and weakens your self-image. In fact, many would argue that verbal abuse is more damaging and more destructive than physical abuse. Physical abuse is, in many cases, easy to recover from; verbal abuse is likely to leave scars for long periods, sometimes throughout one's life. In fact, in a study of 234 battered women (aged 19–64), 159 reported that the verbal abuse (defined in this study as threats of abuse, ridicule, jealousy, threats to change the marriage, the imposing of restrictions, and the damaging of property) had a greater impact than the actual physical abuse (Follingstad et al. 1990).

Research also finds that wives who use verbal abuse—especially attacks on the other person's character, swearing, and attacking the other's competency—also experience greater relationship violence (Infante, Sabourin, Rudd, and Shannon 1990).

Explaining Ideas

How would you explain the difference between face-to-face and online verbal abuse?

Cultural Analysis

Respond to each of these statements:

In general, my culture ignores verbal abuse; it exists, but no one talks about it.
Definitely agree
10 9 8 7 6 5 4 3 2 1
Definitely disagree

In general, my culture encourages members to actively confront and combat verbal abuse.
Definitely agree
10 9 8 7 6 5 4 3 2 1
Definitely disagree

In general, my culture is more accepting of verbal abuse if done by men than if done by women.
Definitely agree
10 9 8 7 6 5 4 3 2 1
Definitely disagree

Do these cultural beliefs influence your current behavior? If so, how?

When in a verbally abusive relationship, it is difficult to feel good about yourself, to maintain a positive self-image, or to feel competent, successful, or worthwhile. Whether it is your physical appearance, intellectual abilities, relational expertise, or emotional stability, it is difficult to maintain a positive self-image when subjected to verbal abuse.

Problems in Recognizing and Combatting Verbal Abuse

Verbal abuse is difficult to recognize and equally difficult to combat. People may be in a verbally abusive relationship and never realize it; the person may simply feel inadequate without realizing that this feeling has been brought on by the partner's constant barrage of criticism and negativity. Or, to take a different example, the partner who refuses to reveal his or her feelings or says "nothing's wrong" while maintaining long periods of silence, can easily make the partner feel at fault or inadequate. Yet, on the surface, "nothing's wrong." In fact, repeated inquiries as to what is wrong often result in intensifying the underlying—and slowly surfacing—hostility: 'NOTHING'S WRONG, DAMN IT!" The conclusion that may easily be reached is "I'm creating problems where none exist."

Similarly, the partner who is evaluated and criticized rather than supported may easily come to believe that he or she is deserving of such criticism. This is more likely to occur in romantic relationships where such criticism is often interpreted against a backdrop of love and sexual attraction. Here the conclusion is likely to be "I must really deserve such criticism; after all, she (he) loves me and wouldn't say that if it weren't true."

Another problem is that any accusation of verbal abuse is likely to be denied and is itself likely to result in an even more pointed attack: "Just because I want to be quiet, I'm being abusive? Are you crazy? Are you paranoid?" Accusations that you are somehow psychologically unbalanced simply because you raised the issue are often enough to keep you quiet.

Still another problem is that verbally abusive statements may deal with trivial issues, for example, the kind of ice cream to buy, being silly, or completing a relatively unimportant task. One abused woman, for example, gave this example: "If he saw that I put the roll of toilet paper on the holder with the paper going under instead of over, he'd lose it. It was always silly things" (*Newsweek*, October 12, 1992, p. 92). Because you conclude that the issues were trivial, the verbally abusive experiences themselves may come to be labeled "trivial." And so, there may be a tendency to attribute little importance to them. The implications, however, as already noted, go far beyond the specific content and attack the person's self-concept and therein lies their importance. It is their relational rather than their content implications that make them significant and potentially damaging.

Dealing with Verbal Abuse

Perhaps the first step in dealing with any troublesome interpersonal behavior is awareness; you first have to recognize it to be able to see it in your own interpersonal interactions. Sometimes, one person is abusive and the other is abused. But, in lots of cases, both partners are abusive. George and

Ethical Judgments

You're convinced that your close friend Jeanne is verbally abused by her boyfriend. His behavior is a classic textbook example of verbal abuse, but Jeanne seems totally unaware that her low self-esteem and negative self-concept stem largely from his constant verbal abuse. As a close friend, what are your ethical obligations?

Communicating Skillfully

Recognizing the dangers that someone might encounter in calling the verbal abuse to the abuser's attention, what would you do if you felt you were being verbally abused by a close friend or romantic partner?

Martha, in Edward Albee's *Who's Afraid of Virginia Woolf?*, are perfect examples of a couple who are equally abusive and equally abused. There is nothing in the definition of verbal abuse that excludes mutuality.

Verbal abuse, as already noted, is frequently denied by the abuser. This need not be because the abuser is particularly adept at defense and denial (although it may be), but rather because it is difficult to recognize in oneself behaviors that are so ingrained. Distinguishing between criticizing because your partner made an important mistake and because your normal tendency is to look for things to criticize is not always easy. A useful guide here is to look at the interpretation of the behavior by the other person. If the behavior is interpreted as abusive then perhaps it is and perhaps it bears closer inspection.

The second step is to recognize the significant consequences of such behavior in your own interpersonal relationship. For example, does frequent criticism lead you to withdraw and fail to express yourself? Does it make you unhappy? Does it prevent you from trying new things or expanding your talents and competencies? Does a lack of empathy create self-doubt? Does negativity lead you to feel depressed? Surely these are not easy questions to consider; but they need to be recognized if the abusive patterns are ultimately to be combated.

The third step is to change the behaviors. Assuming that the verbally abusive patterns are not the product of a severely disturbed psyche, changing these behaviors should prove no more difficult than changing any other behaviors. The techniques for creating and increasing openness, empathy, supportiveness, positiveness, and equality, that are identified in most interpersonal textbooks are especially relevant tools.

If the verbal abuse continues and you continue to suffer and you have no luck in changing the behavior, you may wish to consider seeking professional help. College "student services" personnel will prove a useful source of information on available local facilities. Of course, another alternative is to end the relationship.

Many people of course stay in abusive relationships and to outsiders this may appear incomprehensible. Yet, there are many reasons why people remain in such relationships (Johnson 1993). For example, the person may believe that he or she can change the abuser's behavior or that such abuse is normal. Or, the person may fear for his or her own safety or the safety of children. Or the person may not have a suitable support system or may not know where to seek help. And, of course, abusers are not abusive all the time; during much of their relationship interactions, they may be loving, empathic, and supportive.

Brain Talk

Examining the underlying assumptions that influence your attitudes and behaviors is almost always a useful critical exercise. Try examining your own assumptions about verbal abuse. Ask yourself what you think verbal abuse is and what it isn't. Is it ever acceptable? What are appropriate strategies for dealing with verbal abuse? At the same time, ask yourself where these assumptions about verbal abuse came from—parents, the media, teachers?

Evaluating Ideas

How useful do you feel the suggestions for dealing with verbal abuse are? Would you take issue with any of the suggestions? Would you add suggestions to those offered here?

Bibliography

Follingstad, Diane R., et al. (199). The Role of Emotional Abuse in Physically Abusive Relationships. *Journal of Family Violence 5* (June): 107–120.

Infante, Dominic A., Teresa Chandler Sabourin, Jill E. Rudd, and Elizabeth A. Shannon (1990). Verbal Aggression in Violent and Nonviolent Marital Disputes. *Communication Quarterly* 38 (Fall): 361–371.

Johnson, Scott A. (1993). *When "I Love You" Turns Violent: Emotional and Physical Abuse in Dating Relationships.* Far Hills, NJ: New Horizon Press.

Index